D0975059

TOWARD RATIONAL
EXUBERANCE

TOWARD RATIONAL
EXUBERANCE

The Evolution of the Modern Stock Market

■ ■ ■

B. Mark Smith

Farrar, Straus and Giroux
New York

Farrar, Straus and Giroux
19 Union Square West, New York 10003

Distributed in Canada by Douglas & McIntyre Ltd.
Printed in the United States of America
First edition, 2001

Library of Congress Cataloging-in-Publication Data
Smith, B. Mark, 1953–
    Toward rational exuberance : the evolution of the modern stock market / B. Mark Smith.
        p.   cm.
    Includes index.
    ISBN 0-374-28177-7 (hardcover : alk. paper)
    1. Stock exchanges—United States.   2. Stocks—United States.   I. Title.

    HG4910 .S5633 2001
    332.64'273—dc21

                                                                    00-049477

Designed by Lisa Stokes

CONTENTS

PREFACE

THE STOCK MARKET is big news today. It is covered extensively in the mainstream press and is a topic of great interest to millions of Americans. Economists report that the market influences everything from the personal savings rate to Federal Reserve monetary policy to the size of the federal budget surplus. Accepted wisdom has it that the market will provide retirement security for anyone willing to diligently save and invest. It is easy to accept this state of affairs as unremarkable, as if it has always been so. But it has not always been so.

The American stock market at the beginning of the twenty-first century is vastly different from the American stock market at the beginning of the twentieth century. One hundred years ago the market was a primitive insider's game, lacking in transparency and sophistication and distrusted by the public. The public's negative view was reinforced by the crash of 1929 and subsequent Great Depression. When a prominent United States senator declared that the New York Stock Exchange was a "great gambling hell" that should be closed down and "padlocked," many Americans agreed. Throughout most of the first half of the twentieth century, the stock market was seen as a vaguely ominous thing to be regarded with skepticism and suspicion.

A stunning reversal occurred in the second half of the century. By the 1990s millions of Americans were active participants in the market, buying and selling stocks for their own accounts. Many millions more were involved indirectly, through pension and retirement plans. It has even been suggested that Social Security funds be invested in the market, an idea that, had it been proposed in 1935 when the Social Security system was created, would have been deemed absolutely crazy.

Toward Rational Exuberance tells the story of the American stock market from 1901 to the present, focusing on this remarkable transformation. It is a fascinating story, involving colorful personalities, dramatic events, and revolutionary new ideas. At first glance, the period chosen for examination may seem arbitrary; one hundred years is a nice round number that neatly encompasses the twentieth century. But the choice of 1901 as the starting point for the story is in reality far from arbitrary: 1901 is the year from which it is possible to trace the first manifestations of the major trends that would come to define the modern stock market. Alexander Dana Noyes, longtime financial editor of *The New York Times*, put it best when he wrote, "Probably 1901 was the first of such speculative demonstrations in history which based its ideas and conduct on the assumption that we were living in a New Era; that old rules and principles and precedent of finance were obsolete; that things could safely be done to-day which had been dangerous or impossible in the past."

Why is this story important? It is important because the stock market itself is important—far more important now than ever before. But the market today does not exist in a historical vacuum; it is a product of its past. Virtually all theories of market behavior rely on market history. History is used to provide a convenient benchmark when analyzing present conditions, or is simply extrapolated forward to make predictions about the future. Unfortunately, all too often little or no effort is made to truly understand that history. One recent author has declared that today's market is "irrationally exuberant," while others claim that the market should in fact be trading at a level three times higher than it is. Yet these wildly disparate arguments are based on interpretations of the same market history.

The central thesis of *Toward Rational Exuberance* is that the modern stock market can only be understood in light of the evolutionary processes that created it. The purpose of the book is not to marshal historical evidence to prove that stocks today are either too "high" or too "low"; it is instead to help the reader *understand* that evidence and what it really means. Only in this way is it possible to fully understand the modern stock market and the central role it plays in today's economy.

TOWARD RATIONAL
EXUBERANCE

PROLOGUE: THE EARLY DAYS

THE STORY OF the American stock market actually begins late in the eighteenth century, along a narrow lane at the southern end of Manhattan Island. Given the name Wall Street after a wall built in the 1600s by Dutch authorities administering the colony of New Amsterdam, the seemingly insignificant street would soon come to symbolize the country's financial markets. Eventually, no other street in the world would carry with its name such connotations of wealth and power.

The first marketplace of sorts developed at the eastern end of Wall Street as early as the 1600s; the first items traded were not stocks but commodities and slaves. By the 1790s, after the United States Constitution established a strong federal government, trading in financial instruments became predominant, consisting mostly of U.S. government bonds and the bonds sold by various states to finance internal improvements. A few bank and insurance stocks (totaling no more than half a dozen) were also traded. In the spring of 1792, a group of twenty-four merchants banded together to form an association of "Brokers for the Sale of Public Stock." Called the Buttonwood Agreement because transactions among the brokers were to take place near a buttonwood (sycamore) tree, the regulations establishing the new association were simple. Essentially, all that was required was that the broker-members agree to charge customers a minimum commission and give each other preference in all dealings.

Not long afterward the nascent stock market suffered its first scandal.

The crisis was precipitated by aggressive speculation led by former Assistant Secretary of the Treasury William Duer. In early March 1792, when an audit uncovered a $250,000 discrepancy in the government accounts Duer had controlled in his Treasury job, confidence in him was lost and the prices of securities he was heavily involved in tumbled. On March 10, Duer announced that he would be unable to meet his obligations; he was subsequently thrown into debtor's prison. The market was paralyzed by panic. It was estimated that the total losses ran to as much as $3 million, a fantastic sum at the time, an amount equal to the savings "of almost every person in the city, from the richest merchants to even the poorest women and the little shopkeepers."

One stunned New Yorker commented, "The town here has rec'd a shock which it will not get over in many years." Many leading merchants were ruined, and trade came to a halt as ships languished at wharves with no buyers for their cargoes. Artisans and laborers suddenly lost their jobs, and farmers were unable to sell their produce. Duer was lucky to be in jail, where he was at least protected from angry mobs. But critics turned their attention to what they saw as excessive speculation in the market itself, with even Treasury Secretary Alexander Hamilton denouncing "unprincipled gamblers."

It was a condemnation that would be repeated many times throughout American financial history. Hamilton's caustic remarks anticipated a debate about the nature of the stock market that continues to this day. The economic purpose of a stock market is to raise equity capital for businesses that need it and to provide a mechanism for valuing shares of those businesses on an ongoing basis. But does the market consistently accomplish these tasks in a rational, *efficient* manner? Or do periodic bouts of speculative excess, followed by "panics" like the one in 1792, cause the market to take on the characteristics of a gambling casino?

Fortunately, in the 1790s the stock market was relatively small and, outside New York City, of limited importance in an overwhelmingly agrarian economy. In spite of dire predictions to the contrary, the country soon recovered from the panic of 1792. Subsequent decades would bring the industrial revolution to the United States, with a concomitant increase in the size of the stock market and its importance to the national economy. But the issues raised by Hamilton's comments would not go away.

In 1815 the first stock issued by a business other than a bank, insurance, or canal company—the New York Manufacturing Company—appeared in published quotations. It began trading at $105 per share, then declined steadily into the 60s, finally disappearing in 1817. But other industrial concerns soon followed, as mechanical power, in the form of steam engines, became available to factories. Businesses now often required more capital than a single individual could provide; hence the "joint stock" company (the forerunner of the modern corporation) over time became a popular form of business organization, replacing sole proprietorships and partnerships. And the stock market became the vehicle through which joint-stock companies could raise the capital they needed.

In 1817 the New York Stock and Exchange Board (the predecessor of the New York Stock Exchange) was formed by brokers who felt the market needed more structure than was provided by the original Buttonwood Agreement and its subsequent modifications. The constitution drawn up for the Exchange Board has survived, with various amendments, to the present day. However, the marketplace in 1817 was very different from that which now exists. Trading took place in a restricted format that did not permit a continuous market, and most of the transactions that occurred still involved government bonds, not stocks.

The means by which business was transacted on the Exchange Board appears quite antiquated today. Each business day the president of the board would call out, one by one, the names of the securities listed on the board. After each "call," broker-members could bid for or offer that particular security; when a buyer and seller agreed on a quantity and a price, a transaction would occur and be duly recorded. As soon as activity ceased in a given name, the president would call out the next name, and so on.

From its moment of inception, the board sought to achieve a certain exclusivity of membership, to ensure that members were of appropriate social standing and also to limit competition. After the board was organized, only one new member was admitted in 1817, even though there were numerous applications. The broker-members earned their income as agents, buying and selling securities for their customers, rather than actively trading for themselves. Efforts to manipulate prices were forbidden. One of the first rules promulgated was a ban on "wash" sales, where one individual would effectively sell stock to himself through the board in order to create the false appearance of activity at a particular price. The Exchange Board was a gentlemen's club, and meant to remain one.

One problem that plagued the early stock market was a dearth of information about the companies whose shares were traded. The first recorded instance of the Exchange Board requesting financial data on a listed company occurred in 1825, when the board wrote to the New York Gas Light Company requesting information so that "the public might be informed through us of the existing state of things in relation to this company." This request was refused. Most companies took the position that information on company finances was nobody's business but their own and refused to divulge anything meaningful.

In its early years activity on the Exchange Board was sporadic. Large transactions, when they occurred, would usually be negotiated privately, outside the board itself, despite periodic efforts by board authorities to prevent this from happening. On March 16, 1830, in what would be the slowest day ever, only 31 shares officially changed hands. But this was soon to change. In the fall of 1830, shares of the first railroad to trade on the board, the Hudson and Mohawk, were listed. Many other railroads would follow. The substantial amounts of capital needed to finance the new industry required large numbers of stockholders and greatly increased the importance of an open stock market, accessible to all investors.

By 1837 the United States had more miles of completed railroads than any other country. But in that year the nation experienced a very unpleasant shock—a severe stock market crash. The nation's unstable banking system, consisting of poorly regulated state-chartered banks, collapsed under the burden of rampant speculation in western lands and in the new railroads. The banking crisis pulled down the stock market and left a bitter hangover in the form of a depression that would last six years. The rapid stock price fluctuations of the period also brought to the fore a new type of professional market participant, more interested in exploiting short-term moves in share prices than in executing orders for outside investors. A former clerk named Jacob Little was the most prominent of the new breed, and was soon almost universally despised in the small Wall Street community.

Little was a tall, slender man, with a slight stoop and a curt, cold manner. He dressed carelessly and made no real effort to fit into the clubby atmosphere of the Exchange Board. He profited from the 1837 market collapse through a technique he is credited with inventing—the "short sale" of stock. As practiced by Little, short-selling involved the sale of stock for delivery at a future date, often six to twelve months later. Little would gamble that share prices would fall in the interim, allowing him to buy back at a lower price the stock he would be required to deliver in the future. While this method of short-selling differs mechanically from the way in which short sales are transacted today, the objective is the same—to profit from a decline in the market. Needless to say, in a time of crisis such as the 1837 panic, a short-selling market operator who openly profited from the distress of others could be (and was) quite unpopular.

Little was the first professional "bear" in the history of the American stock market. The term "bear," as applied to a speculator who believed prices would fall, was derived from the well-known proverb "to sell the bear's skin before one has caught the bear"—in other words, to contract to sell something one does not yet own. "Bears" were opposed in the market by "bulls"—strong, powerful animals who would push prices higher. Little's practice of aggressively trading stocks to profit from short-term fluctuations did not sit well with the gentlemen members of the Exchange Board. Over the next two decades Little would be forced into bankruptcy four times, at least partly as a result of organized efforts by other brokers who reviled him. He was able to recover and resume his activities three times but was finally done in by the panic of 1857. There would be many others to replace him. As much as the leading members of the Exchange Board wished to preserve the genteel character of their business, economic realities did not allow them to do so. The stock market was now a fundamentally different game, with a different set of players.

By the 1850s stock market speculation had become so prevalent that crowds of 200 to 300 men often gathered at the corner of Wall and William Streets, outside the New York Stock and Exchange Board. Railroad securities, many of them quite speculative, were by far the most actively traded instruments, having long since eclipsed government bonds. A *New York Tribune* journalist described the market as a place "where millions of diamonds lay glistening like fiery snow, but which was guarded on all sides by poisonous serpents, whose bite was death and whose contact was pollution." Some newspapers preached against "stock gamblers," but others began to report actively on the new phenomenon. Horace Greeley, editor of the *New York Tribune*, started a column devoted entirely to the stock market, the first of its kind in America.

Perhaps no man better typified the new environment than Daniel Drew, a semiliterate former cattle drover who by the 1850s had come to control more liquid wealth than any other American. Drew was a self-defined "spekilator," who, like Jacob Little, made his money by trading (and quite frequently manipulating) stocks. Nicknamed the "speculative director," Drew frequently obtained positions on the boards of directors of various companies solely for the purpose of obtaining inside information that he could use in the market. Outwardly austere, with a cadaverous appearance, Drew was by all accounts deeply religious but saw no conflict between his religion and his market machinations.

Drew was to come into frequent conflict with another man who would loom large in the stock market and who personified the rollicking, unrestrained capitalism of the era—Cornelius "Commodore" Vanderbilt. Where Drew was simply a craven manipulator of stocks, Vanderbilt was a builder, creating an empire of steamboat and railroad lines. A great hulk of a man, square-jawed with piercing blue eyes, Vanderbilt was contemptuous of government laws and regulations that were often used corruptly by competing economic factions. He was often quoted as saying, "What do I care about the law? H'aint I got the power?" Whether Vanderbilt actually made this remark or not, there is little question that it accurately reflected his view.

The panic of 1857, precipitated by the unexpected collapse of a major insurance company, abruptly checked the frenetic growth of the stock market. But the setback was only temporary; by 1862 stocks were caught up in a "war boom" as the conflict between Union and Confederate forces showed no signs of an early resolution. The boom was fueled by massive government spending and the rapid expansion of the money supply that resulted from the Treasury's issuance of "greenbacks" (paper money not backed by gold) and was marked by some of the most frenzied stock trading in history.

The members of the Exchange Board, who quickly declared their loyalty to the Union cause, sought to chart a middle course between rampant speculation (which was perceived to be unpatriotic at a time of national crisis) and the need to maintain free, open capital markets. The issue came to a head when an active market in gold sprang up shortly after the Treasury issued the new greenbacks. Since greenbacks were not immediately convertible into gold, their value expressed in gold fluctuated daily, based on the fortunes of the Union. It was assumed that if the North won the war, the greenbacks would eventually be redeemed in gold at face value, but if the North lost, the greenbacks could potentially be worthless. Thus every Union battlefield defeat caused the price of gold expressed in greenbacks to shoot up. Speculators who traded in gold were perceived as benefiting from Northern reverses in battle and were angrily condemned. (Gold traders were often referred to as "General Lee's left wing on Wall Street.")

The Exchange Board severed its connection with the gold traders, refusing to allow transactions in gold to occur on its premises. Government bonds were also now traded in a separate facility. Reflecting these changes, with stocks now the primary instrument dealt in, the New York Stock and Exchange Board in January 1863 changed its name to the New York Stock Exchange.

The Exchange still attempted to rigidly control membership; unfortunately, the effect was to encourage competing exchanges to spring up. In the boom years of the war, these new exchanges flourished. Transactions occurred in venues ranging from the so-called Coal Hole (a dingy basement on William Street) to an exclusive hotel on Broadway. Trading often continued far into the night; as one observer put it, "Mammon is worshipped from daylight in New York until midnight."

Speculative profits available in the market had a corrupting influence on government at all levels. It was not uncommon for army telegraph operators to be bribed to send battlefield news to Wall Street before the Department of War itself was notified. But nowhere was market-related corruption worse than in New York City and New York State, where the legislative and judicial branches of government in the 1860s were in the thrall of market operators. In one of the most egregious instances, Daniel Drew and Commodore Vanderbilt engaged in a bitter struggle over the stock of the Harlem Railroad, which bounced up and down as the New York City Common Council and the New York State Legislature at various times approved, then disapproved, the railroad's application for a lucrative streetcar franchise. The legislators themselves actively played Harlem stock, first buying it to side with Vanderbilt, then selling it short to side with Drew. Eventually Vanderbilt emerged victorious, "cornering" the stock by acquiring all the outstanding shares, and bankrupting many of the legislators who had opposed him.

Daniel Drew survived to do battle with Vanderbilt again, this time over control of the Erie Railroad. Drew was assisted by Jay Gould and Jim Fisk, two unscrupulous young men who would soon surpass even their mentor in the shameless application of overtly manipulative techniques to the stock market. At one time or another several New York State judges, as well as many members of the New Jersey and New York legislatures, were bribed, either by the Vanderbilt or the Drew faction (and sometimes by both). The contest ultimately ended in a draw of sorts, but it established Gould and Fisk as preeminent operators in the market, positions they would cling to tenaciously until their deaths.

The unprecedented demands of government wartime finance greatly stressed the nation's jerry-built network of scattered state-chartered banks; it soon became clear that the banking system was inadequate to the task. The politically connected Philadelphia-based investment banking house of Jay Cooke and Company stepped in to sell more than $2 billion in government bonds necessary to finance the war. For the first time in history, a nationwide network of salesmen was employed to solicit funds from previously ignored small investors. Many new investors were introduced to the financial markets through these Jay Cooke & Company salesmen.

The Civil War is usually seen by economic historians as a watershed event, separating the primitive antebellum period from the postwar industrial era. The American economy, and the stock market, grew at a hectic pace in the postwar years. Railroad mileage doubled between 1865 and 1870, from 35,000 to 70,000 miles. The aggregate capital invested in manufacturing in 1870 was nearly four times the amount that had been invested in 1850. Improved communications for the first time began to create a truly national (and international) market for stocks. The first stock ticker was installed in 1867 in the Wall Street brokerage firm where Daniel Drew made his office, the same year that the new transatlantic cable began operating.

Some of the traditional practices of the New York Stock Exchange were clearly obsolete in the new environment. To accommodate the increased volume of trading, the Exchange leased additional space, which came to be called the Long Room, in which location trading could continue after the specific "calls" of each stock were made under the old rules. In 1868 the Long Room was rearranged so that specific stocks would trade in specific places, a forerunner of the modern system. Within a few years, the practice of "calling" stocks individually was abolished entirely, and continuous trading of all listed securities during Exchange hours was permitted. Memberships (known as "seats") were made transferable, and the New York Stock Exchange merged with other exchanges, doubling its size to more than 1,000 members.

Unfortunately, the rapid growth of the Exchange outpaced the ability of Exchange authorities to prevent abusive practices. Neither federal nor New York State officials exercised any real regulatory control over stock trading, leaving such matters to the Exchange, which was notably reluctant to act. But occasionally abuses occurred that were so egregious, and so threatening to the broad interests of Exchange members, that some form of institutional response was inevitable.

Jay Gould was at the center of several such incidents. Probably the most notorious Wall Street operator in the second half of the nineteenth century, Gould was a small, frail man, totally devoid of scruples, possessing the cunning intelligence and relentless determination to win at all costs that had served him so well in his earlier battle with Commodore Vanderbilt over the Erie Railroad. (Joseph Pulitzer, who knew Gould personally, described him as "the most sinister figure ever to flit bat-like across the vision of the American people.") Gould and his associates used the Erie Railroad treasury as if it were their personal plaything, financing multitudinous schemes that ranged from a plot to constrict the nation's money supply and thus cause a stock market crash, to a disastrous attempt to corner the market in gold in 1869. To raise money, Gould flooded the stock market with secretly issued Erie shares. Brokers who were members of the New York Stock Exchange became concerned; they were frequently called upon in the normal course of business to make loans to clients to finance the purchase of stock, holding the stock itself as collateral. What was the value of that collateral if an unlimited number of new shares could be printed up and sold without warning?

Thus a new rule went into effect in February 1869 requiring all companies listed on the Exchange to provide a public registry of outstanding shares. The companies were also required to give thirty days' notice before issuing new shares. Gould initially resisted the change and actually attempted to create a competing stock exchange on which the registration rules would not apply. But it was to no avail; the Erie Railroad needed the New York Stock Exchange more than the Exchange needed the Erie. When Gould finally did comply with the new regulation, publicly registering the Erie shares then outstanding, it was revealed that during his tenure as head of the railroad the number of Erie shares had increased from 250,000 to 700,000.

It is important to note the motivation for the new Exchange regulation. Ultimately, it was the self-interest of the broker-members of the Exchange, not a concern for the interests of the investing public, that caused the Exchange to act. While the two may have coincided in this instance, there was no guarantee that they would always do so in the future. (In fact, the rule the Exchange enforced most zealously was the minimum commission rate of 12.5 cents per share its broker-members were required to charge clients. Penalties for undercutting the minimum could be quite severe, ranging from lengthy suspensions to expulsion.)

As the nineteenth century progressed, additional rules were imposed by the Exchange, often following a particularly nasty scandal. Eventually, corporate directors were forbidden to sell short the stock of their own companies, and minimal reporting requirements were established so that rudimentary information about each listed company would be available to investors. Repeated efforts (not wholly successful) were made to eliminate "wash sales," which had theoretically been banned ever since the formation of the original New York Stock and Exchange Board in 1817. But for every two steps forward, there was a step backward.

Corporate insiders who were not directors could still sell short, and there were no real prohibitions against purchases of stock on inside information. Two or more operators, acting in concert, could arrange "wash" sales back and forth between themselves, circumventing the prohibition against such sales if carried out by only one individual. Perhaps most important, competitive market conditions forced the Exchange to back off from even the limited reporting requirements it had established.

In 1885, concerned that many new "industrial" companies were not applying for listing because of the requirement that they make certain financial data public, the Exchange created an Unlisted Department. (An "industrial" is defined here as anything other than a railroad, utility, bank, or insurance company.) The reporting requirements for listed companies were hardly onerous; essentially, all that was expected was that they submit annual income statements and balance sheets. But even this was too much for some companies, and thus the Unlisted Department required virtually nothing at all.

Stock market crashes were distressingly common in the second half of the nineteenth century. Devastating panics occurred in 1857, 1869, 1873, 1884, and 1893, and often ushered in severe downturns in the nation's economy. (The panic of 1873, touched off by the collapse of the venerable Jay Cooke & Company, eventually resulted in the bankruptcy of 89 railroads.) In each instance the story was similar. During a boom period, individuals and firms would become overextended and thus vulnerable to any unexpected slowdown in business. When one major firm failed, it would often set off a chain reaction of related failures, snowballing into a financial calamity. With government a passive player in the economy, there was no mechanism by which these panics could be arrested. The forces unleashed were allowed to play themselves out, often wreaking havoc on the economy as a whole.

Between crashes, the stock market continued to grow. Telegraph and telephone lines were first installed at the New York Stock Exchange in 1878, and the Exchange experienced its first million-share day in 1886. The method by which stocks were continuously traded—the "open outcry auction," which had replaced the old system of "calls" for individual stocks—proved to be quite effective. Orders to buy or sell stocks were sent to broker-members of the Exchange, who executed those orders for a fee. All brokers seeking to transact in a given stock came together at a central location specific to that stock, known as a post. They bid for or offered shares to the other brokers clustered there, with all orders given an equal chance to participate. The purpose was to ensure that the best possible price was obtained for each order. So efficacious was this system that it is still in use today.

In 1896 the decisive presidential election victory of pro-business William McKinley over populist William Jennings Bryan signaled that the government would not take actions considered by the business community to be inimical to economic growth. The economy roared ahead, pulling the stock market along with it. The large majority of shares traded were still those of railroads, but, increasingly, "industrials" began to appear on the list. New technologies were creating entire new industries, to be dominated by companies like General Electric and American Telephone and Telegraph. In 1896 the Dow Jones Average of Twelve Industrial Stocks was launched to provide an index monitoring the shares of these new companies. Charles Dow, its creator, had earlier predicted, "The industrial market is destined to be the greatest speculative market of the United States." (By 1896, however, Dow was still able to find only twelve industrial companies that he deemed sufficiently "seasoned" to merit inclusion in the new index.) Much as in the 1830s, when the first railroads were organized, the nature of the stock market was to be dramatically altered by radical changes occurring in the economy.

At the threshold of the twentieth century the economy was booming, driven by a pro-business political environment and new technologies. The stock market had played an indispensable role in facilitating the economy's growth, but was a far from perfect mechanism. Little had been done to make the market less susceptible to periodic boom-and-bust cycles that dangerously destabilized stock prices and jeopardized the entire economy. The market lacked transparency, with accurate financial data often unavailable. Unsavory manipulative practices by market insiders were commonplace, unrestrained by effective regulation. The issues raised by Hamilton's denunciation of "unprincipled gamblers" remained. How would those issues be resolved? Could the stock market perform its vital economic function without debilitating distortions caused by speculative excess? The answers to these questions would be instrumental in shaping the evolution of the stock market in the coming century and in defining its role in the modern economy.

1
STEEL

"**I** ACCEPT."

These words, spoken by John Pierpont Morgan in early 1901, would soon reverberate throughout Wall Street. A piece of paper had just been handed to Morgan by the energetic young president of Carnegie Steel, Charles Schwab. Written on the paper was a number representing Andrew Carnegie's asking price for Carnegie Steel, the biggest producer of crude steel in the world. After a quick glance, Morgan signaled his acceptance of Carnegie's terms. With that gesture he acquired the essential building block for what would in a few weeks become the world's largest industrial corporation: United States Steel. In the rush of events that followed, Morgan did not actually get around to instructing his attorneys to draw up the contract with Carnegie for over a week. But it didn't matter; both men had given their word, and the deal was done.

U.S. Steel was a giant—or a monster, depending on one's perspective. With a capitalization of more than $1.4 billion, it dwarfed even the federal government (with an annual budget of approximately $350 million and a total national debt of slightly more than $1 billion). Senator Albert Beveridge of Indiana hailed Morgan as "the greatest constructive financier yet developed by mankind."[1] But even normally pro-business spokesmen such as the editors of *The Wall Street Journal* acknowledged some "uneasiness over the magnitude of the affair." Others rendered harsher verdicts. Henry Adams, financial gadfly and descendant of two Presidents, stated bluntly,

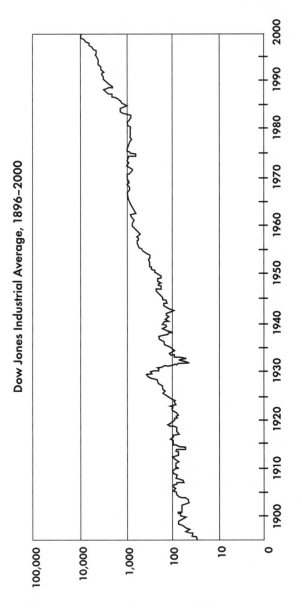

Dow Jones Industrial Average, 1896–2000

© *Dow Jones & Company Inc.*

"Pierpont Morgan is apparently trying to swallow the sun."[2] President Arthur T. Hadley of Yale, referring to the great "trusts,"* like U.S. Steel, that were controlled by a few imperious financiers, such as J. P. Morgan, declared that if such business combinations were not "regulated by public sentiment," the country would have "an emperor in Washington within 25 years."[3]

Some observers on Wall Street were also critical of the new "trust," although for reasons different from Hadley's. U.S. Steel was made up of dozens of smaller firms, besides Carnegie's, that had been amalgamated into the new entity. Many analysts felt that Morgan and his associates, in their eagerness to form U.S. Steel, had paid too much for its constituent parts. According to their calculations, the $1.4 billion capitalization of U.S. Steel (representing the face value of the U.S. Steel stock and bonds to be sold to the public and issued to the owners of the acquired companies) greatly exceeded the actual value of the new corporation's assets. The whole, the critics alleged, should not and could not be worth more than the sum of the parts.

The cry of "watered stock" was raised. Legend has it that the term originated in the early decades of the nineteenth century. Daniel Drew, in his years as a cattle drover before he became a notorious Wall Street operator, is said to have hit upon the idea of plying his scrawny "critters" with salt, then depriving them of water as he drove them down the length of Manhattan to the butcher shops on Fulton Street. As the story goes, Drew would finally instruct his drovers to "let them critters drink their fill" immediately before the cattle were to be inspected by potential buyers. He knew that a thirsty cow could easily drink 50 pounds of water; he was counting on it. The Fulton Street butchers, enthused about the apparently fat cattle Drew had for sale, would pay top dollar for the bloated animals, a price that effectively included thousands of pounds of water. When Drew

---

*The term "trust," as applied to large industrial combinations, originated from the need to circumvent state laws forbidding corporations to own stock in other corporations. Thus a "trust" would be established to hold the shares of acquired companies, and shares of the trust would be issued to the former owners of those acquired companies. The officials of the trust would be "trustees," rather than officers and directors of a corporation.

later hung out his shingle on Wall Street, he was frequently accused of "watering" the stock of companies he controlled, meaning that he would secretly sell stock in quantities far in excess of the amount justified by the assets of the company. The term "watered stock" stuck in the Wall Street lexicon.

J. P. Morgan was no Daniel Drew. To the extent that an aristocracy existed in the United States, Morgan was a charter member. His ancestors on both his mother's and father's sides had come to America shortly after the *Mayflower*, and his father had been the leading American investment banker in Europe. Morgan looked and acted the part; he was a large, physically imposing man with a gruff manner and a penetrating stare that could be very intimidating. Born to wealth and influence, Morgan was openly disdainful of the unsavory tactics employed by operators like Drew who sought to claw their way to success on Wall Street. For J. P. Morgan to water stock was unthinkable.

The debate over the capital structure of U.S. Steel had a broader significance, reflecting the first inklings of changing standards for valuing stocks. Those critics who alleged that a substantial quantity of water existed in the new trust were in a way correct, given the essentially static analysis prevalent at the time. It was customary to speak in terms of a company's "intrinsic" worth, usually defined as its "book value"—the total of assets minus liabilities. The Federal Commissioner of Corporations, later looking back on the birth of U.S. Steel, made use of the traditional valuation approach in attempting to calculate the true worth of the corporation at the time of its formation. Adding together the values of its constituent parts, he calculated that U.S. Steel at the time of its creation had actually been worth about $700 million, meaning that the other $700 million of the $1.4 billion initial capitalization was water.[4]

The commissioner's report included one important disclaimer. It explicitly did not take into account any additional profits that would flow from the presumably great efficiencies to be reaped by the new combination. But of course it was those efficiencies that were the primary rationale for forming the giant trust in the first place. Morgan and his associates were anticipating that profits would be greatly enhanced by economies of scale and other advantages the new entity would possess; they were looking to the future, and rejected the notion that U.S. Steel was properly valued simply by summing up its constituent parts. (History seems to suggest they were correct. With the exception of a difficult period in 1903–1904, the corporation was solidly profitable for decades to come.) But conventional standards of stock market valuation did not take into account future earnings growth, which was assumed to be unpredictable. Conservative investors would not speculate on developments they believed they could not foresee. Hence the disagreement over the amount of watered stock.

The founders of U.S. Steel had unwittingly touched on a controversy that would recur repeatedly during the twentieth century—the clash between new and traditional methods for valuing stocks. Many years later, Alexander Dana Noyes, longtime financial editor of *The New York Times*, suggested that 1901 marked a crucial turning point. He wrote, "Probably 1901 was the first of such speculative demonstrations in history which based its ideas and conduct on the assumption that we were living in a New Era; that old rules and principles and precedent of finance were obsolete; that things could safely be done to-day which had been dangerous or impossible in the past."[5] The events of 1901 may have marked the first such instance, but they would certainly not be the last.

The basic question asked by any investor is, What is the right price for a given stock? At the turn of the century, this question was answered by traditionalists in a very straightforward fashion. The price an investor was willing to pay for a stock reflected what he would receive from his investment—his share of the company's earnings in the form of dividends paid out to him from those earnings. Dividends were all-important, and stock prices tended to fluctuate with the level of dividend payments.

The tool most commonly used today to value stocks, the price-earnings (P/E) ratio,* had its origins in this analysis, although in a way that would now be considered somewhat backward. At the turn of the century, appropriate P/E ratios for stocks were derived from dividends. For example, for most of the decade preceding 1901, the average dividend yield of industrial stocks traded on the New York Stock Exchange varied between 5% and 6%.[6] As a standard rule of thumb, it was assumed that a mature industrial

---

*The price-earnings ratio is simply the price of a share of a company's stock divided by the annual earnings per share of the company.

company should pay out between 50% and 60% of its earnings in dividends. Thus, if a company's annual dividend was between 5% and 6% of its stock price, and was to represent between 50% and 60% of its earnings, the earnings per share must equal 10% of the stock price. Put in the form of the price-earnings ratio, the price of a share of stock should be ten times the company's earnings per share—a P/E ratio of 10 to 1.

Simple enough. In fact, the 10-to-1 P/E ratio had become something of a standard by the turn of the century. An industrial stock trading at a 10-to-1 P/E ratio was arbitrarily considered by many analysts to be fully valued. This standard had certainly held true in the decade preceding 1901; in only one year of that decade did the composite P/E ratio for the New York Stock Exchange industrials rise significantly above 10 to 1. (In 1896 it touched 11.7 to 1.)[7]*

Price-earnings ratios were calculated on the basis of the current year's earnings. Richard Schabacker, financial editor of *Forbes* magazine, wrote later about accepted valuation standards in the early twentieth century: "Since it is generally impossible to prophesy what earnings the stock will show in any future time, it is necessary to base this [P/E] ratio on the probable earnings for the current year."[8] Anything else was speculation, not investment.

This rigid, static mode of analysis yielded results that would today appear to be perverse. Since stocks were presumably riskier than bonds (which had fixed interest rates and guaranteed the return of principal on

---

*P/E's presented in this book are for industrial stocks, unless otherwise noted. It should be understood, however, that in 1901 industrial stocks were far outnumbered by railroads. Railroads were seen by investors to be more stable, predictable (less risky) businesses than industrials; hence P/E ratios on rail shares were generally higher, and dividend yields were generally lower, than those for industrials. Some market observers, such as Robert Shiller in *Irrational Exuberance*, have argued that P/E ratios were too "high" in 1901. Part of the problem is that Shiller calculates market P/E ratios using ten-year trailing earnings in the denominator, a dubious approach that divides 1901 stock prices by the average of the very depressed earnings generated during the depression of the mid-1890s, thus ballooning the P/E's. Shiller also uses market P/E numbers that primarily reflect railroad, not industrial, valuations. While this may be representative of the market in 1901, it does not facilitate "apples to apples" comparisons with the industrial stocks that would dominate the market for most of the twentieth century.

maturity), investors expected to receive dividends on stocks that were greater than the interest rates available from bonds, so as to be compensated for the extra risk. Dividend rates at the turn of the century were in fact higher than bond interest rates, and had always been so, going back as far in time as data are available. Investors, unable or unwilling to estimate future growth but cognizant of the fact that stocks were riskier than bonds, demanded a higher yield from stocks than bonds. This is the precise opposite of the relationship between stock dividends and bond yields that prevailed throughout most of the second half of the twentieth century.

The arbitrary derivation of appropriate P/E ratios from current dividend payouts resulted in relatively low stock prices. Since stock prices fluctuated with dividends, and dividend rates were relatively high, by definition stock prices had to be relatively low to produce the required high dividend rates. (The dividend rate is simply the dividend per share divided by the price per share of the stock—hence the lower the share price, the higher the dividend rate.)

In short, stocks were typically viewed by turn-of-the-century investors very differently than they are viewed today. They were valued primarily on the basis of the current income—dividends—they produced. This conservative approach resulted in stock dividends that were higher, and stock prices that were lower, than modern methods of analysis produce.

The proponents of trusts like U.S. Steel implicitly challenged these standards by citing presumably enhanced future profits as a justification for the giant business combinations. But it was only a mild challenge; once created, the shares of the trusts were still typically valued on the basis of the dividends they paid. However, some serious students of the market were exploring significantly more unorthodox ways of evaluating stock prices. In 1900 two such men, separated by thousands of miles and coming at the problem from very different disciplines, proposed theoretical approaches to analyzing the market that were fundamentally different from traditionally accepted methods.

One of these men was none other than Charles Dow, creator of the Dow Jones averages and editor of *The Wall Street Journal*. Dow developed an entirely new way of looking at the stock market that would later form the basis of what would be called technical market analysis. In a series of articles in the *Journal* between 1900 and 1902, Dow put forth a theory for predicting stock prices that had nothing to do with earnings or dividends but was based simply on the price action of the stocks themselves. His ideas were taken up by William P. Hamilton, who succeeded Dow as editor at the *Journal*. Hamilton refined Dow's approach, giving it a name—the Dow theory.

The Dow theory assumed that the stock market at all times accurately reflected the sum total of all knowledge as to the future course of business activity much better than any individual could possibly hope to. Therefore, little advantage could be gained by analyzing business fundamentals. But Dow and Hamilton claimed that certain patterns could be discerned in the action of stock prices that could be used to predict the market's future course. In effect, they argued that an investor should read the market as a "barometer" of business conditions, but a barometer that not only measured the present but sometimes provided clues to the future as well.

Dow believed that at any given time there were three movements present in the market—the primary trend, a secondary (or reactive) trend counter to the primary trend, and essentially random daily fluctuations. He believed that the price action of the market itself would provide signals as to when a primary trend (which could last for years) was reversing, and that these signals could be very valuable to investors. In perhaps his best-known article on the subject, in *The Wall Street Journal* in 1901, he compared the action of the market to waves on a beach:

> *A person watching the tide coming in and who wishes to know the exact spot which marks the high tide, sets a stick in the sand at the points reached by the incoming waves until the stick reaches a position where the waves do not come up to it, and finally recede enough to show that the tide has turned.*
>
> *This method holds good in watching and determining the flood tide of the stock market . . . The price-waves, like those of the sea, do not recede at once from the top. The force which moves them checks the inflow gradually and time elapses before it can be told with certainty whether the tide has been seen or not.*

Coincidentally, as Charles Dow was propounding his theory of stock price movements, a young French mathematician, starting with a similar conception of the market, reached profoundly different conclusions. Louis Bachelier completed his doctoral dissertation at the Sorbonne in Paris in 1900. Entitled "The Theory of Speculation," it was the first work to employ mathematical techniques to explain stock market behavior. Bachelier, like Dow, believed that the stock market at all times accurately represented the collective wisdom of all participants. He wrote, "Clearly the price considered most likely by the market is the true current price: if the market judged otherwise, it would quote not this price, but another price higher or lower." But Bachelier, unlike Dow, did not discern any means by which future prices could be predicted. In the opening paragraphs of his thesis he argues that market movements are not only impossible to predict but often hard to explain even after they have occurred:

> *Past, present, and even discounted future events are reflected in the market price, but often show no apparent relation to price changes . . . artificial causes also intervene: the Exchange reacts on itself, and the current fluctuation is a function, not only of the previous fluctuations, but also of the current state. The determination of these fluctuations depends on an infinite number of factors; it is, therefore, impossible to aspire to mathematical predictions of it . . . the dynamics of the Exchange will never be an exact science.*[9]

Bachelier had another important insight—that stock price fluctuations tend to grow larger as the time horizon lengthens. The formula he developed to describe the phenomenon bears a remarkable resemblance to the formula that describes the random collision of molecules as they move in space. Many years later this process would be described as a random walk, a key concept underlying much of the academic work on the stock market in the second half of the twentieth century.

A great deal of Bachelier's work was revolutionary. He laid the groundwork upon which later mathematicians constructed a full-fledged theory of probability, and made the first theoretical attempts to value options and futures. All this was done in an effort to explain why stock prices were impossible to predict.[10]

Bachelier was not modest about his work. He stated openly, "It is evident that the present theory resolves the majority of problems in the study of speculation by the calculus of probability."[11] Sixty years later a leading finance scholar agreed, saying, "So outstanding is [Bachelier's] work that we can say that the study of speculative prices has its moment of glory at its moment of conception."[12] Bachelier anticipated by half a century the efforts of mathematicians and economists to develop rigorous models of stock market behavior. Unfortunately, Bachelier was a frustrated unknown in his own time. His dissertation was awarded "honorable mention" rather than the "very honorable mention" that was essential to finding employment in the academic world. After years of trying, he finally secured an appointment at an obscure French provincial university. The quality of his dissertation was simply not appreciated at the time, in part because he had chosen such an unusual topic for his research. One of his professors wrote, "M. Bachelier has evidenced an original and precise mind," but also commented, "The topic is somewhat remote from those our candidates are in the habit of treating."[13] Over fifty years were to pass before anyone took the slightest interest in his work.

J. P. Morgan and his associates undoubtedly never heard of Louis Bachelier and were probably quite unfamiliar with the Dow theory. The problem they faced as they attempted to bring U.S. Steel to market was much more immediate: how to ensure that the market could absorb the heavy weight of the new securities to be issued. Fortunately, the tone of the market in 1901 was good, even exuberant. The volume of trading on the New York Stock Exchange for the year would total a record 265 million shares, a number that would be exceeded only three times before 1925. Turnover would be an incredible 319%, meaning that the average share traded on the Exchange would change hands more than three times during the year. (As a comparison, in 1929 the turnover figure for the New York Stock Exchange would be 119%, and by 1940 it would fall to 12%, the lowest of the century.)

Ready buyers had been found for shares in other large trusts that had recently been formed; by 1900 there had been no fewer than 185 such amalgamations, with total capitalization in excess of $3 billion. (This represented one-third of all capital invested in American manufacturing enterprises.) The stock market had absorbed all these new issues without flinching. If ever there was a moment to bring to market a huge new batch of stock, 1901 was the time to do it.

It is tempting, looking back at the ebullient state of the market in 1901, to draw parallels with the booming Wall Street environment that would exist toward the end of the twentieth century. But today's market is vastly different. The New York Stock Exchange trading volume for the entire year of 1901 (265 million shares) was only a fraction of a single *day's* volume today. Public participation in the market in 1901 was tiny; it is difficult to estimate how many Americans actually owned stocks, but it could not possibly have been more than a small fraction of the total population. (The difficulty of estimating the fraction of the population that holds stocks will be discussed in greater detail in subsequent chapters.) The majority of Americans in 1901 still lived and worked on farms, without telephones or electricity. Outside New York City, most newspapers did not even print stock quotations, because of a lack of interest. The public, to the extent that it was even aware of the stock market, viewed it with a mixture of skepticism and indifference.

Such an attitude was well justified. The market in the first years of the twentieth century was still an insider's game, much as it had been throughout the nineteenth century. It was an era of caveat emptor, when a paucity of publicly available information effectively precluded potential investors from making informed choices. The information that companies listed on the New York Stock Exchange were required to make public was sketchy at best; companies whose shares traded in the so-called Unlisted Department, or on other, smaller exchanges, frequently made public nothing at all. (In 1901, 15% of the trading on the New York Exchange was still in unlisted securities. American Sugar Refineries, the most actively traded stock in the Unlisted Department, had not made public any income statements for ten years.)

The Wall Street Journal took note of the dearth of reliable information available on stocks in an 1899 article, stating that "very few figures are published and those figures are usually in such form that it is impossible to canvass the integrity of net earnings . . . Consequently, in ninety-five cases out of a hundred the stockholder in an industrial company is obliged to take the word of the managers—with all that implies—for the company's net earnings."

"With all that implies" was a phrase pregnant with meaning. The average shareholder was almost entirely at the mercy of management, deprived of reliable information and unprotected by any real regulatory authority. All too often the men who controlled the new industrial corporations at the turn of the century made use of their positions to manipulate the stock of their companies for their own benefit, not to enhance shareholder value. One particularly egregious example occurred in April 1900 and involved a man who would be a key player in the U.S. Steel transaction, John "Bet a Million" Gates.

Gates was regarded by friends as a "good character," but he could be ruthless in dealing with adversaries. Frederick Lewis Allen described him as "the sort of man who will sit up all night at a friend's bedside and then destroy the man financially the next day."[14] As his nickname Bet a Million implies, Gates was an inveterate gambler. One story about Gates described how, sitting in a railroad car on a rainy day, he repeatedly bet an associate on which raindrops would first reach the bottom of a window. The terms of the bet: $1,000 per drop. Another story had it that in one of his marathon bridge-playing sessions at the Waldorf-Astoria, his game was joined by a young man who was told that the stakes were "ten a point." Thinking this meant ten cents per point, the young man played for several hours and won. The next day he was shocked to find a check in the mail from Gates in the amount of $33,000, which represented his winnings.

In 1898, Gates formed the American Steel and Wire Company. Business seemed to be good and growing, but suddenly, in April 1900, the company announced that it was closing 13 of its plants. The stock tumbled on the unexpected news. The reason for the shutdown, however, had nothing to do with business conditions. Gates had first sold the stock short, then ordered the plant closings simply as a means of causing the price to collapse. He then bought back ("covered") his short, creating a sizable profit for himself at the expense of hapless investors unaware of his machinations.

J. P. Morgan did not have a high opinion of Gates, but had no choice but to deal with him in the formation of U.S. Steel. The new trust needed Gates's company. As might be expected, Gates waited until the deal was almost done, then at the last minute tried to demand an outrageous price for his holdings. Morgan, however, was not to be bluffed. He curtly told Gates, "I am going to leave this building in ten minutes. If by that time you have not accepted our offer, the matter will be closed. We will build our own wire plant." Gates capitulated.[15]

Once agreement had been reached with Andrew Carnegie, John Gates, and the other owners of the companies to be acquired, the Morgan syndicate took steps to launch the massive creation without disrupting the stock market. Carnegie, ever distrustful of the market, had insisted on receiving U.S. Steel bonds in exchange for most of his holdings of Carnegie Steel. The stockholders of the other constituent companies, however, received U.S. Steel common and preferred stock* worth over $1 billion. In addition, J. P. Morgan & Company and the Wall Street firms underwriting the new issue were to be paid in Steel common stock for their services, in the amount of nearly 1.3 million shares. A huge overhanging supply thus imperiled the market in the new Steel shares; it was assumed that many of those who had received Steel stock in the transaction would soon want to dispose of it.

J. P. Morgan & Company was not a member of the New York Stock Exchange. The most influential investment banking house in the world would not deign to do the work of a "stockjobber." But Morgan and his partners could not ignore the cross realities of the marketplace; someone would have to be found to do the messy job of facilitating trading in the new Steel shares.

The man selected was James R. Keene, known as the Silver Fox of Wall Street. At an early age Keene had made his fortune in California mining stocks; he then came east to Wall Street with $6 million in search of bigger game. According to legend, he quickly ran afoul of Jay Gould. Allegedly Gould said of Keene, "He came east in a private [rail] car. I'll send him back in a boxcar."[16] In 1884, when Keene overextended himself seeking to corner the market in wheat, Gould and his allies were ready to pounce.

---

*Preferred stock is a class of stock that ranks higher in the capital structure of a corporation than common stock, but lower than debt. In case of the liquidation of the company, preferred stockholders will be paid off before common holders but after bondholders. Preferred stock dividends must also be paid before any common stock dividends can be paid, but preferred dividends are usually fixed and do not increase, as can common dividends, if the earnings of the company improve.

Keene soon lost his entire fortune, actually ending up in debt to the tune of $1.5 million.

Keene would make and lose several more fortunes over his Wall Street career. But beginning in the late 1880s, when he handled the market operations of the "sugar trust," he established a reputation as a broker skilled in managing the trading of large new issues. In essence, Keene's task was to manipulate trading of the new stocks in such a way as to draw in buyers, allowing the promoters to unload their holdings. He did so quite skillfully, buying and selling stock to create the impression of activity and an upward trend in prices.

Keene's experience prepared him well for his most challenging task— handling the trading of U.S. Steel for the Morgan-led syndicate of investment banking firms that underwrote the offering. It is unlikely that Morgan himself ever talked with Keene; the Great Man would customarily delegate such tasks to others. But everyone involved recognized the importance of what Keene would attempt to do.

The backers of U.S. Steel left nothing to chance. All the principals made themselves available for frequent interviews in which they extolled the prospects of the new combination. Positive stories were fed to sympathetic journalists. Perhaps most important, Morgan very publicly attached his own prestige to the transaction, announcing that J. P. Morgan & Company, along with its fellow syndicate members, stood ready to subscribe to as much as $200 million of Steel stock if necessary.

It wasn't necessary. Demand for the new issue was huge. Steel common stock commenced trading at $39 per share, and the preferred first traded at $85; the prices of both began to rise steadily on heavy volume. Within a few weeks Keene was able to dispose of 750,000 shares of the 1.3 million the investment bankers had received as compensation for the underwriting, and many of the former owners of the companies that had been merged together to form U.S. Steel were able to unload their holdings as well. By late April, two months after the first trades, the common stock hit $55 and the preferred traded at $100.

The U.S. Steel offering was an unqualified triumph for Morgan and his partners. Keene, basking in the success of the deal, found himself portrayed in the press not as a craven manipulator of stocks but as a "sportsman." *The New York Times* opined, "So persistent a stock speculator was Mr.

Keene that none of the Wall Street veterans considered him a money-seeker at it, but rather a sportsman, who found in manipulating stocks and bonds the same excitement other sportsmen might get from a roulette wheel or a poker game . . . He could find no contentment in life except that which came from taking his money off the tape." (The muckraking era of journalism had not yet arrived; when it did a few years later, Keene and other market operators would find the press far less sympathetic.)

The syndicate underwriting U.S. Steel eventually recognized a profit of $62.5 million from the sale of its Steel shares, of which J. P. Morgan & Company received $12.5 million. Morgan himself immediately set sail for his customary European vacation, well satisfied with the results of his efforts. Keene, now regarded as the premier broker on Wall Street, continued to represent Morgan interests but also devoted an increasing amount of time to his other passion: breeding and racing thoroughbred horses. Andrew Carnegie, with more than $300 million in U.S. Steel bonds secure in a specially constructed vault in Hoboken, New Jersey, went off to live in baronial splendor in a castle he had built on the coast of Scotland, complete with medieval battlements, covered swimming pool, and miniature waterfall. There he entertained distinguished guests, and commenced the task of giving away most of his fortune. John Gates, furious at Morgan's decision to keep him off the U.S. Steel board of directors, tangled with the Great Man in a dispute over the Louisville & Nashville Railroad a few years later. Although Gates emerged from that confrontation unscathed, his gambler's luck would soon run out, forcing him to retire from Wall Street to a small Texas town.

The young (thirty-eight-year-old) president of Carnegie Steel, Charles Schwab, had so impressed Morgan that he was chosen to be the operational head of U.S. Steel. "Judge" Elbert H. Gary, a pillar of Methodist moral rectitude and a trusted Morgan associate, was selected as chairman. Gary quickly moved to impose tight ethical standards on the Steel directors; to prevent them from speculating on the basis of inside information, he refused to make them privy to any important news except at formal directors' meetings, which were invariably held after the stock market closed and were followed immediately by press releases disclosing any significant information. U.S. Steel would not become a vehicle for insider speculation if Gary could help it.

Unfortunately, Gary's attitude was atypical. Machinations like those of John Gates were the norm on Wall Street in 1901, not the exception. Much as Morgan and Gary might like to change things, even the vast power they held was insufficient to do so. A year of great turmoil, 1901 marks the beginning of what would prove to be revolutionary changes in the stock market. But the "game" as it was played on "the Street" was still fundamentally an insider's game, played by men who were unrestrained by rules or concern for the small investor. Even as Morgan sailed off for a long vacation in Europe, a dispute was brewing between two such men that would soon break into open, ugly conflict—a conflict that would devastate the Street and claim many innocent victims.

AN INDIAN GHOST DANCE

IT WAS SAID that Edward H. Harriman actually enjoyed stock market crashes. These events, appropriately referred to as panics, were distressingly frequent in the second half of the nineteenth century. Harriman was reputed to have profited from several of them; in one instance, he was described as being "very cheerful through it all, as though indeed he liked it."[1]

At five foot four, weighing at most 130 pounds, Harriman was nearly as small in stature as Jay Gould. Slender, balding, with wire-rimmed glasses and a drooping mustache, he resembled a clerk more than a captain of industry. Harriman's interest in trading railroad stocks soon led him, like Gould, into the management of the railroad companies themselves. After gaining control of the Union Pacific in 1895, he rebuilt the bankrupt line into one of the leading railroads in the country. By 1900, he was much respected for his acumen, both on Wall Street and in the boardrooms of competing railroads. The press began to apply the nickname Little Giant to him, and he reveled in the publicity. But Harriman was confronted by another railroad magnate, equally small in stature and driven by great ambition, who had also been christened the Little Giant. James Jerome Hill, of the Great Northern and the Northern Pacific lines, was not about to be outdone by Edward Harriman.

Hill, like many other so-called robber barons of his era, made his career in industry but was not wholly unfamiliar with the ways of Wall

Street. He possessed a startling intelligence, incredible willpower, and a relentless work ethic. Unfortunately, he was also quick-tempered, willful to the point of ruthlessness, and capable of coldly calculated manipulations of allies and adversaries alike. Both Hill and Harriman desperately wanted to expand their large regional railroads into transcontinental lines. The problem was that they would have to trample over each other to do it.

Conflict was inevitable, and the instrument of that conflict was to be another railroad, the Chicago, Burlington, and Quincy, often known simply as the Q. The Q offered a vital link between the eastern terminuses of both the Hill and Harriman roads and Chicago, where connections could be made to the East Coast. Whoever controlled the Q would be well on his way to creating a truly transcontinental rail network. Without the Q, either Hill or Harriman would be relegated to the position of also-ran.

Concerned that Harriman might attempt to buy the Q, Hill turned to his investment banker, J. P. Morgan, for assistance. Morgan and Hill promptly set about negotiating a deal with the Q, eventually paying a stiff price to buy the vital line. Better to overpay than to run the risk that such an important property would fall into the hands of Harriman and the Union Pacific.

Surprised by Hill's aggressive move, Harriman asked to be let in on the deal. He offered to pay one-third of the purchase price in exchange for a one-third interest in the Q and the right to use the Q to connect his Union Pacific to Chicago. Hill summarily refused. He saw no reason to give away the spoils he had just bought fairly in the marketplace. Upon hearing this, Harriman answered, "Very well, it is a hostile act and you must take the consequences."[2]

Harriman's warning notwithstanding, Hill and Morgan undoubtedly believed that the matter had been resolved and that they had won. Hill left New York for an extended trip to the Northwest to tour his railroads, while Morgan was preoccupied with the formation of U.S. Steel. Harriman was left sitting on the outside looking in, bitter yet determined.

Harriman then decided upon a daring gamble: since he had effectively lost the Q to the Hill-controlled Northern Pacific Railroad, why not after the Northern Pacific itself? If he could wrest that road from Hill's control, he would gain the Northern Pacific's interest in the Q, thus accomplishing his original objective. But beyond that, by adding the Northern Pacific to his Union Pacific, he would control the largest railroad empire in the country and, at the same time, inflict an embarrasing defeat on the Hill-Morgan axis. It would later be said of Harriman that "he feared neither God nor J. P. Morgan." In early 1901 he was prepared to prove it.

Harriman and his investment banker, Jacob Schiff of Kuhn, Loeb & Company, estimated that between $80 million and $100 million would be required to gain control of the Northern Pacific through open market purchases of stock. To raise the needed funds, they assembled a syndicate that included William Rockefeller. There was no love lost between the Rockefellers and Morgan; at one point during the formation of U.S. Steel, Morgan had refused to meet with John D. Rockefeller, stating simply, "I don't like him."[3] The feeling was mutual; Rockefeller often said of Morgan that he could not see "why any man should have such a high and mighty feeling about himself."[4]

In late March 1901, Schiff began to buy Northern Pacific. Orders to purchase shares were parceled out carefully to unrelated brokers so as to disguise the buying—to avoid alerting Hill and Morgan. Schiff bought shares of Northern Pacific preferred stock in addition to the common. The preferred, unlike the common, was a fixed income security, paying a set dividend that would not rise or fall with the company's earnings. This distinction, however, was not important to Schiff. The Northern Pacific preferred shares carried with them the same rights to elect the board of directors as did the common shares; thus Schiff bought preferred and/or common stock whenever he could without dramatically disturbing the respective prices. At first, all went well.

Northern Pacific common stock rose 7⅝ to $96 per share during the week ending April 1, 1901. Trading was active. Normally this action would attract attention, but it came at a time when the entire market was rising on heavy volume. The common stock of U.S. Steel, initially issued at $38 per share, quickly rose to $55. Sentiment on the Street was very bullish; it was widely believed that the formation of gigantic trusts like U.S. Steel (as well as Borden's Condensed Milk, Corn Products, Eastman Kodak, National Distillers, and United Fruit) would usher in a new wave of prosperity for the country, and for Wall Street. The action in Northern Pacific shares was lost in the excitement.

By April 15, Schiff had accumulated 150,000 shares of Northern Pacific common stock and 100,000 shares of the preferred. The financial press noted the activity but assumed it was related to the prospect of enhanced earnings associated with the upcoming merger with the Chicago, Burlington, and Quincy. Nobody suspected the truth.

In fact, at the same time Northern Pacific common and preferred shares were rising under the accumulation by the Harriman syndicate, the common stock of Harriman's own Union Pacific was rising even more, on an even greater volume of trading. Press speculation centered on the activity in Union Pacific, not Northern Pacific. Who was behind the buying in Union Pacific? Very few market players possessed the resources that would be required. Rockefeller interests, as well as George Gould, were known to be friendly to Harriman and thus were ruled out. Morgan seemingly had no interest in the line. It was thought that only one possible operator with the funds necessary to carry out such a buying program existed: William K. Vanderbilt, grandson of Cornelius "Commodore" Vanderbilt. The Street buzzed with rumors of a Vanderbilt raid on Union Pacific.[5]

Such rumors were the stuff of what passed as financial journalism at the turn of the century. Because of the dearth of reliable data, relatively little hard economic analysis was published. Columns written about the market generally portrayed stock price movements in highly personal terms, as clashes between bull and bear factions led by major market operators. Many poorly paid reporters actually supplemented their incomes by taking bribes from the very operators they reported on. A favorable or unfavorable newspaper story about a particular stock at just the right time could be quite helpful in furthering a manipulative scheme. Of course, the average investor, who was not privy to the secret deals between market operators, and between market operators and compliant journalists, was at a tremendous disadvantage.

If Harriman was concerned about the rumored raid on his own Union Pacific, he did not show it. In a way, the rumors helped him, by distracting attention from his play for Northern Pacific. Schiff continued to buy Northern Pacific stock carefully, but as the month of April wore on, the price rise in the common shares accelerated. On May 1 it hit 115.

Ironically, the first man outside the Harriman syndicate to suspect anything untoward was James Hill, three thousand miles away from Wall Street in the Pacific Northwest. Suspicious of the activity in Northern Pacific stock, and hearing that Jacob Schiff's Kuhn, Loeb & Company was somehow involved, he immediately ordered a special train to rush him across the country to New York on tracks cleared in advance. Arriving on Wall Street on May 3, he went directly to Kuhn, Loeb & Company to confront Schiff.

The meeting did nothing to calm Hill's fears. Instead, Hill was angry and apprehensive when he left Schiff's office, hurrying the short distance to J. P. Morgan & Company. The Great Man himself was in Europe, but Hill vented his displeasure on any other Morgan partner he could find. How could the premier investment banking house on the Street have been caught so unawares?

The pace of events quickened. Schiff, surprised by Hill's visit, immediately contacted Harriman. He assured Harriman that even though their secret was now out, they were still in a very good position. Although they owned only 370,000 shares of Northern Pacific common (slightly less than a majority of the 800,000 outstanding), they did own a majority of the preferred, and, most important, a majority of the two classes of stock combined. Schiff was certain Hill and Morgan could do nothing to thwart their plan. Harriman was not so sure.

That night Harriman felt sharp pains in his abdomen that would soon be diagnosed as symptoms of appendicitis. Even as he suffered the physical pain, however, he could not help worrying about his Northern Pacific campaign. True, he and his allies controlled a majority of all voting stock outstanding (common and preferred together). But he knew that the preferred could be legally retired on January 1 of each year by a decision of the common stockholders. Just conceivably, if the Hill-Morgan group could obtain a narrow majority of the common, they could then vote to retire the preferred and retain majority control of the company.

Harriman did not want to leave anything to chance. On Saturday, May 4, he sent orders from his sickbed to Schiff, instructing him to buy an additional 40,000 shares of common in the short Saturday trading session. That amount would give them a clear majority of the common outstanding and clinch control of the Northern Pacific. Only then could they be absolutely certain they had won.

Unfortunately, Harriman had not counted on divine intervention, in the form of the Jewish Sabbath, to obstruct his plans. When Harriman's urgent instructions reached Jacob Schiff, he was worshiping in his synagogue and refused to act on them. He would not do business on the Sabbath and, frankly, didn't consider it necessary anyway. He was quite confident that Harriman's syndicate had won control of the Northern Pacific; any details that remained to be resolved could be dealt with on Monday morning.

James Hill scrambled to recoup his position. A hasty calculation showed that his group held only 260,000 shares of Northern Pacific common stock. Hill pressed Robert Bacon, the senior partner left in charge in New York in Morgan's absence, to cable Morgan in Europe, requesting permission to buy 150,000 additional shares, enough to secure a majority. The cable was sent; Morgan responded in the affirmative, and the war was on.

The Street was completely unaware of the impending Northern Pacific struggle. Instead, the press continued to focus on rumors of a Vanderbilt raid on Harriman's Union Pacific. *The New York Times* reported that a Vanderbilt-led takeover was inevitable, stating bluntly that "nothing but a panic can avert this end."

As brokers and traders arrived at their offices on Monday morning, May 6, most expected that the day's action would be in Union Pacific, not Northern Pacific. Little notice was taken of the Morgan forces girding for battle. James Keene, Morgan's chief broker after his successful efforts in U.S. Steel, established his headquarters in the office of an independent broker, so as to hide the Morgan connection. From there he would send orders to other brokers who would not be identified with J. P. Morgan & Company. Keene faced a difficult task; he was required to buy stock as quickly as possible without betraying his intent.

Jacob Schiff, prodded by Edward Harriman, also assembled his forces that Monday morning, although his task was seemingly much easier than that facing the Hill-Morgan faction. Fewer than 40,000 shares would be required to give Harriman a clear majority of Union Pacific common. Schiff proposed to buy it quickly and be done with it.

The market as a whole opened higher on heavy volume. At first, the activity in Northern Pacific was not unusual. Both the Morgan and the Kuhn, Loeb forces sought to disguise their intent by both buying and selling, never forcing the price up too quickly. But inevitably, as the day wore on, the price jumped. By midafternoon it hit $125 per share, up $15 on the day.

The sharp run-up in Northern Pacific began to attract attention. Even though the entire market was strong, the gains in Northern Pacific seemed excessive. Many short-sellers appeared, seeking to take advantage of the high prices, betting that Northern Pacific would soon fall back to more reasonable levels. Most likely, as the afternoon progressed, much of the selling in the stock came from these "shorts."[6] But the shares continued to move higher under relentless accumulation, closing the day at 127½.

The Morgan forces transacted more than 200,000 shares of Northern Pacific that day, which would have been more than sufficient for control if all their trades had been purchases. But because they had often been required to sell stock to hold down the price, they were still well short of a majority. Schiff and his brokers, however, apparently thought they had finally bought enough to secure control.

On Tuesday, May 7, the Morgan brokers again entered the market. The supply of available stock was very thin and the price rose rapidly. More short-sellers sold stock, with the Morgan brokers snatching everything offered. The shares closed the day at 143½, up $16.

When totaling their purchases after the close of business, the Morgan brokers calculated that they finally owned a majority of the common shares outstanding. They were not aware that the Schiff forces also thought they had a majority. The seeming anomaly resulted because many of the shares both sides had purchased during the previous two days had been sold short to them. The short-sellers did not actually own the stock they had sold; they planned to borrow the shares necessary to make good on their sales, with the intention that they would later buy the stock back cheaper in the market. In effect, the stock sold by the short-sellers did not exist. When later called upon to actually deliver the shares to the buyers, the "shorts" would be unable to do so. No one realized it Tuesday night, but a fuse had been lit that would soon touch off an explosion of unprecedented violence.

Northern Pacific traded sharply higher Wednesday morning, even though neither Morgan nor Schiff brokers were buying. The short-sellers began to realize that they could not borrow any stock to cover their original sales and frantically tried to buy back the shares on the Exchange. Rumors of the Hill-Harriman contest to control the Northern Pacific circulated freely, eclipsing the now discredited rumors of a Vanderbilt raid on the Union Pacific. A "corner" of Northern Pacific existed, but it was very different from previous corners. In the past, corners had been created by speculators seeking to profit specifically by trapping unwary short-sellers. Those who had cornered the stock would negotiate a settlement allowing the shorts to buy back the stock they owed; then the losers and winners would settle up and go on to speculate again. But in the Northern Pacific "corner," the stock was owned not by speculators but instead by groups contending for control of the company, who needed every share if they were to achieve their majority. They had no intention of selling any stock to the shorts, regardless of price. Northern Pacific closed Wednesday at 160, rising $23 on the day.

From the opening Thursday morning it shot straight up, trading, incredibly, at 320, then 700, and eventually 1,000. There was virtually no stock available, yet the short-sellers had to buy stock back to fulfill their contracts or be ruined. As *The New York Times* described it, "The thing was so sudden that conservative men lost their heads, and language was heard from reputable churchgoing members of society that would not bear repetition under ordinary circumstances in a barroom of even the second class." The shorts scrambled madly for any shares that could be had. Upon hearing that a few hundred shares were available in Buffalo, a desperate speculator hired a special train to bring the stock quickly to New York.[7]

The panic spread to other stocks, but in reverse, with heavy selling pounding down prices as the Northern Pacific short-sellers were forced to liquidate their other holdings to raise money. The *Times* described the scene: "When the full impact of [the Northern Pacific] quotation was realized, a roar akin to a hurricane arose, and all effort to preserve anything like order was abandoned . . . Brokers acted like insane men . . . Big men lightly threw little men aside, and little men, fairly crying with indignation, jumped anew into the fray, using hands and arms, elbows, feet—anything to gain their point . . . To spectators . . . it was something incomprehensible, almost demonic—this struggle, this Babel of voices, these wild-eyed excited brokers." At one point mammoth U.S. Steel, which had started the week near $40, fell to $24. Hundreds of millions of dollars were lost and a wave of bankruptcies resulted. Rumors of suicides were common; that afternoon, a Troy, New York, businessman, facing ruin in the market, killed himself by jumping into a vat of hot beer.

Both J. P. Morgan & Company and Kuhn, Loeb recognized that quick action was necessary to stem the panic, before it engulfed and destroyed their other interests. Neither had anticipated the extent of the debacle their actions would inflict on the Street. They quickly conferred and agreed that the best solution would be to temporarily put aside their struggle for Northern Pacific and instead lend out Northern Pacific shares to the short-sellers, enabling them to fulfill their contracts.

Al Stern, a broker for Kuhn, Loeb, was the first man to reach the floor of the New York Stock Exchange with the news. He forced his way through the crowd to the post where Northern Pacific was traded and shouted, "Who wants to borrow Northern Pacific? I have a block to lend."

A thunderous roar erupted as a mob of brokers grabbed for Stern, shoving, pummeling, and gouging in frantic attempts to get to him. Several men fell to the floor, desperately scrambling over each other. One broker pulled off his hat and repeatedly hit Stern over the head with it to get his attention. Stern, known as one of the best dressed men on Wall Street, hastily beat a retreat, his elegant suit in tatters.[8]

In spite of Al Stern's travails, his message was received by the Street. The shorts withdrew their bids, allowing Northern Pacific common to fall back, closing at 325. It was still up 165 for the day, but down 675 from its high. Fewer than 12,000 shares actually traded. Other stocks recovered from their lows, but the damage had been done.

Reporters sought out the principals in the Northern Pacific struggle, seeking an explanation for the chaotic events. A stunned James Hill, far more experienced in operating railroads than in speculating on Wall Street, responded by comparing the scene to what he called an Indian ghost dance:

The Indians begin their dance and don't know why they are doing it. They whirl about until they are almost crazy. It is so when these Wall Street people get the speculative fever. Perhaps they imagine they have a motive in that they see two sets of powerful interests which may be said to be clashing. Then these outsiders, without rhyme or reason, rush in on one side or the other. They could not tell you why they

*make their choice, but in they go, and the result is such as has been
seen here for the past few days.*[9]

Hill disclaimed responsibility for the fiasco, stating, "The truth is, that
I have been engaged in no fight—although there are some people who have
been throwing stones into my yard."[10] Later, speculating on the motives of
those who supported Harriman, he commented, "I am sure that the main
motive was truly expressed by [those] who said that they would show the
world that Morgan was not the only banker in America . . . and that all
other banking houses were nothing more than his clerks . . ."[11] Hill went
further in private; three years later, in a letter to a friend, he wrote, "All
they [Harriman and his allies] want to make them crooked is the opportunity to cheat somebody."[12]

J. P. Morgan was forced to cut short his European vacation, traveling
instead to his firm's Paris office. He was in a bad humor, and when ac-
costed by a crowd of reporters he barked at them, allegedly threatening to
"kill" one man who was in his way. An American journalist shouted out a
question: "Don't you think that since you are being blamed for a panic that
has ruined thousands of people and disturbed a whole nation, some statement is due to the public?"[13]

In response, Morgan is said to have growled, "I owe the public nothing." Much like William Vanderbilt's oft-quoted remark, "The public be
damned," Morgan's words would repeatedly be used against him in the increasingly important arena of public opinion. Morgan's most recent biographer, Jean Strouse, casts doubt on the authenticity of this account,
questioning whether Morgan actually uttered these words. But perception
mattered more than reality. Accurate or not, reports of Morgan's comment
were widely believed.

Most major newspapers lambasted Wall Street brokers and bankers.
The New York Times criticized Wall Streeters for "behaving like cowboys
on a spree . . . shooting wildly at each other in entire disregard of the safety
of bystanders." However, the performance of the press itself in the affair
was far from exemplary. Right up to the moment the Northern Pacific
"corner" exploded into reality, the newspapers completely missed the true
story, instead speculating about an entirely illusory raid by William Vanderbilt on the Union Pacific. Vanderbilt was actually out of the country at

the time, only returning from Europe on the afternoon of May 9, at the height of the panic. As he disembarked from his ship, reporters asked him for his opinion of the day's events on Wall Street. He described those events with one word: "Silly."[14]

Strong rumors do not arise out of thin air; it is likely that the Vanderbilt story was planted by someone seeking to gain advantage from it. Perhaps independent players in Union Pacific wanted to force the stock higher for their own speculative purposes. Or perhaps one of the factions in the Northern Pacific struggle planted the story, thinking it would somehow aid their cause. Whatever the case, the press was sent off on a wild-goose chase by the anonymous rumormongers. It seems the Northern Pacific factions were not the only ones "shooting wildly."

The day after stock was made available to the squeezed short-sellers, the market returned to something resembling normality. Northern Pacific fell back to 150, and most other stocks recovered their losses. Setting aside a number of bankruptcies and suicides, it was almost as if nothing had happened. But the battle for Northern Pacific remained to be decided. Both sides now recognized that some sort of compromise would be required.

Harriman, recovering from his appendectomy, initiated negotiations. On May 31 a solution was announced. Morgan would designate men to be elected to the Northern Pacific board of directors, with the understanding that he would name Harriman and two individuals friendly to Harriman to that board. Union Pacific interests would also gain representation on the board of the Chicago, Burlington, and Quincy, and the Union Pacific would gain trackage rights on some Northern Pacific lines. Morgan and Harriman were required to swallow their dislike for each other to reach the settlement, but ultimately business necessity outweighed personal animus.

James Hill then advanced a proposal designed to solidify the new management structure and prevent any unwanted market raids in the future. He proposed that a large holding company be created that would own all the Hill-Morgan northwestern railroad interests. To be called the Northern Securities Company, it would be capitalized at $400 million and thus be too large to fall victim to any hostile takeover attempt. Morgan agreed, and the new company was duly chartered. All the principals viewed the new entity simply as another large trust, like so many others being formed in huge mergers around the turn of the century. But they underestimated the depth of public outrage resulting from the Northern Pacific fiasco on Wall Street. They would soon confront a different adversary, one that posed a far greater threat than the Little Giant Harriman and his Union Pacific—the United States government.

On September 6, 1901, President William McKinley was shot in an assassination attempt. One week later he died of his wounds. Wall Street was uneasy about the new President, Theodore Roosevelt, called by some a "wild man" and "that damned cowboy."[15] In his first message to Congress, Roosevelt voiced his disapproval of speculators who sought gain not by honest work but by "gambling." He was critical of the chaos caused by Harriman's raid on Northern Pacific, and hinted opposition to the formation of Northern Securities.

Shortly thereafter, Roosevelt decided to attack the Northern Securities Company head-on, using the rarely enforced Sherman Antitrust Law of 1890. He kept his decision secret from all in his cabinet except Attorney General Philander C. Knox, apparently fearing that some cabinet members might inform Morgan.[16] The decision to prosecute was officially announced on February 19, 1902; Morgan received the news while dining with his wife and a few friends. Flushed red, his hands shaking, he angrily denounced Roosevelt to his guests. The public announcement of the action, without advance notice or an opportunity to work out a compromise, was an infuriating affront. It was not the way the Great Man was accustomed to being treated. "And I regarded him as a gentleman," Morgan commented sarcastically.[17]

The stock market sold off on the news, but other observers, such as Henry Adams, were openly exultant. Adams wrote that President Roosevelt, "without warning . . . hit Pierpont Morgan, the whole railway interest, and the whole Wall Street connection, a tremendous whack square on the nose. The wicked don't want to quarrel with him, but they don't like being hit that way . . . The Wall Street people are in an ulcerated state of inflammation."[18] (Adams's references to a "whack square on the nose" and "an ulcerated state of inflammation" could not have been accidental; for years Morgan had suffered from a rare skin condition, acne rosacea, which scarred and deformed his nose, causing it to swell grotesquely. Morgan was quite embarrassed by the condition. Adams's remarks could not have been better calculated to infuriate him.)

Morgan arranged a personal meeting with the President, to voice his objections to what he viewed as unfair treatment. The contrast between the two men was striking. Roosevelt, of smaller stature than Morgan, was possessed of tremendous physical energy; he could rarely sit still, often pacing back and forth in important meetings. Morgan, older and much heavier, moved slowly, with an almost august presence. In the truest sense it was the collision of an irresistible force with an immovable object.

Morgan complained to the President that he should have been warned of the action against Northern Securities. Roosevelt responded bluntly, "That is just what we did not want to do." Unable or unwilling to recognize Roosevelt's purpose, Morgan offered a proposal that to him must have seemed perfectly straightforward. He said, "If we have done anything wrong, send your man to my man and they can fix it up." The President stated simply, "We do not want to fix it. We want to stop it."[19]

Roosevelt's "man" to whom Morgan referred was apparently the Attorney General. Morgan was suggesting that the Attorney General go to New York and work out the details of the dispute with Morgan's lawyers, much as lawyers representing parties in any contract dispute would get together and reach a compromise. To Roosevelt, Morgan's attitude was "a most illuminating illustration of the Wall Street point of view," as the President later remarked to Attorney General Knox. He went on to observe that Morgan apparently regarded him, and the United States government, "as a rival operator, who either intended to ruin all his interests or else could be induced to come to an agreement to ruin none."[20]

Northern Securities lawyers contested the government's antitrust case all the way to the Supreme Court, where, two years later, the government finally won by a 5–4 vote. The landmark decision served notice that big business could no longer operate in a vacuum, free from the restraints of government and public opinion. What had started as a struggle between two Wall Street operators for control of a railroad developed into a precedent-setting case that helped establish government antitrust policy for decades to come.

But what of the stock market itself? More than any other incident, the Northern Pacific panic starkly portrays the true nature of the market in 1901. The American stock market was not the *efficient* mechanism for allocating equity capital that today's economic textbooks describe, with prices set by the impersonal interaction of supply and demand. Instead it often became a battlefield on which highly personalized conflicts between financial titans such as Hill, Harriman, and Morgan, as well as dozens of lesser combatants, were played out. The consequences for individual investors caught by accident in the resulting maelstroms could be quite severe. For those unlucky "outsiders," the stock market in 1901 was a very risky place indeed.

As a parody of public sentiment, *Life* magazine published an imaginary dialogue between a teacher and student:

TEACHER:

Who made the world, Charles?

STUDENT:

God made the world in 4004 B.C., but it was reorganized in 1901 by James J. Hill, J. Pierpont Morgan, and John D. Rockefeller.[21]

3
LENDER OF LAST RESORT

JOHN PIERPONT MORGAN rose from his seat to sing "O Zion, Haste, Thy Mission High Fulfilling." It was one of his favorite hymns, and he belted it out in a deep bullfrog voice. Gradually his fellow delegates to the Triennial Convention of the Episcopal Church in Richmond, Virginia, joined in. It was October 1907, and the convention had been rent asunder by a bitter dispute. As always, Morgan spoke for moderation and compromise whenever possible. He sought to bring the contending factions together, seeking cooperation, not confrontation, much as he did in the world of finance. The other delegates appeared to respond to his gesture; by the time the echoes of the last "Amen" died away, harmony seemed to have been at least temporarily restored.

Morgan was 70 years old and semi-retired. He had spent most of the summer touring Europe and was now as much concerned with religious matters and his art collection as with Wall Street. But he could not escape the Street's problems. With increasing frequency, telegrams arrived in Richmond from the New York office of J. P. Morgan & Company. Stock prices had been sliding lower for most of the year; the markets were uncertain, uneasy. Morgan sensed trouble but was not really sure what to do about it.

Business conditions appeared to be good. The economy was growing rapidly, and that growth seemed likely to continue for the foreseeable future. Granted, the administration of Theodore Roosevelt had attacked major trusts, with the President calling the gigantic corporations subjects

Dow Jones Industrial Average, 1896–1909

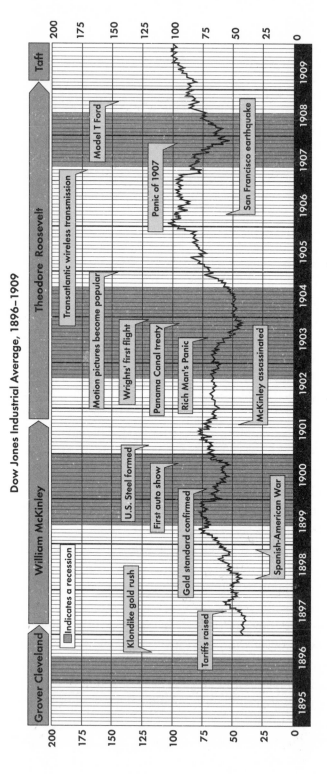

Grover Cleveland | William McKinley | Theodore Roosevelt | Taft

■ Indicates a recession

Klondike gold rush

Tariffs raised

Gold standard confirmed

U.S. Steel formed

First auto show

Spanish-American War

McKinley assassinated

Rich Man's Panic

Panama Canal treaty

Wrights' first flight

Motion pictures become popular

Transatlantic wireless transmission

Model T Ford

Panic of 1907

San Francisco earthquake

1895 1896 1897 1898 1899 1900 1901 1902 1903 1904 1905 1906 1907 1908 1909

0 25 50 75 100 125 150 175 200

© *Dow Jones & Company Inc.*

without a sovereign. The Justice Department had brought antitrust indictments against the biggest trust of all—the Rockefeller-dominated Standard Oil Company—as well as the sugar and tobacco trusts and E. H. Harriman's Union Pacific. But Roosevelt had not proved to be the dangerous radical that many on Wall Street had feared. In fact, Morgan and most of the Street had supported him in his reelection campaign in 1904. The country continued "to enjoy a literally unprecedented prosperity." Why then were the markets so nervous?[1]

Money was tight in the fall of 1907. The world economy was growing faster than the supply of gold, which, since most major nations were on the gold standard, determined the supply of money. Wall Street had also been sucking in huge amounts of capital, both to finance the creation of the new trusts and for speculation. For well over a year, warnings had been voiced of a crisis to come if the monetary stringency was not relieved. Kuhn, Loeb's Jacob Schiff cautioned, "If the currency conditions of this country are not changed materially . . . you will have such a panic . . . as will make all previous panics look like child's play." James J. Hill warned of a "commercial paralysis" that would result if the supply of capital did not keep pace with the expanding economy.[2]

Rarely do financial panics arrive when they are expected; almost by definition, a market crash must come as a surprise and shock to most of the players. The panic of 1907 could have been triggered by any one of a number of incidents. But the essential elements of the crisis were distressingly similar to most of the panics of the nineteenth century: a key bank or broker fails because of financial chicanery or imprudent speculation, setting off a chain reaction of other business failures, a rapid contraction of available credit, and a collapse in stock prices. Although the specific players involved in each instance are different, the results are usually the same.

The crisis of October 1907 was instigated by the machinations of Frederick Augustus Heinze, a Brooklyn native of Irish and German-Jewish extraction, who had emigrated to Montana at 18, making his fortune in the rough-and-tumble mining industry. An energetic man possessing great physical strength, Heinze was described as having "the torso of a Yale halfback, lighted up with a pair of large blue eyes."[3] He fought a bitter battle against Amalgamated Copper, the new copper trust, eventually forcing Amalgamated to buy him out for the inflated price of $10.5 million.

Heinze might have faded into comfortable obscurity, but he was determined to take his hard-won money to speculate on Wall Street. Perhaps emboldened by his success in Montana, Heinze was not content to play the game on the Street with his $10 million; he required much more capital to realize his ambitions. He set out looking for allies and soon found one in the person of Charles W. Morse. Morse was a short, barrel-shaped man who had worked his way through Bowdoin College by getting paid a clerk's salary in his father's company and then hiring another man to do the actual work for less money.[4] Morse had merged many small suppliers of ice to form one large entity, the American Ice Company. He hoped to create an ice trust. The project, however, fell short of expectations, and by 1906 Morse was looking for other opportunities. Heinze soon convinced him that copper was a promising alternative.

Morse, through his other activities, had already acquired control of the Bank of North America. Despite its name, the bank was not among the larger institutions in New York, but it provided a base from which Morse and Heinze could operate. The two men moved quickly, using Bank of North America money to purchase control of the Mercantile National Bank, and then using Mercantile assets to acquire control of Knickerbocker Trust Company. The resources of these institutions would be used to finance copper speculations.

Trust companies such as Knickerbocker existed as entities separate and distinct from banks because of a quirk in New York State law that prohibited commercial banks from handling estates and administering trusts held for the benefit of others. Trust companies were organized to provide these services and were originally intended to be conservative institutions making long-range investments. Unfortunately, the law was poorly drawn and effectively allowed trust companies to engage in activities similar to those of banks without being subject to the same restrictions as banks. Much like many savings and loans in the 1980s, trust companies soon began to be used as speculative vehicles by those who controlled them. Knickerbocker Trust was to become one of the worst.

Knickerbocker was a good-sized institution, with assets of $65 million and eighteen thousand depositors. Its president, Charles T. Barney, was himself not averse to making speculative investments with the company's assets. He quickly fell in line with the new owners. Knickerbocker money helped finance a new Heinze-Morse venture, United Copper, which was capitalized at $80 million, selling stock in a public offering in early 1907. With their control of Knickerbocker Trust and United Copper in place, Heinze and Morse were prepared to make their fortunes on the Street.

Their scheme was not new—they set out to corner the stock in the newly created United Copper and squeeze any short-sellers foolish enough to be caught in the trap. But on Tuesday, October 15, something went badly wrong. The price of United Copper collapsed. Heinze and Morse were in trouble; banks financing their holdings demanded more collateral. Heinze and Morse struggled to come up with the money but were unable to do so. They would be forced to sell their United Copper stock.

The next day United Copper plummeted, costing Heinze and Morse millions. Even worse, the financial institutions they controlled were now in grave jeopardy. Rumors circulated that Mercantile National Bank funds had been lost in United Copper, jeopardizing the bank's financial position. Since no form of deposit insurance existed at the time, rumors of this type were taken quite seriously by depositors, who could lose their money if a bank failed. Worried depositors rushed to withdraw funds from Mercantile National, starting a run on the bank. It soon became apparent that Mercantile would not be able to meet the unexpected demand for cash. On Friday, October 18, both Heinze and Morse resigned their positions at the bank, but not soon enough to save it. Mercantile was forced to close its doors.

When J. P. Morgan, still in Richmond, was informed of the United Copper crash and the Mercantile Bank failure, he deemed the events serious enough to hasten his return to New York. Upon reaching Manhattan, Morgan immediately went to confer with associates in the new library he had built next to his house on East Thirty-sixth Street. They met in the West Room, a comfortable study furnished with plush, dark red couches and armchairs, crimson damask wallpaper, stained-glass windows, and a high, parqueted ceiling. Along the walls stood lead-lined glass bookcases, and above the bookcases hung masterpieces from Morgan's art collection. The trappings of tradition and prestige associated with the House of Morgan were everywhere. The men gathered in the study quickly brought Morgan up to date; their reports on the state of the New York banks and trust companies were ominous indeed. Once he had digested the facts, the

Great Man sent his advisers away. He sat alone by the fire, smoking a cigar, playing solitaire, and considering his options.[5]

Morgan's instincts and experience told him that he confronted a very serious crisis. There would almost certainly be more bank and trust company failures in the coming days; the question was how best to contain the resulting panic. Morgan cared nothing for United Copper or Knickerbocker Trust. He was determined, however, that the manipulations of a few speculators not be allowed to tear apart the essential core of the banking system, if he could prevent it.

Sunday evening a steady procession of leading Wall Street figures filed into the Morgan library. Bankers from strong institutions pledged to support weaker ones, subject to Morgan's direction. The secretary of the treasury, who had hurried to New York from Washington, announced that the federal government would deposit an additional $6 million in New York banks and that more would be forthcoming if Morgan deemed it necessary. A pool of money was established, controlled by Morgan, to be used to provide aid to imperiled financial institutions. All parties, even the federal government itself, deferred to him. In the absence of a central bank of the United States, J. P. Morgan & Company had assumed the role of "lender of last resort."

There were some people whom the Great Man refused to see. Morgan consistently avoided E. H. Harriman; he had never really altered his opinion of Harriman after the Northern Pacific panic and was furthermore irritated to learn that the Day and Night Bank, a twenty-four-hour banking facility that Harriman controlled, was reportedly seeking to profit from the distress of endangered banking institutions by sending runners to solicit deposits from people lined up outside those institutions waiting to withdraw money. Morgan also refused to meet with President Charles Barney of the Knickerbocker Trust, suspecting correctly that Barney had been intimately involved in the Heinze-Morse speculations. His decision proved fateful; denied an audience with the Great Man, Barney resigned his position and later shot himself through the head.

The remaining Heinze-Morse interests were savaged when business on Wall Street resumed Monday. Shares of Morse's American Ice plummeted, and a run on Knickerbocker Trust developed. Even though Knickerbocker was the third largest trust company in New York, and even though the tainted Charles Barney had been replaced by a much more respectable chief executive, Morgan determined that the institution was too far gone to be salvaged. When Knickerbocker's request for assistance was turned down, rumors swept the Street that the trust company would soon be declared insolvent. It finally failed at two o'clock Tuesday afternoon. Far from stopping there, however, the contagion quickly spread to other trust companies. Suddenly, in the minds of fearful depositors, every trust company was unsafe.

By Wednesday morning, October 23, the situation was desperate. One of the largest trust companies, the Trust Company of America, was teetering on the brink of failure. Morgan and the Wall Street bankers could not ignore the threat posed to the rest of the banking system by the weakness of the trust sector. As Morgan partner George Perkins put it, "Indeed, we hadn't any use for their management and knew they ought to be closed, but we fought to keep them open in order not to have any runs on other concerns."[6]

Depositors were withdrawing money from the Trust Company of America at a fearsome pace. Morgan received periodic bulletins by telephone listing the amount of cash in the company's vaults; at 1 p.m. there was $1,200,000; at 1:20, $800,000; at 1:45, $500,000; by 2:15, only $180,000 was left. Aides from J. P. Morgan & Company had hastily examined the books of the company and agreed that it was fundamentally sound if it could survive the panic. Morgan listened to their evaluation, then nodded, stating firmly, "Then this is the place to stop the trouble."[7] He ordered that money from the bankers' pool be sent to the trust company. It barely arrived in time.

Unfortunately, each crisis that was stanched was quickly replaced by another. A massive run developed at another major trust company, Lincoln Trust. Money from the bankers' pool was quickly dispatched to save it. Worse, on Thursday a decline in stock prices on the New York Stock Exchange accelerated into a free fall. Markets in stocks virtually disintegrated; major stocks dropped ten points or more, often with no significant bids showing at any price. The president of the New York Stock Exchange, R. H. Thomas, hurried to Morgan's office, reporting that at least two dozen brokers faced failure unless $25 million could be made available in loans within the next 15 minutes. Thomas said that if the money was not forthcoming, he would be forced to close the Exchange. Morgan quickly called the leading bankers participating in his pool and was just able to raise the required money in time. When word of the emergency loan reached the Exchange, a roar went up that could be heard across the street in Morgan's Wall Street office. George Perkins later remarked that without "the whiff of oxygen" provided by the loan, "the Exchange and a hundred or more firms would have gone up."[8]

But even the Great Man could not work miracles. Morgan was rapidly exhausting the resources available to him. The U.S. Treasury had deposited an additional $35 million into New York banks; that money had quickly been loaned out and was unlikely to be followed by more funds from Washington. The public confidence upon which the banking system depended was fast eroding, as millions of dollars were pulled out by depositors. People sat outside troubled institutions overnight on folding chairs, crates, and blankets, seeking to be near the head of the line at the next morning's opening. Exhausted depositors sometimes paid young men to stand in line for them; in some cases, policemen gave out numbers to people to hold their places overnight. A Morgan confidant, Benjamin Strong of Banker's Trust, later described a long line of depositors outside an endangered trust company: "The consternation of the faces of the people in the line, many of them I knew, I shall never forget. I know . . . a sense of dejection and defeat which it is quite impossible for me to describe." The fear fed upon itself, and even J. P. Morgan began to doubt his ability to stop it.[9]

Far from slowing, the runs on trust companies worsened. In addition, more stockbrokers were threatened with failure and required emergency loans. On Friday, October 25, Morgan was forced to hastily assemble another loan for cash-strapped brokers. He pressed the banks for $15 million, but was able to raise only $13 million. They simply had no more money to lend. Morgan had pushed the banking system to its limits.

But where no real money existed, could not substitute money be created? Morgan and his advisers hit upon a stopgap measure first employed during the panic of 1884: "scrip" would be issued in lieu of cash, to be redeemed after the crisis was over. Morgan placed the full prestige of "the House of Morgan" behind the plan. Anyone who refused to accept the scrip would be implicitly questioning the integrity of J. P. Morgan himself. No one chose to do so.

That evening Morgan called in religious leaders and asked them to pray and to reassure their congregations on the Sabbath. Archbishop Farley himself led a special mass for businessmen. Beyond spiritual assistance, however, the financial community required cold, hard cash. Morgan knew that confidence must be restored if individuals were to be persuaded to put their savings back into the banks and trust companies. Although a number of smaller banks and trust companies had failed, so far no large institution other than Knickerbocker Trust had closed its doors. If Morgan and his colleagues could prevent a major failure, perhaps the panic could be confined and would eventually run its course.

The new week saw more runs, with both the Trust Company of America and Lincoln Trust still under siege. Stock prices continued to fall. It seemed as if every time one leak in the dike was plugged, another would appear someplace else. Money was so tight that there was no margin for error. Any entity, public or private, that was required to borrow in the normal course of its activities could suddenly find itself facing a crisis. Wall Street existed on borrowed money; as long as the monetary stringency continued, there would always be the risk of more failures.

By November 1, Morgan was determined to resolve the problem of the trust companies once and for all. Both the Trust Company of America and Lincoln Trust needed additional cash infusions to meet depositor withdrawals, and other, smaller trust companies faced similar problems. All the previous efforts to support the weak trust companies had been made by commercial bankers led by Morgan; the Great Man now decided that it was time the stronger trust companies provided the means to save themselves. A meeting of top officials from the major trust companies was set for Saturday, November 2, in Morgan's library. Morgan planned to put an ultimatum to the men who assembled: either they would contribute to a new pool of reserves large enough to save the weaker institutions or he would let them all fail.

Just as Morgan was preparing for the Saturday-night meeting, a new crisis threatened to disrupt all his hastily improvised efforts to achieve stability. The respected Wall Street firm of Moore & Schley reported that it would be unable to meet its obligations come Monday. Like many firms, Moore & Schley had borrowed heavily to finance its activities, expecting that the short-term loans could always be refinanced when necessary. Suddenly, like so many other firms, Moore & Schley found that in spite of its excellent reputation on the Street, there was no money available to "roll over" the loans. The partners faced the disastrous possibility that they would be forced to quickly liquidate their holdings in an extremely weak market. Another stock market collapse could easily result, and they knew that Moore & Schley would not survive it.

Two groups of financiers arrived at the Morgan library Saturday night. In the West Room, Morgan collected the chief executives of the major trust institutions, pressing them for contributions to his pool for the support of the weaker trust companies. In the East Room, he assembled leading commercial bankers to deal with the Moore & Schley crisis. After bluntly informing each group of the situation they faced and what action he proposed, Morgan retired to a small side office, where he smoked cigars and played solitaire. It would be a long night.

The trust company officials probably did not have time to admire the lavish surroundings of the library. In particular, there is no record that they took note of a sixteenth-century Flemish tapestry by William van Pannemaker that hung over them, *The Triumph of Avarice*, portraying one of the seven deadly sins. They made every effort to avoid agreeing to the plan Morgan demanded. They pleaded that they did not have the authority to commit the funds. They claimed that the plan was not prudent, and that it would only enable those institutions that had badly mismanaged their affairs to avoid the consequences of their actions. They objected that the contributions demanded of them were excessive. Much of the dialogue between the trust company officials and Morgan was carried out by means of notes carried back and forth by a Morgan aide. As the hours passed, Morgan became more disdainful of the excuses and evasions, often crumpling the notes in his hand and disgustedly tossing them into a wastebasket. He rejected all objections. He stated bluntly that if the emergency loan was not made, the "walls of the other [trust companies] might come crumbling down about their ears."[10] And he would do nothing further to prevent it.

To the bankers gathered in the East Room, Morgan proposed a straightforward solution to the Moore & Schley difficulties. Moore & Schley owned a controlling interest in the Tennessee Coal, Iron, and Railroad Company, which was pledged as collateral against loans. Given the unstable stock market, Moore & Schley's lenders were no longer willing to accept TC&I stock as collateral. Morgan recommended that U.S. Steel buy Moore & Schley's interest in TC&I in exchange for U.S. Steel bonds. Moore & Schley's lenders would undoubtedly accept Steel bonds as good collateral, thus resolving the problem.

The principals of Moore & Schley agreed to the deal, but one important objection was immediately raised by others present at the meeting. The Roosevelt administration up to that point had not challenged U.S. Steel on antitrust grounds, but an acquisition as large as that of Tennessee Coal and Iron would surely raise concern in Washington. If the government objected, the deal could not possibly be consummated in time to save Moore & Schley. Morgan reluctantly acknowledged the concern; he admitted he would have to determine Roosevelt's reaction before they proceeded.

The meeting of the commercial bankers in the East Room then broke up, to be resumed the following day. However, the trust company executives in the West Room were not so lucky. When one of them attempted to leave after midnight, he found that the massive bronze doors to the library had been locked. He was told that Morgan himself had the key.

Finally, at 4:45 a.m. on Sunday, the trust officials gave up and agreed to Morgan's plan. The Great Man entered the West Room with a document creating the emergency fund and presented it to the exhausted men. Waving his hand toward the paper, he said, "There you are, gentlemen." The gathered executives shifted uneasily, but no one stepped forward to sign. Morgan waited a few moments, then pressed his hand on the shoulder of the elderly president of Union Trust, Edward King, urging him forward. "There's the place, King," he said, pointing to the signature line, "and here's the pen." Morgan placed a handsome gold pen in King's hand. King signed, followed by the others.[11]

After a Sunday afternoon meeting on the Moore & Schley crisis, Morgan dispatched Elbert Gary and Henry Clay Frick of U.S. Steel to Washington to sound out President Roosevelt about the possible acquisition of TC&I by U.S. Steel. In an early-morning meeting on Monday, November 4, Gary and Frick presented a bleak picture, one in which the prospect of a Moore & Schley bankruptcy threatened to bring down the stock market and the banking system. The U.S. Steel–TC&I merger was the only viable solution, they argued.

Roosevelt, fearing the consequences of an uncontrolled panic as much as Morgan, quickly agreed to allow the merger, stating that he "would not advise against the proposed purchase."[12] Gary immediately telephoned the news to the offices of J. P. Morgan & Company in New York. Word reached the Stock Exchange only minutes before the scheduled opening at 10 a.m. The market rose dramatically that day.

The panic was finally over, and it was clear to everyone who had saved the day. J. P. Morgan's prestige was never higher than in the period immediately following the 1907 crisis. Irresponsible speculation by operators such as Frederick Heinze and Charles Morse, as well as the reckless behavior of many trust companies, had created the panic. J. P. Morgan, almost single-handedly, had stopped it. Morgan now ruled Wall Street. As Frederick Lewis Allen wrote in *The Lords of Creation*, "there was now one kingdom, and it was Morgan's."

Frederick Heinze soon left Wall Street and went back to more familiar territory in Montana. When he died in 1914 he was nearly broke. Charles Morse, convicted of malfeasance and misappropriation for his role in the management of the banks he had controlled, served a term in the Atlanta Federal Penitentiary. The 1907 panic, like those that had preceded it, exposed dangerous defects in the financial system. More and more, voices began to be heard urging some sort of governmental response to avoid a repetition of the crisis. Prominent Republican Senator Nelson W. Aldrich said, "Something has got to be done. We may not always have Pierpont Morgan with us to meet [another] banking crisis."[13]

Morgan himself did not disagree. His aide and son-in-law Herbert Satterlee summed up Morgan's attitude: "It was not a good pattern—no one knew that as well as he—but it was the pattern in which he had found it. From that moment he worked to make it better and less vulnerable in bad times or periods of overspeculation. He realized that it must be buttressed against disclosures of dishonesty or irregularity and consequent loss of prestige and the confidence of the public. Security should not rest on any one man."[14]

In the years following 1907, muckraking journalism and progressive politics took their toll on the public's perception of Morgan and Wall Street bankers and brokers. In 1912, Morgan and other leading financiers were summoned to testify before the Pujo Committee of the House of Representatives; the proceedings quickly took on the look of an inquisition. In response to questioning, Morgan said that while he did not approve of short-selling or speculation in the stock market, such practices were unavoidable if an active marketplace for stocks was to be maintained. The committee was much less willing than Morgan to condone the machinations of stock market operators. It concluded in its official report that "the facilities of the New York Stock Exchange are employed largely for transactions producing moral and economic waste and corruption." It was Alexander Hamilton's denunciation of "unprincipled gamblers" all over again.

John Pierpont Morgan died shortly after the Pujo hearings. His passing symbolized the end of an era. No one person could even begin to assume Morgan's position in the economy—only the federal government could hope to do so. Within weeks of Morgan's passing, the administration of the newly elected Democrat Woodrow Wilson began to assert the government's newfound role.

Perhaps the most significant reform enacted during the Wilson administration was legislation authorizing the Federal Reserve System. Designed to be the American central bank, disguised for political purposes as a system of regional banks ostensibly operated by private bankers, the Federal Reserve began operations in 1914. It was hoped that the new institution could better regulate the nation's money supply and banking system, and if necessary perform the role taken on by J. P. Morgan in the panic of 1907— acting as a lender of last resort to support endangered banks in a time of crisis. Wall Street professionals were cautiously optimistic; despite inevitable misgivings about governmental involvement in the economy, many recognized that if the new central bank could prevent the monetary instability that had so often been associated with stock market crashes in the past, the market would be on a much less risky footing. More than a few agreed with the words of the first governor of the Federal Reserve, Charles Hamilton, who predicted in his initial address that stock market panics "generated by distrust of our banking system" would be relegated to "the museum of antiquities."[15]

Most of the other Wilson reform initiatives were directed at tariff and antitrust issues having little direct bearing on the stock market. As it turned out, the Stock Exchange, and Wall Street brokers in general, were not greatly affected by the reform movement. The newly created Federal Trade Commission did require that corporations issue annual financial statements, but the New York Stock Exchange already mandated such reports, having finally eliminated the notorious Unlisted Department in 1910. The Pujo Committee had made specific recommendations for regulating the stock market, including the incorporation of stock exchanges so that they might be regulated, empowering the government to determine what percentage of a stock's purchase price could be borrowed by the purchaser (margin requirement), making manipulation illegal, and mandating federal supervision of new securities issues. However, none of these proposals were enacted. For the moment, at least, the Street seemed to have escaped unscathed.

The market itself languished directionless for much of 1914; average daily trading volume on the New York Stock Exchange in the first half of the year would be the lowest of the entire century. Then suddenly, in July 1914, events in a small country thousands of miles away shocked the market out of its doldrums. Very few people foresaw the coming worldwide conflagration. And no one could have predicted the surprising impact it would have on the stock market.

4
WAR

RARELY IN ECONOMIC history have external events, completely unan ticipated at the time, so radically affected the stock market as did the gunshots fired by a Serbian assassin in the summer of 1914. Those shots quickly exploded into a general European war. The burgeoning conflict, with direct American participation beginning in 1917, would cause government to intrude into the American economy as never before. War would touch off dramatic changes in the stock market; it would prove to be the instrument by which the market was altered in ways not even imagined by the reformers. Surprisingly, the war would create conditions that would reverse the negative image of Wall Street held by many Americans and lay the groundwork for vastly increased public investment in stocks.

The first reaction on Wall Street to the outbreak of war, however, was fear. The governors of the New York Stock Exchange passed a resolution to suspend trading indefinitely; the resolution was approved on a voice vote, without debate. For only the second time in its history (the other having occurred during the panic of 1873), the Exchange shut its doors.

There seemed to be good cause for concern. The market sold off sharply the day before the closing was announced, in near-panic conditions, as war became imminent. Conventional wisdom had it that European investors would rush to dump American securities in order to repatriate their funds at a time of crisis. Markets could collapse. Economist Irving Fischer declared that "this general depreciation of investment securi-

Dow Jones Industrial Average, 1910–1919

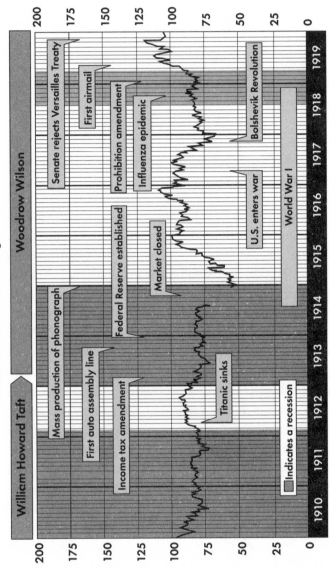

William Howard Taft

Woodrow Wilson

Mass production of phonograph

First auto assembly line

Income tax amendment

Federal Reserve established

Market closed

Titanic sinks

Senate rejects Versailles Treaty

First airmail

Prohibition amendment

Influenza epidemic

U.S. enters war

Bolshevik Revolution

World War I

Indicates a recession

1910 1911 1912 1913 1914 1915 1916 1917 1918 1919

0 25 50 75 100 125 150 175 200

ties will doubtless lead to many bankruptcies, if not a general crisis."[1] Of equal importance, a run on gold was anticipated; with the nation on the gold standard, foreigners had the right to demand gold in exchange for American currency, and appeared likely to do so. There might not be enough gold in the nation's banks to meet the sudden demand, thus imperiling the banking system. Prominent experts foresaw severe dislocations due to the closure of European markets to American exports and the disruption of imports of raw materials. All sorts of unpleasant scenarios were envisioned. Nothing like this had ever happened before, and the members of the Exchange were in no mood to take chances.

Seldom have so many experts proven so wrong. The war, and eventual American participation in the conflict, would have a dramatic impact on the economy, but not in the way the pessimists feared. While gold did flow out of the country in the first month after the war began, that flow soon reversed as foreign investors realized that the United States was in fact a haven, safe from the rapidly expanding conflict. Demand for American exports by the Allied powers, as well as by nonbelligerent nations, rose dramatically. A war boom was on, and the booming economy eventually took hold of the stock market. When New York Stock Exchange trading fully resumed in 1915, the market stabilized, then soared. The Dow Jones Average of Twenty Industrial Stocks rose from a low of 67.88 in 1915 to break 100 by the fall of 1916, cresting above 110 in late November.

Impressive as these gains were, however, they failed to keep pace with the spectacular growth in corporate earnings driven by wartime demand. For example, Du Pont's profits before bond interest had been $5.5 million in 1914, but jumped to $57 million in 1915, and $82 million in 1916. A leading shipping line, International Mercantile Marine, earned in 1915 a profit ten times greater than its average annual profit in the preceding decade. Bethlehem Steel saw earnings after depreciation go from $5.5 million in 1914 to $17 million in 1915 and $43 million in 1916. U.S. Steel, which actually lost money in 1914, experienced an increase in earnings per share to $9.96 in 1915, then to a staggering $48.46 in 1916.

Because earnings grew so rapidly, P/E ratios declined, even though stock prices rose. (The denominator of the P/E ratio, earnings, rose faster than the numerator, stock prices.) The composite P/E ratio for the New York Stock Exchange industrials, which had averaged approximately 11 to

1 over the preceding five years, fell to 7.42 to 1 in 1915, and to an all-time low of slightly over 4 to 1 in 1916.[2] *The Commercial and Financial Chronicle* reminded readers that the boom in war stocks was not "based on an enduring condition." Most investors seemed to agree.

Periodic "peace" rumors caused sudden sell-offs in the market as investors feared the war boom might be abruptly terminated. Perhaps the most famous (or infamous) peace rumor was circulated in December 1916 and became the source of a scandal involving two established market operators, Bernard Baruch and Jesse Livermore.

Baruch and Livermore were probably the most famous stock market traders in the early decades of the twentieth century. They could not have been more different. Baruch, a tall man with a patrician appearance, was the consummate insider. He had attained a partnership in an eminently respectable investment banking firm at an early age and later served as a governor of the New York Stock Exchange. He went on to hold a number of influential government positions, directly advising several Presidents. Livermore, on the other hand, was an outsider much like the notorious nineteenth-century cattle drover–turned–Wall Street operator Daniel Drew, of "watered stock" fame. (Livermore was often called Daniel Drew's successor.) Both Baruch and Livermore achieved successes in the market using tactics that would be illegal today. Baruch often profited by trading on inside information provided by his countless contacts, while Livermore, less well connected, was frequently forced to resort to heavy-handed manipulations. Baruch usually managed to avoid stepping across the poorly defined line between what was considered to be ethical behavior versus unethical behavior; Livermore seemed unaware such a line existed.

On December 20, 1916, while attempting to evade his New York–based creditors, Livermore was enjoying the balmy weather of Palm Beach, Florida. Apparently by chance, while idly observing the action of the markets from a local brokerage office, he received advance word of a diplomatic message President Woodrow Wilson was to send that evening. The gist of the leak was that Wilson planned to make a public plea to the warring European nations to cease hostilities and seek a negotiated end to the war. Livermore, as the story goes, instantly recognized the impact such a development would have on the stock market. He immediately contacted brokers in New York, instructing them to sell short stocks aggressively.[3]

Baruch was already heavily short the market, although his trading was entirely unrelated to Livermore's. The following day, after the story behind the leak had been confirmed, stock prices fell precipitously. As *The Wall Street Journal* put it, "Prices melted like the snows of the Pacific Northwest before the Chinook wind."

Among the big losers was Thomas Lawson, a part-time author and unsuccessful speculator. Lawson happened to be heavily invested in stocks when the peace rumor market break occurred; he cried foul, claiming that short-selling market operators had profited from improperly obtained official information. In his customarily lurid style, he declared, "The good old Capitol has been wallowing in Wall Street leak graft for forty years, wallowing hale and hearty."[4]

Lawson already bore a grudge against Livermore, resulting from a business dispute a decade earlier. He thus made the most of his opportunity to accuse Livermore of wrongdoing in the leak scandal. But he also singled out Bernard Baruch. Baruch could not afford the negative publicity, having taken on an official public role after his appointment by President Wilson to an advisory commission for the Council of National Defense. Baruch was chagrined to find himself denounced on the floor of the House of Representatives by a congressman who stated, "The rumor is that Mr. Barney M. Baruch . . . was the man responsible for this information getting to Wall Street, and that thirty minutes before the President's message was made public, he sold, on a rising market . . . fifteen thousand shares of Steel common short."[5]

These sensational charges led to an official congressional investigation, but nothing much came from the proceedings. It turned out that the source of the leak had been White House reporter William W. Price, who moonlighted as a stringer for several brokerage firms, including the firm that Livermore traded through in Florida. Price, along with the rest of the White House press corps, had been made aware of the Wilson peace move in advance but had been sworn to secrecy. Either intentionally or inadvertently, however, Price had sent out the story to his brokerage house clients before the scheduled time of release. Livermore acted on the information; it is not clear Baruch was even aware of it.

The reaction of the press to the peace rumor scandal is instructive. The boom psychology of the market seemed to have infected the news media, dissipating the harshly critical sentiments so common in the earlier muck-raking era. Livermore and Baruch, far from being condemned for profiting from improperly released information, actually received accolades in the financial press. *The New York Times* was seduced by the pair of speculators, describing them as representative of a "new breed of trader . . . more of a student and economist than the sensational manipulator of other years . . ." Specifically discussing Livermore's willingness to short the market (albeit using leaked inside information), the *Times*'s panegyrics continued: "He [Livermore] sensed the market tendency and stood unmoved amid a shower of optimistic utterances . . ."

There is no question that the war boom in stock prices, and favorable press coverage of the likes of Baruch and Livermore, enhanced public interest in the market. Reports of sensational market gains became front-page news for the first time since the early years of the century. Newspaper stories told of a broker who had staked everything on shares of Electric Boat and was now worth $500,000, and of a man who had bought 1,000 shares of Bethlehem Steel at 18 for his baby and now thought it was worth $364,000.[6] In addition to such anecdotal accounts, however, there was solid statistical evidence of increased public interest in the market.

This hard evidence came from data compiled by the Treasury Department from income tax returns filed under the new income tax law. Beginning in 1916, when the first data from tax returns became available, dividend income received by American taxpayers could be tabulated and analyzed. Since most stocks paid dividends, and since a taxpayer had to be a stockholder to receive dividends, counting the number of people who reported dividends on their tax returns became a means of estimating the number of people who owned stocks.

Subsequent studies derived from income tax data and other sources showed that two surprising developments occurred during the war years and the immediate postwar period. First, the number of Americans who owned shares rose dramatically, and second, the distribution of shareholding in the United States shifted significantly from higher-income to middle-income individuals. One of the scholars who compiled the data, Gardiner C. Means, wrote, "This represents a shift of almost revolutionary proportions, and of great social significance."[7]

Means was commenting on the first evidence of what would prove to be an enduring trend in the twentieth century—the democratization of the stock market. In 1917 people with annual incomes over $20,000 received 79% of all dividends; by 1921 the percentage of dividends received by these "high-income" individuals had fallen to 47%. Big increases in the share of dividend income were shown by taxpayers in the $1,000 to $5,000 income group; in 1917 this group had received 9.5% of all dividends, but by 1921 they took in almost 23%.[8]

Even though the aggregate dollar amount of dividends paid by corporations increased roughly 25% from 1917 to 1921, the dollar amount received by persons with annual incomes over $20,000 actually declined. This suggests that high-income people were divesting themselves of stocks over this period, while middle-income individuals were aggressively acquiring stocks. No other period of similar duration in the twentieth century shows such a startling shift.

Unfortunately, because only the wealthiest Americans were required to file tax returns, it is not possible to determine precisely from the income tax data how many Americans were actually shareholders at that time. Other estimates have been made from a different source—the shareholder records maintained by corporations. This method contains inevitable duplications; each corporation reports the number of people who own its shares, but there is no precise way of knowing how many of these stockholders also own shares in other corporations. Thus the total number of shareholders reported by all corporations (to the extent such a figure can be obtained or estimated) would overstate the actual number of people who own shares unless every stockholder owned shares in only one company. For example, if the average shareholder owned stock in two corporations, the total number of reported shareholders would overstate the actual number by a factor of two to one. If the average shareholder owned stock in four corporations, this method would overstate the total number of shareholders by a factor of four to one, and so on.

Given this limitation, it is useful to examine the data, if only to observe trends. When the United States formally entered the Great War in 1917, there were an estimated 8.6 million corporate shareholders in the United States (with no adjustment made for the double-counting problem). By 1922 that number had increased to 14.4 million, representing an 11% annual rate of increase. This rate of increase is more than twice as high as the rates that prevailed before 1917 and after 1921. Stock ownership surged from 1917 through 1921; the increase is even more astounding when it is remembered that stockholdings by upper-income individuals actually declined during this period.

The explanation of this phenomenon remains something of a mystery. Granted, the war boom and resulting favorable press coverage of the market undoubtedly attracted new investors. But there had been other such periods before (and would be again), in which the rate of increase in shareholding was much lower. Something other than a strong stock market and positive press coverage must have been responsible for the unique events of 1917–1921.

One plausible explanation advanced by scholars of the period is that the massive government Liberty Loan campaigns, designed to encourage Americans to buy the government bonds needed to finance the war, also introduced many people to the idea of owning securities, which in turn made them more receptive to investing in stocks. Four separate Liberty Bond issues were floated during the war, financing roughly two-thirds of the $32.8 billion the war cost the Treasury. (This staggering expenditure was twice the entire amount spent by the federal government from its creation in 1789 until 1917.) Intended to be a broad-based appeal to small investors, the Liberty Loan campaigns set up a network of Liberty Loan committees and were assisted by organizations ranging from local chambers of commerce to Boy and Girl Scout troops. In one campaign in 1918, twenty-four trains crisscrossed the country, staffed with soldiers and celebrities, to publicize the bond drive. Liberty Loan posters appeared everywhere and became something of a new form of art. Impassioned pleas were made in theaters and virtually all public forums. The loan campaigns were ubiquitous; they were also extremely successful.

The first campaign raised money from 4 million separate individuals. The second was subscribed to by 9.4 million, the third by nearly 18.4 million, and the fourth received support from almost 22.8 million.[9] Most of the subscribers had never invested in a bond, or any type of security, before. If only a relatively small fraction of these people also decided to take a flier in stocks, much of the large increase in shareholdings that occurred during this period can be accounted for.

One reason middle-class investors had the money to purchase both Liberty Bonds and stocks was that the war created an employment boom for wage earners, which also lessened income inequality. The National Bureau of Economic Research reported that the share of national income going to the top 5% of earners declined from 33% in 1913–1916 to about 25% in 1918–1919.[10] Nominal hourly wage rates (not adjusted for inflation) more than doubled between 1916 and 1920.

Another important reason new money was available for investments was that much more money was circulating in the economy during the war years. To keep interest rates low in the face of the massive financing needs of the government, the Federal Reserve pumped money into the banking system. This effort was successful in holding down the interest rates the government had to pay on the war debt; the huge Liberty Loan issues were floated at the very reasonable rates of 3½%, 4%, and 4¼%. Undoubtedly, the easy money policy had the unintended effect of making more funds available for stock investments as well.

Thus the booming economy, successive Liberty Bond campaigns, and an expansive Federal Reserve monetary policy seem to have induced many middle-class people who had never before invested in securities to become stockholders. But what of upper-income investors, who appear to have divested themselves of stocks at the same time? The explanation of their behavior is straightforward: the very high marginal rates of income taxation imposed during the war made income-producing corporate securities (such as bonds and dividend-paying stocks) unattractive to high-income individuals. They therefore sold stocks, investing either in tax-exempt securities (state and local bonds and some U.S. government bonds) or in other vehicles, such as real estate and life insurance policies, that were treated more favorably by the tax laws. When the high marginal tax rates began to come down after 1921, the shift out of stocks by upper-income individuals abruptly halted.

The Pujo Committee reformers had not "cleaned up" the game on Wall Street as they had wanted; the legislation the committee proposed had not been enacted, and abusive behavior by market insiders still occurred. But an important trend had been initiated by events entirely unrelated to the reformers' efforts, a trend toward much broader public participation in what had been essentially an insider's game. This democratization of the market would continue throughout the century, fundamentally reshaping the role the stock market played in the American economy.

Even as new investors flocked into the market, however, the New York Stock Exchange itself still operated like an exclusive club. Members usually came from the same social class, attended the same prep schools, and were graduates of Harvard, Yale, or Princeton. Ambitious outsiders could aspire to attain a position as a clerk with a Wall Street brokerage firm and occasionally, with the right patron, actually acquire a seat on the Exchange. But in general the doors at the top were closed.

Serano Pratt, himself a member of the Wall Street establishment, described the typical broker this way in *The Work of Wall Street*:

> *The broker is usually a gentleman and dresses and lives well . . . On the whole, brokers as a class compare well, mentally and morally, with other businessmen. They are always patriotic, if for no other motive than that of self-interest, for if the Government went down or suffered from domestic revolt or foreign invasion, the whole structure of Wall Street credits and values would collapse like a house of cards . . . The broker is proverbially generous. When he makes money, he spends it freely, and his contributions to charity are liberal.*

Whatever the moral characteristics of the typical broker, the financial community was still a world apart from the average American. Wall Street and Main Street did not intersect. The new money flowing into the market from middle-class investors still passed through mechanisms controlled by the old Wall Street elite. It would be many years before the "democratization" of market participants would begin to influence the institutional structure of the Street.

The war boom in stocks ended abruptly in late 1916 (roughly at the time of the so-called leak scandal). Stocks fell broadly throughout most of 1917, and by the end of that year the market was back to where it had been in July 1914, before the war began. All the gains of the war boom had been wiped out, even though the war was still very much on.

The action of the market was puzzling, to say the least. As Alexander Dana Noyes described it, "Easy money, and industrial activity wholly unparalleled in the country's history, were accompanied by financial markets such as in other days would have indicated financial panic."[11] Of all the possible explanations of this paradox, the high wartime tax rates imposed when the United States formally entered the war in 1917 seem the most plausible. It has already been shown how high marginal tax rates on individuals probably caused upper-income taxpayers to divest themselves of stocks. In addition, the heavy excess-profits taxes imposed on business had the effect of drastically reducing after-tax profits. Pretax profits were high, but the ability of corporations and investors to retain those profits after taxes was limited. The logical result was lower stock prices. P/E ratios remained remarkably low; in 1917 the composite P/E ratio for the New York Stock Exchange industrials was 4.57 to 1, and in 1918 only 6.3 to 1. Along with the all-time low P/E ratio of 4.04 to 1 in 1916, the ratios for 1917 and 1918 remain the lowest in the century.[12]

Stock prices (and P/E ratios) rebounded in 1919 as the postwar economy boomed, fed by unsatisfied consumer demand built up during the war. In early November, however, the stock market was hit with a rude shock. For the first time in its short history, the Federal Reserve slammed on the economic brakes. The central bank's expansionary monetary policy during the war had created an inflationary hangover, with consumer prices advancing at double-digit annual percentage rates. The rapid price increases were quite unsettling, in that inflation in the United States had been virtually unknown since the Civil War. Finally, on November 3, 1919, the Federal Reserve was forced to abandon its easy money policy, increasing its discount rate (the interest rate at which member banks could borrow from the system) from 4% to 4¾%. The days of easy credit and low interest rates were over.

The discount rate would eventually rise to 7%, forcing up other interest rates as well. In 1920, for the first time in history, the yield on long-term government bonds exceeded 5%. The impact on the stock market was devastating. As measured by the Dow Jones Industrials, the market fell 44% from its 1919 peak to its eventual bottom in 1921. The mechanism through which rising interest rates affected the market was quite simple. Since investors expected to receive dividends on stocks that were higher than the interest rates available on bonds (to compensate for the presumably higher risk of owning stocks), when interest rates rose, dividend rates were also required to rise. And since the dividend rate is simply the annual dividend per share paid by a company divided by the company's stock price, the only way the market could quickly adjust to create the required higher dividend rates was for stock prices to fall.

As might be expected, the Federal Reserve's high-interest-rate, tight-money policy was quite unpopular, both on Wall Street and in the country at large. There were many critics, and calls for a congressional investigation were heard. The antipathy toward the central bank was exacerbated when the economy fell into a steep recession (some called it a depression) in mid-1920. Although the central bank quickly reversed course, bringing its discount rate back down to 4½% by November 1920, the damage, according to the critics, was already done. The recession-depression of 1920–1921 was widely believed to have been the work of the central bankers.

Ironically, as the critics of the Federal Reserve focused their attention on the discount rate, another action taken by the central bank, which would have profound implications for the economy and the stock market, went almost unnoticed. Sluggish loan demand throughout 1921 left the member banks of the Federal Reserve System with large cash surpluses. Looking around for other ways to utilize their funds until loan demand picked up, the banks began to invest in government securities by purchasing them in the open market. From October 1921 through May 1922, Reserve bank holdings of government obligations increased from less than $200 million to more than $600 million. This had the unintended effect of pumping money into the economy as the sellers of the securities deposited the amounts paid to them into the banking system. Unwittingly, what would later become the most powerful tool of Federal Reserve policy (and the Fed action watched most closely today by market participants) was discovered. Formally recognized in April 1923, when the Fed established its Open Market Investment Committee, such "open market operations" would become the means by which the Federal Reserve controlled the nation's money supply.

Economists would later agree that industrial overexpansion, creating large inventory buildups, and the postwar recovery of European agriculture, which lessened demand for American farm exports, were the most likely causes of the economic slowdown of 1920–1921. But in the short term, perception is often more important than reality, and the perception that the Federal Reserve's interest rate decisions had throttled the economy was reinforced when the economy began to quickly recover during the second half of 1921 in the face of lower rates. It would not be the last time the Federal Reserve was made a scapegoat for unpleasant economic developments.

Concerns about the effect of central bank monetary policy on the stock market were obviously something quite new, in that there had been no American central bank at all before 1914. But otherwise, despite the influx of new investors during and immediately after the war years, the market itself had changed little since the beginning of the century. As has been seen, the reform effort of the early Wilson administration had largely overlooked the stock market, concentrating instead on the creation of the Federal Reserve and on antitrust and tariff issues. And in spite of the inklings of new, forward-looking valuation standards during the trust boom at the turn of the century, by 1920 surprisingly little was different in the way most investors looked at the market. Future growth in earnings was still considered to be largely unpredictable; current (after-tax) dividends were what mattered most. For the prewar years of the twentieth century (1901 through 1914), the composite P/E ratio of the New York Stock Exchange industrials had averaged slightly above 10 to 1, with no real definable trend in the ratio, either up or down. Stock dividends remained higher than bond interest rates in every year of the first two decades of the twentieth century, just as they had in the nineteenth century. The rules of thumb that had prevailed in 1901—that an industrial stock was fully valued at a P/E ratio of 10 to 1, and that stock dividends should always be higher than bond yields—still held. If anything, the war boom valuations (with very low P/E ratios) reinforced the pattern.

The conservative, essentially static approach used to value stocks had an important side effect. Equity financing was very difficult for new, unproven businesses to obtain, and very expensive when it was available. If investors and investment bankers were reluctant to attempt to predict future earnings growth, why would they be willing to buy or underwrite stock in any sort of unproven venture, except on extremely cheap terms? As innovative new technologies (such as automobiles, electric power, and aviation) made possible new industries in the early decades of the century, tension frequently developed between aggressive entrepreneurs and the conservative, risk-averse Wall Street investment bankers who controlled access to the capital the entrepreneurs desperately needed. Potential new stock offerings of immature businesses were shunned, not sought out— very unlike what happens in the proactively risk-taking environment of today.

Bernard Baruch ran into just such a problem when he approached J. P. Morgan with a proposal for a sulfur mining venture in Texas. Stating his engineers' estimate that modern mining techniques gave the prospective mine a fifty-fifty chance of success, Baruch told Morgan that he would be willing to "gamble" on the outcome, if Morgan would as well. Morgan replied peremptorily, "I never gamble." The discussion was closed, and Baruch was left to fend for himself.[13] The reception granted his idea was not at all atypical; established Wall Street firms had little interest in financing ventures that in any way appeared to be speculative.

Entering the third decade of the twentieth century, the stock market, buffeted by war, high taxes, and inflation, was caught in something of a paradox. The surge of new investors who entered the market during and immediately after the war had dramatically changed the character of the "players" of the game on Wall Street and significantly increased the importance of the market to the broader economy. The rapid growth of new industries based on new technologies required that equity capital be made available for inherently risky, speculative ventures. But the conservative standards used on Wall Street to value stocks had actually changed little since the nineteenth century. The growth of the market was straitjacketed by primitive ideas and patterns of behavior. Those binding restrictions would have to be torn off before the modern American stock market could begin to emerge.

5

A NEW ERA

M OMENTS AFTER NOON on September 16, 1920, the bustle of activity at the corner of Broad and Wall Streets in lower Manhattan
was blotted out by a devastating blast. Shrapnel-like pellets of iron exploded through narrow streets, shattering windows and hurling bodies
helter-skelter, instantly igniting anything flammable. Within seconds a thick
cloud of greenish smoke enveloped the intersection, snaking its billowing
tentacles down side streets and alleys.

The corner of Broad and Wall was the epicenter of American finance.
On one side stood the United States Sub-Treasury building, where most of
the country's gold reserves were stored. On another stood the New York
Stock Exchange, and on a third, the solid marble edifice of J. P. Morgan &
Company. A hail of broken glass rained down on the interior banking floor
of the Morgan building. Two Morgan employees were killed, but only one
partner, Junius Morgan, grandson of the legendary John Pierpont, was injured. (Apparently he suffered a scratch on the buttocks, which was tact-
fully reported in the press as a minor injury to one hand.) Upstairs in a
conference room, fortuitously protected from the explosion by a solid
stone wall, a visiting French general was meeting with several Morgan
partners. As the last reverberations of the blast faded away he turned to
one of the Morgan men and inquired, "Does this happen often?"[1]

Across the street in the New York Stock Exchange building the president of the Exchange walked quickly (running was forbidden) to the ros-

Dow Jones Industrial Average, 1920–1928

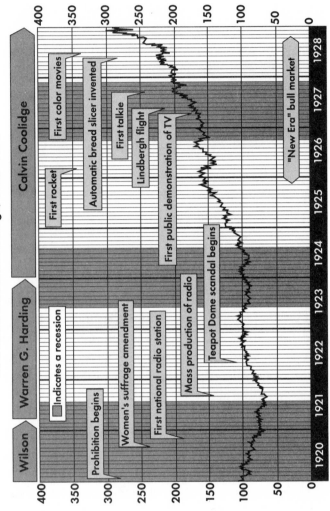

© Dow Jones & Company Inc.

trum and rang the bell that suspended trading. Outside, 30 people had been killed instantly, and several hundred injured, ten of whom would later die. Accounts from witnesses were confusing and often contradictory, but it was generally assumed that "Red" radicals were responsible for the bombing. Earlier that year bombs had been mailed to a number of prominent people; most of the devices had failed to reach their targets for the mundane reason that they were sent off with insufficient postage. Federal authorities, led by the virulently anticommunist Attorney General, A. Mitchell Palmer, orchestrated a massive crackdown on suspected radicals, but it did not now appear to have been sufficient to stop the subversive onslaught. *The New York Times* reported that after the Wall Street bombing, "federal, state and city authorities agreed that the devastating blast signaled the long-threatened Red outrages."

Instead the explosion marked the beginning of the end of radical political disturbances. The perpetrators of the blast were never caught, but, contrary to popular fears, there would be no more such incidents. There was to be no real challenge to the ascendancy of American business. Finance capital, and the markets that were essential to modern capitalism, had presumably been the target of the bombers of September 16. But the markets were unscathed. The day after the bombing the Stock Exchange opened at the normal time, and traded higher.

The market's short-term resilience in the face of the bombing was misleading. To many knowledgeable observers the market seemed to be languishing. One such man was the estimable Charles Schwab, who had become chairman of Bethlehem Steel after years as the president of U.S. Steel. A self-appointed spokesman for the business community, Schwab never passed up an opportunity to proselytize on behalf of big business and his belief that the scientific management of large, modern corporations would bring a revolution in living standards for the entire population. In December 1920 he gave a speech calling for the liquidation of labor (the term "liquidation," as Schwab employed it, meant a reduction in wages necessary to adjust for anticipated deflation). Attributing much of the then-current economic malaise to the high tax rates introduced during the war and not yet repealed, Schwab vigorously voiced the Wall Street consensus that if the federal government would only get out of the way, business leaders would bring about a quick return to prosperity.

Schwab went on to complain about the stock market. Asking a rhetorical question, "What's wrong with the market?" he argued that stock prices did not adequately reflect the condition of American business. Schwab pointed out that the stock of his own Bethlehem Steel was trading at a price-earnings ratio of only 2 to 1, and that even the stock of massive U.S. Steel (still the largest industrial corporation in the world) was trading at the bargain P/E ratio of 6 to 1.[2] The P/E ratio for the industrial stocks listed on the New York Stock Exchange stood at only 8.3 to 1.

Schwab seemed to recognize that changes were occurring in the economy that were not reflected in stock prices. The traditional methods of valuing stocks based on current dividend rates dictated low valuations in 1920. Those methods assumed that a mature company would pay out the majority of its earnings in dividends to its shareholders each year. Yet many companies were beginning to abandon that practice; during the war some utility companies had adopted a policy of constant dividend payments, with any "surplus" earnings to be retained for future contingencies. This practice spread to industrial companies after the war and by the early 1920s was generally accepted. The idea was that the "retained earnings" of the company would be used to finance expansion.

As Charles Schwab may have recognized, such important changes occur only rarely in business history and can have dramatic implications for stock prices. The booming economy that developed later in the 1920s would have propelled stock prices higher anyway. But when combined with a newly accepted notion that allowed an upward revaluation of companies based on future earnings prospects rather than current dividend payments, the rally in stock prices could, and did, become an explosion.

Occasionally periods in history come to be identified in the popular imagination with certain institutions or events that seem symbolic of the era. The 1920s, or the Roaring Twenties, as the decade came to be known, would be one of these periods. It would be the era of *The Great Gatsby*, and of flappers and speakeasies. But one institution, perhaps more than any other, would provide a metaphor for the entire decade. That institution was the stock market.

Thus the great bull market that would begin in 1921 would later be seen as synonymous with hedonistic excess, a tempestuous orgy of speculation. Inevitably, as if in a biblical morality tale, the intoxicated speculators would first taste success, only to be dashed on the rocks of harsh reality in the form of the crash of 1929 and the subsequent Great Depression. In this view, the crash and Depression were inextricably linked, and the inevitable result of the preceding speculative excess. It was a view that came to be widely accepted in the 1930s and is still believed by many today. And it is dead wrong.

In 1921, however, what would occur later in the decade was well beyond the imagination of most observers. A few farsighted men, such as Charles Schwab, did recognize that the stock market was misjudging the potential of the American economy and misvaluing corporate earnings. They foresaw the possibility of boom times ahead, and there actually was substantial reason for optimism. In 1920 only 10% of households were electrified; obviously as electrification spread it would open up vast new markets for appliances ranging from refrigerators to radios. Likewise, the steadily falling prices of automobiles held out the prospect that car ownership would soon spread beyond the one family in three that then owned a vehicle. In fact, consumer spending on autos and appliances would power the upcoming boom. Seemingly much of this could have been foreseen by analysts in 1921, but, besides Schwab and a few like-minded individuals, it was not.

One of the like-minded individuals was the financial journalist Clarence Barron. In May 1921 he commenced publication of *Barron's Financial Weekly*, which he declared would provide a "weekly review of the application of money to practical ends." Barron argued that the principal problem plaguing the economy (and thus the stock market) was a "lack of confidence." He believed that "a fresh financial publication based on sound sources of information and policy should be a helpful factor in assuring the return of confidence in the world of business."

Barron moved quickly to address an issue he believed was undermining confidence in the stock market: the fact that market "insiders" frequently engaged in manipulative practices. He ran several articles in late 1921 that directly addressed the matter. While admitting that manipulative activity was present in the stock market, he claimed it had only a short-range effect. Major, long-term price movements were caused by broad economic trends and by the changing fortunes of individual companies, not by manipulation. Barron was willing to concede the obvious existence of manipulation to make a larger point: outside investors could invest successfully in stocks and not be adversely impacted by the machinations of market operators as long as the investors made solid, long-term investment decisions based on economic fundamentals and stayed away from short-term speculation.

Barron's argument anticipated what would become conventional wisdom later in the century—the notion that investors could manage risk by adopting a long time horizon that ignored short-term fluctuations. Over a long horizon, the growth of the economy and corporate profits would pull stock prices higher, swamping short-term volatility in the market, whether that volatility was caused by manipulation or other factors. In effect, Barron was claiming that the market was less risky in the long run than it appeared to be in the short run.

An empirical basis for this important conclusion was provided by the publication in 1924 of *Common Stocks as Long Term Investments* by Edgar Lawrence Smith. The thesis of the book, unremarkable from today's perspective but revolutionary in the early 1920s, was that a diversified portfolio of common stocks would consistently outperform bonds over long time horizons. Smith argued that the increasingly common practice of retaining earnings to finance future expansion created a "compounding effect" that gave the stocks of modern corporations an "upward bias." His book caused something of a sensation, both among academics and the financial press. Prominent economist Irving Fischer commented: "It seems, then, that the market overrates the safety of 'safe' securities and pays too much for them, that it underrates the risk of risky securities and pays too little for them, that it pays too much for immediate and too little for remote returns . . ."[3]

In a nutshell, Fischer encapsulated the radical conclusion implicit in Smith's results—that investors, in a misguided quest for safety, were paying too little attention to future returns relative to current income. This idea had been slowly crystallizing for a number of years; now Smith's book provided a solid foundation for the new theory of stock valuation. Obviously Smith's work did not, by itself, cause the spectacular rise in the stock market in the years following its publication. But the wide acceptance it received indicates that there was a general willingness to embrace the new methods of valuing stocks. And those methods would stand the test of time. In the later decades of the century it would be accepted as a given that stocks should be valued based on future earnings prospects. Successive refinements to this approach over the years would be used to justify higher and higher stock prices.

Clarence Barron's notion that stock manipulation need not trouble long-term investors may have made sense in theory, but in practice manipulation was so prevalent in the 1920s that it was difficult to ignore. Jesse Livermore was one of its leading practitioners. Livermore did not really look the part of a major market operator; he was slightly cockeyed, and his slim build made him look younger than he was. His hands were very soft, almost womanly, and his blond hair ran straight back from a tufted crest above his high forehead. The pince-nez supported by his nose gave him a somewhat owlish appearance.[4]

His appearance notwithstanding, however, Livermore made quite a reputation for himself by effectively manipulating the press as well as stocks. Several times over his career, Livermore lost millions and was wiped out. But each time he would return chastened to what he really did best—convincing wealthy backers to give him another chance. To Jesse Livermore, Wall Street was a "giant whorehouse," where brokers were "pimps" and stocks "whores" on which customers threw their money away. Livermore—a "madam" who for a percentage arranged it all—wanted only a chance to play the game. He usually got it.[5]

In 1923, Livermore strayed into a serious quagmire. He had helped form a selling group to distribute and support in the marketplace shares of a new Sinclair Oil subsidiary, Mammoth Oil. Mammoth controlled lucrative oil properties leased from the U.S. Navy, including some parcels in the so-called Teapot Dome formation in Wyoming. One of Livermore's functions was to "maintain an orderly market" in the new stock, which basically meant he had to find buyers for the shares his partners wanted to sell. Suddenly Livermore, a perennial bear, became very bullish. He opined to the press, "Stocks of the better-managed and conservatively capitalized corporations should be bought for substantial profits . . ." *The New York*

Times took note of Livermore's changed stance with the headline BEARS TAKE A DRUBBING: "Jesse Livermore who led them six months ago joins ranks of the bulls . . ."

However, no amount of optimistic rhetoric could protect Livermore from the stench of the corruption scandal that erupted in Washington when it was revealed that some Mammoth Oil leases had been improperly obtained through the mendacious intervention of Interior Secretary Albert Fall. Livermore was soon dodging subpoenas and was finally forced to testify before investigators. Attorney Samuel Untermeyer, interrogator of J. P. Morgan and others in the Pujo Committee hearings of 1912, commented caustically about Livermore: "As this gentleman is not in the business of manipulating stock markets for his health it is to be hoped the committee will give him a little attention . . ."[6]

The committee gave Livermore a great deal of attention but received little useful information. Not directly involved in the oil lease transactions himself, Livermore escaped any consequences for the criminal activity uncovered at Mammoth Oil. Two of his associates, however, were indicted for bribery. One, Harry F. Sinclair, went to prison. Commenting afterward on the disgrace of Interior Secretary Fall, Livermore said that "men of higher caliber should be sent to Washington."[7]

Despite Livermore's repeated brushes with scandal, he continued to receive positive press coverage (paid or otherwise). As his fame increased, a new expression entered the common lexicon: "If only I had Livermore's money." Far from expressing disgust at Livermore's unsavory antics, more and more people came to be fascinated by him and his fellow market operators.

One of those operators was a young man from Boston by the name of Joseph P. Kennedy. Kennedy had begun his career in the market when he took a job at the brokerage firm of Hayden, Stone in 1919 and had made his first market killing by trading on inside information gleaned from one of the managing partners, Galen Stone. Stone was chairman of Pond Coal Company, which Ford Motor wanted to buy. Acting on this information, Kennedy purchased 15,000 shares of Pond Coal at 16, putting up only $24,000 of the purchase price and borrowing the rest. When the acquisition of Pond Coal was consummated, Kennedy sold his stock for a profit of $675,000. Commenting to his Harvard friend Tom Campbell, Kennedy exclaimed, "Tommy, it's so easy to make money in the market we'd better get in before they pass a law against it."[8]

No stranger to many of the pools* organized to manipulate stocks in the mid-1920s, Kennedy skillfully managed several. In 1924 he was summoned to New York by John D. Hertz, who was concerned that bears were forcing the share price of his Yellow Cab Company lower for their own speculative purposes. Hertz wanted Kennedy to manage a bull pool in Yellow Cab stock, to be funded by Hertz and his associates. Kennedy ensconced himself in a suite in the Waldorf-Astoria Hotel, equipped with a stock ticker and a battery of telephones, and went to work. His carefully timed buying, combined with a generally rising market, soon accomplished his objective, and the mysterious "bear raiders" were forced to desist.

A few months later Yellow Cab stock abruptly fell again, and this time Hertz suspected that Kennedy himself was responsible for the decline. He publicly threatened to punch Kennedy in the nose the next time the two men met. If Kennedy actually double-crossed his former partners, it could never be proven. However, his biographer Richard J. Whelan stated that "it would not have been unthinkable." Encouraged by his successes, Kennedy later moved his family (including his young sons John and Robert) from Boston to New York so that he could be closer to the market.

Meanwhile, the long-term trends *Barron's* had urged investors to identify were all pointing upward. The boom in consumer spending was fueled by a new element: credit. For the first time in history, financing was made available on a large scale for middle-class customers purchasing consumer durables. Usually the financing was provided directly by manufacturers, who recognized correctly that they could greatly enhance demand for their product by allowing installment buying. By the mid-twenties, a majority of all furniture, phonographs, washing machines, radios, sewing machines, vacuum cleaners, and refrigerators were sold on time.

Nowhere was the use of consumer credit more important than in the sale of automobiles. Auto production in the United States more than dou-

---

*The term "pool," as used here, refers to a group of speculators who each contributed money to a fund to be managed by one of the participants with the objective of manipulating a stock or stocks to make profits for all the pool participants.

bled from 1921 to 1925, from 1.5 million units to 3.6 million. Two-thirds of new cars were purchased on credit, usually in the form of 24- to 36-month installment loans. The automotive industry provided the driving impetus for rising stock prices. General Motors, Du Pont (which owned a substantial interest in GM and also produced products for the auto industry), Fisher Body, and Yellow Cab of Chicago were often referred to as the Four Horsemen of the Boom, leading the market upward. The market itself was said to be "a product of General Motors."

As the bull market advance continued in 1924, the ascendancy of probusiness sentiment in both the White House and popular culture was virtually unchallenged. President Harding, before dying unexpectedly of apoplexy in 1923, had repeatedly called for "less government in business and more business in government." His successor, Calvin "Silent Cal" Coolidge, went him one better, stating bluntly that "the business of America is business." In keeping with the times, Bruce Barton, a consummate salesman and pioneer of modern advertising techniques, published a book entitled *The Man Nobody Knows*. Barton's subject, surprisingly, was none other than Jesus Christ. Barton argued that Christ, far from being a dreamer only interested in otherworldly affairs, had been "the first businessman," whose parables were "the most powerful advertisements of all time." Christ was, according to Barton, a man who "picked up twelve men from the bottom ranks of business and forged them into an organization that conquered the world." *The Man Nobody Knows* became the best-selling book of 1924.[9]

According to conventional wisdom, the bull market of the mid-1920s was fueled in part by the low interest rate policy of the Federal Reserve. European central bankers had expressed concern that large quantities of gold were flowing from Europe to the United States, a trend that, if continued, would ultimately imperil their ability to keep their nations on the gold standard. Reluctantly, the Federal Reserve Bank of New York sought to lower interest rates so as to make American-based deposits less attractive to foreigners. Through open market operations and discount rate cuts, domestic interest rates were pushed down by 1½%. These moves proved effective, and by early 1925 gold flows reversed, so that England was again importing gold from the United States. The Federal Reserve had resolved the immediate problem of international monetary instability, but only at the price of pursuing an easy money policy.

It was this easy credit that allegedly provided the fuel for the "speculative boom" of the late 1920s. In this view, the unprecedented rise in stock prices was not justified by growth in the economy and in corporate earnings, but was instead symptomatic of the type of "overspeculation" that periodically plagues the stock market, causing stocks to rise well above their "intrinsic" values, only to come crashing down when investors return to sanity. The most recent proponent of the "overspeculation" explanation for the 1920s boom is Edward Chancellor, author of the history of speculation *Devil Take the Hindmost*. Chancellor specifically cites the late 1920s "bubble" as an example of excessive speculation and goes on to argue that the history and culture of the United States make Americans uniquely susceptible to this type of speculative mania. According to Chancellor, the experience of colonizing a wild continent and pushing the frontier of civilization ever westward in the face of very real dangers fostered a willingness to take risks. A people who were willing to uproot themselves from their homes and travel long distances to settle in a hostile wilderness would presumably think nothing of risking mere money in speculation.

Another authority who subscribes to the overspeculation explanation is John Kenneth Galbraith. In his best-selling book *The Great Crash, 1929*, Galbraith cites numerous manifestations in the 1920s of a "national passion to get rich quickly with a minimum of effort." Both Chancellor and Galbraith believe that a tendency toward speculative excess infected the stock market after 1925.

There certainly were specific occurrences that appear to support their argument. One such instance took place in midsummer 1926, when Thomas Cochran, a J. P. Morgan & Company partner, granted an interview to a reporter on board the ocean liner *Olympic* as it prepared to depart for Europe. The gist of the interview was reported on the Dow Jones news ticker shortly after noon on July 31, quoting Cochran as saying that "General Motors running at its present rate is cheap at the price, and it should and will sell at least one hundred points higher."[10]

Partners at the august J. P. Morgan & Company were not accustomed to issuing stock market predictions; the elder J. Pierpont Morgan, when asked once what the market would do, responded imperiously by stating simply, "It will fluctuate." For a Morgan partner to issue a specific prediction for a specific stock was unheard of. *The New York Times* later declared that "there was no precedent on Wall Street for such an episode." Everyone knew that J. P. Morgan & Company was the investment banker for General Motors and that some Morgan partners were GM directors. Instantly the assumption was made that Cochran was speaking on the basis of inside information. He must know something, the reasoning went, and by chance or intent had communicated it to the mere mortals on the Street.

Minutes after the story hit the news ticker, more than half the brokers on the New York Stock Exchange floor crowded around the post where General Motors traded. The stock shot up from 189½ to 201. The following day it spiked another 12½ points. Cochran, responding with a radiogram from the middle of the Atlantic, denied that he had "authorized" a statement predicting a future price for the stock but did not disclaim the thrust of his quoted remarks. When General Motors continued to soar, *The Wall Street Journal* went so far as to praise Cochran for his frankness, congratulating him for sharing his inside information with the public. The *Journal* opined that it would be better if all corporate insiders were so "public spirited," making available to everyone their information rather than simply keeping it for their own use.

Inside information or not, Cochran's assessment was correct. GM stock attained his price target within a year. Over that same period the stock market as a whole rose a spectacular 50%. Critics of overspeculation cite such sharp advances as a priori evidence of speculative excess. But was that necessarily so? Were there not economic fundamentals that could justify such impressive moves?

Ten years earlier there had been over a hundred separate manufacturers of automobiles in the United States, most of them small. As time passed, the industry consolidated, with dominant companies such as General Motors and Ford winning out. Even many of the larger competitors were forced to merge or go out of business. The market leaders, especially GM, experienced rapid growth and greatly enhanced profitability resulting from economies of scale. (GM's profits more than doubled between 1925 and 1928.) What stock price properly values a company in this enviable position, soon to become the largest industrial concern in the world? The question that should be asked by market historians is not why GM's stock price was so "high" in 1927, but why it had been so "low" earlier in the decade.

The same could be said for the overall market. The P/E ratio of industrial stocks listed on the New York Stock Exchange stood at 13.9 in 1927. This was up substantially from the depressed levels of 1920, but the rise does not seem excessive in view of the greatly improved prospects for the economy. Slowly the market was beginning to reflect the new standards of valuation based on future earnings growth, but even by the middle of the decade this revaluation had been modest indeed. The "speculative mania" identified by Chancellor and Galbraith was largely an illusion.

On November 17, 1927, President Calvin Coolidge made a speech that would be memorable for only one line. He declared that America "was entering upon a new era of prosperity." Immediately the phrase "New Era" was picked up by commentators, who used it as a catchword for what many believed promised to be a period of permanent prosperity. According to the believers, the scientific management of business and the implementation of sound economic policies by government would eliminate the troublesome boom-and-bust cycles of the past. The future would bring steady growth and rising wealth for all Americans. And, it went without saying, rising stock prices as well.

In many ways Coolidge was preaching to the converted. It took little to convince most Americans that the New Era had already arrived. An increasing number (although still a small fraction of the total population) were willing to bet on it in the market, both with their own money and with that which they borrowed. The truly explosive growth in broker's loans (loans made to investors to enable them to buy stock, with the stock itself used as collateral for the loans) that would characterize the late 1920s began in earnest in 1927. The dollar amount of such loans rose from $2.6 billion at the beginning of the year to $4.4 billion at year-end. (It would reach $6.4 billion one year later, and peak at $8.6 billion in 1929.) Concerned observers such as Alexander Dana Noyes would frequently point to these figures with alarm. But Noyes had been very cautious about the market for some time, and had been wrong. He and the dwindling number of bears on Wall Street faced the prospect of being marginalized by the powerful market advance. Every time the market seemed to pause, the bears would proclaim that the end of the boom was near; when the market turned sharply upward again, as it invariably did, the bears were made to look very foolish indeed.

The stock that John Kenneth Galbraith and others have labeled the speculative darling of Wall Street in the late 1920s was Radio Corporation of America (RCA). Radio, as it was called, was ideally positioned to exploit both sides of the new industry of radio broadcasting—it manufactured radio receivers and owned broadcast stations as well. Originally only a producer of radio sets, the company had expanded into broadcasting as a means of providing a programming product that would stimulate sales of receivers. But as the decade wore on and the commercialization of radio programming became more acceptable to the public, analysts recognized that profits in broadcasting might actually exceed those from manufacturing.

"Radio" stock took off. From a low of $32 per share in early 1926, it would hit $101 in 1927 and eventually top out at nearly $574 (adjusted for a split*) in 1929. Perhaps no stock better symbolized changing standards of valuation. Even as it hit its high in 1929, RCA had never paid a dividend.

Critics of presumed overspeculation in the market point to Radio as a prime example. But a closer look at the spectacular growth of RCA (as in the case of GM) is revealing. In 1925, RCA earned $1.32 per share. In subsequent years its earnings skyrocketed; in 1928 it earned $15.98 per share, a twelvefold increase. At the end of 1928 the stock was trading at 420, yielding a P/E ratio based on the *preceding* year's earnings of 26 to 1. Was

---

*A stock "split" occurs when a company issues new shares to stockholders in exchange for, and in a number greater than, the shares they already own. The effect is to increase the number of shares outstanding while proportionately reducing the price those shares trade at. For example, a two-for-one stock split would mean that shareholders received two new shares for each old share, but the market price of the new shares would likely be only half that of the old shares. In theory, no new value is created; the purpose of a split is usually to reduce the price of high-priced stocks, making them more affordable to small investors.

that ratio unreasonable, given the fantastic growth the company had exhibited? Certainly not by the standards that would prevail later in the twentieth century, given the obvious potential for future growth. (In the late 1920s, not only was RCA an important player in both radio manufacturing and broadcasting, but it was actively pursuing the new technology of television.)

In the spring of 1927 the governors of the central banks of England and Germany, along with the deputy governor of the Bank of France, came to the United States to meet with officials of the Federal Reserve. Their mission was to urge a repetition of the credit easing the Fed had adopted in 1925 to halt the flow of gold from Europe to the United States. A similar problem existed in 1927 and had as its cause a 1925 decision by Winston Churchill, Britain's chancellor of the exchequer, to restore the pound to its prewar value of $4.86. This exchange rate was too high and was set more as a sop to British pride than as a reflection of reality; the result had been that the overvalued currency priced British goods out of the world market and led to a series of foreign exchange crises as traders sold overpriced pounds to invest in assets denominated in other currencies. The European central bankers believed in 1927 that the problem could be alleviated if interest rates fell in the United States—this would make dollar holdings less attractive and thus presumably dampen the flight from the pound.

The Fed obliged, cutting the discount rate from 4% to 3.5% and engaging in open market operations to increase the money supply. The move was controversial, with one dissenting member of the Federal Reserve Board, Adolph Miller, terming it "the greatest and boldest operation ever undertaken by the Federal Reserve System . . . [that] resulted in one of the most costly errors committed by it or any other banking system in the last 75 years."[11] According to Professor Lionel Robbins of the London School of Economics, who wrote extensively on the subject, "From that date, according to all the evidence, the situation got completely out of control."[12]

The reasoning of the critics was simple: the easy money policy of the Fed in 1927 threw more fuel on the fires of speculation already burning in the American economy. Thus the final frenzied upward thrust of the stock market (and its subsequent collapse) at the end of the decade was thought by these critics to have been caused by the ill-advised actions of the Federal

Reserve in attempting to defuse a foreign exchange crisis. In 1921 the central bank had been made the scapegoat for a recession; now it was to be held responsible for creating an unsustainable boom.

Unfortunately, this conventional interpretation, drawing heavily on the excess speculation argument, has very significant flaws. First, easy money alone does not necessarily create a stock market boom. There had been many times before the 1920s (and there would be others afterward) when credit was cheap and plentiful and stock prices did not rise precipitously. Clearly, other factors were also at work.

Second, in spite of the well-publicized instances of Federal Reserve easing cited earlier, there is reason to believe that monetary policy was not really all that loose in the 1920s. Milton Friedman and Anna Schwartz in their classic work, *A Monetary History of the United States: 1867–1960*, state that "the stock of money . . . failed to rise and even fell slightly during most of the expansion—a phenomenon not matched in any prior or subsequent cyclical expansion. Far from being an inflationary decade, the twenties were the reverse." (Consumer prices over the decade actually declined at a .9% annual rate.) If Friedman and Schwartz are correct, an expansionary monetary policy on the part of the Fed could not have been responsible for the stock market rise, because there was in fact no such expansionary monetary policy.

If not easy credit, what did trigger the sharp increases in stock prices? In the simplest sense, it was rapidly growing corporate profits and a revaluation upward of the methods by which the stock market capitalized those profits. Those analysts who continued to base their market forecasts on traditional standards were left behind.

One of the leading proponents of the new valuation theory was William R. Biggs. Projecting future moves in the stock market would run in his family; William Biggs was the father of Barton Biggs, who would himself become a prominent market strategist for the investment banking firm Morgan, Stanley later in the century. The senior Biggs attacked traditional standards of valuation in an article in *Barron's*; citing historian James Harvey Robinson, he declared that while radical thinkers were usually wrong, ultraconservative thinkers were always wrong. Admitting that it was impossible to consistently predict the future, Biggs reasoned that one thing was certain: whatever happened, it would undoubtedly be different from what had happened in the past. Thus the traditionalist who rigidly applied old benchmarks in an effort to anticipate future market moves would inevitably be disappointed.

Biggs decried the tendency of market observers to complain that stock prices were too high simply because they were higher than in the past. Making an argument that would be heard many times throughout the century as successively more liberal standards of stock valuation became accepted, Biggs claimed that conditions existing in the mid-1920s made the period different from earlier eras. He had a litany of reasons; most seemed quite reasonable. He noted that rapidly growing corporate earnings had enabled many companies to boost their dividends substantially, resulting in very respectable dividend yields even for stocks that had appreciated substantially. In addition, many companies had used their increased earnings to build up significant cash reserves, so that they would be better able to weather any normal downturn in business. But most important, Biggs said, was the fact that the newly created Federal Reserve System would prevent the instability in the banking sector that had so often accompanied (and sometimes precipitated) major stock market declines, such as the panic of 1907. Steady management of the nation's money supply would mean that future fluctuations in the economy would be less pronounced than in the past. (So often the target of criticism, the governors of the Federal Reserve System must have been heartened by the faith Biggs placed in them.)[13]

Many other explanations of the bull market were advanced by New Era advocates. The publisher of *The Magazine of Wall Street* even suggested that the fact that investors could now buy stocks in companies that made products familiar to them, such as autos, refrigerators, and radios, gave them greater confidence in the stock market. But most of the believers of the New Era based their arguments on the radical transformation that seemed to be occurring in the economy and its implications for stock prices.

And the facts were with them. For example, in 1919, 32% of the machinery in American factories had been powered by electricity; by the late 1920s that figure had risen to nearly 50% and was continuing to climb, with concomitant increases in productivity. The replacement of horse-drawn wagons by trucks and automobiles traveling a network of newly built highways was revolutionizing transportation. And other, still newer industries, based on radical new technologies (such as broadcasting and aviation), held out the prospect of even greater gains in the future. The statistics on productivity for the decade reflect these technological advances; in the ten-year period beginning in 1919, productivity grew at an annual pace of 3.7%, one of the highest rates on record. In the face of this undeniable progress, who could really dispute the optimistic outlook of the New Era proponents?

Beginning in March 1928, for no immediately obvious reason, the market broke out decisively on the upside. Stocks moved higher not in steady increments but in great vaulting leaps. Volatility increased as well, with sizable run-ups being frequently punctuated by sharp downdrafts, which were followed again by more run-ups. The action of Radio is indicative. On March 12 the stock gained 18 points. The following day it opened for trading 22 points above its previous close, dropped 20 points on rumors that trading was being investigated, then gained back 15 before falling 9. A few days later it jumped another 18 points.

Near-breathless press accounts of this activity included rumors (often carefully planted, sometimes simply guesswork) about pools and other manipulative activity. Pools in Radio were legendary; one such operation in 1929 would be reported on a daily basis by *The Wall Street Journal*, which obviously had access to some of the pool participants. However, while the machinations of pool operators undoubtedly affected short-term moves in specific stocks, most of the stocks involved would have gone up anyway, with or without the pools. And far from discouraging outside investors who presumably would be disadvantaged by the machinations of market insiders, the often lurid stories of manipulation actually served to enhance interest in the market. More and more individual investors thought that they could mimic the actions of the big players, tagging along to profit themselves.

Sometimes recognized market titans came into conflict with each other; in such instances the press and public would eagerly observe from afar, much like mythical ancients witnessing a clash of the Gods. In particular, nothing interested the news media more than the frequent run-ins between Jesse Livermore and his alleged archrival, Arthur Cutten. Cutten had been a farm boy who, like Livermore, left his family's farm to make his fortune in the markets. He first went to Chicago, where he took a job as a clerk in a grain-trading firm. Slowly husbanding his meager resources, he patiently awaited his chance. When he was ready, he opened a grain-trading account and soon surprised his employer by making enough money to purchase a seat on the Chicago Board of Trade. Like Livermore, Cutten then quit his clerical job to become a professional speculator. He never looked back.

Cutten achieved his greatest fame in 1924, when he "bulled" wheat over the two-dollar-per-bushel threshold for the first time in history. The press was full of reports of amateur investors reaping large profits from small investments; the fact that options could be purchased on grain contracts for as little as $12.50 encouraged people of very limited means to "take a flier" in commodities. Cutten was the high priest of commodity speculators, labeled the Wheat King by the press. When asked to predict the movement of prices, his inevitable response was one word: "Higher."

Jesse Livermore could not help noticing Cutten's growing fame. He looked with skepticism on the ever-upward course of grain prices—particularly wheat, corn, and rye. Believing that "gravity works in the market as well as in science," he determined to sell grain short, opposing Cutten. It would be the first of several clashes between the two.[14]

Livermore had no basis for believing grain prices would fall other than instinct, and, as had often happened before, instinct failed him. By the end of 1925 he had lost more than $3 million on his commodity play and was again broke. Cutten apparently made nearly $5 million over the same period. Referring contemptuously to men like Livermore, Cutten scoffed, saying, "They know the game in and out; they trade for other people, but they can't trade for themselves . . ." He attributed his own success to "nerve," saying, "It takes nerve to speculate in the market . . ."[15]

Cutten then transferred his base of operations from Chicago to New York, and his speculation from the commodity market to the stock market. He met with phenomenal success in the booming market of the late twenties. An inveterate bull, he made millions in the stocks of Montgomery Ward, Baldwin Locomotive, and Radio Corporation of America, among others, in the process becoming the darling of the New York press. In an era of well-known operators, Cutten was pronounced the most influential. *The New York Times* devoted a full-page feature article to him, headlined CUTTEN CRACKS WHIP OVER THE STOCK MARKET.

The last years of the 1920s bull market seem to blur together into one long, exuberant binge. But a careful reading of the financial press at the time does not support this monochromatic interpretation. Many voices sounded cautionary notes in 1928, warning that the market had advanced too far too fast. The respected financial editor of The New York Times, Alexander Dana Noyes, consistently expressed caution. He was not alone. A major brokerage firm ran prominent ads asking "Will You Overstay the Bull Market?" while Moody's Investment Service warned that high stock prices had "overdiscounted anticipated progress."[16] Bernard Baruch advised friends to watch economic statistics with care; he was concerned that a crash might be in the making.

Critical rumblings also emanated from Washington, D.C. In February and March 1928 the Senate Committee on Banking and Currency held hearings on stock market speculation, the immediate issue being the spectacular growth in broker's loans used to finance stock investments. The respected Senator Carter Glass of Virginia, who had authored the enabling legislation for the Federal Reserve System fifteen years earlier, reflected the concerns of most of the committee members when he asked, "What percentage of the public speculating in stocks of the stock exchange understand the real intrinsic value of the stocks in which they deal?" Senator Glass went on to give an example of what he meant by speculation, referring to a particular stock that "was selling at 108 in January" but was "selling in the market yesterday at 69," asking, "Now what is that but gambling?" Another committee member, Senator Robert La Follette of Wisconsin, went further, denouncing "the great American evil of stock exchange speculation."[17]

Herbert Hoover, commerce secretary in the Coolidge administration and soon to be elected President, was also quite concerned about what he perceived to be excessive speculation. Hoover claimed in his memoirs that as early as 1925 he had become concerned about the "growing tide of speculation." Referring to such speculation, Hoover wrote, "There are crimes far worse than murder for which men should be reviled and punished." Hoover said that as commerce secretary he had "sent individually for the editors and publishers of major newspapers and magazines and requested them systematically to warn the country against speculation and the unduly high price of stocks. He also said he had pressured Treasury Secretary Andrew Mellon and a governor of the Federal Reserve Board,

Roy Young, "to strangle the speculative movement."[18] The stock market seemed to ignore Hoover's concerns; when he won election to the presidency in a landslide in November 1928, stock prices rallied sharply. But the views he expressed were not at all unique. To suggest that no one was preaching caution in the heady days of 1928 is to badly misconstrue what actually occurred.

Over the course of 1928, as the market rose more than 40%, the P/E ratio for the Dow Jones Industrials increased from 12 to 14. The market closed on the last trading day in December 1928 at its high for the year. The advocates of a New Era were firmly in the driver's seat. As has been seen, there were reams of economic data to justify their optimism. The future looked very bright indeed. Yet shortly, in one of the greatest cataclysms in stock market history, the New Era was to come crashing down. What happened? What went wrong? And could anyone have reasonably foreseen the coming disaster?

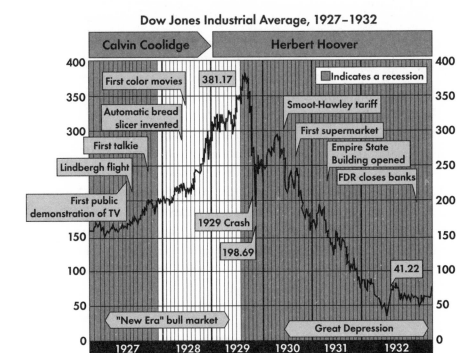

Dow Jones Industrial Average, 1927–1932

Calvin Coolidge | Herbert Hoover

First color movies | 381.17 | ■Indicates a recession

Automatic bread slicer invented | Smoot-Hawley tariff

First talkie | First supermarket

Lindbergh flight | Empire State Building opened

First public demonstration of TV | FDR closes banks

1929 Crash

198.69

41.22

"New Era" bull market | Great Depression

1927 1928 1929 1930 1931 1932

© *Dow Jones & Company Inc.*

6

CRASH

CERTAIN YEARS, SUCH as 1066, 1492, and 1789, stand out in history, important because of a single, seminal event. Nineteen twenty-nine is such a year. It was not a year of conquest, discovery, or revolution; rather, it was defined by something much more arcane—a stock market crash. In many ways, the crash was not much different from other panics that had preceded it. But while most of those earlier events have long been forgotten by all but market historians, the crash of 1929 still looms large in the popular consciousness. In a visceral, almost palpable sense, something about the 1929 collapse makes it seem different from all the panics that had gone before.

Writing in the 1950s, John Kenneth Galbraith declared, "On Jan. 1, 1929, as a matter of simple probability, it was most likely that the [stock market] boom would end before the year was out." Of course, Galbraith had the benefit of twenty-twenty hindsight. Other scholars have not claimed such prescience. Economist Paul Samuelson wrote in 1979 that "playing as I often do the experiment of studying price profiles with their dates concealed, I discovered that I would have been caught in the 1929 debacle . . . The collapse from 1929 to 1933 was neither foreseeable nor inevitable."[1]

Samuelson was not alone. Noted economist John Maynard Keynes lost heavily in the crash, as did other leading members of the academic community. Apparently the warning signs so obvious to Galbraith were somewhat more obscure to other students of the market.

This is not to suggest that the warning signs were invisible. Cautionary notes were frequently voiced by market analysts in early 1929 and can be divided into two broad categories. First was concern over "high" stock prices, and second was the worry that too many people were speculating with borrowed money.

By historical standards, stock prices certainly did appear high in 1929. P/E ratios on most stocks had climbed well above the traditionally accepted 10 to 1 ratio that had been the rule ever since industrial stocks began to trade on the New York Stock Exchange in the late nineteenth century. Perhaps more important, the spectacular rise in the stock market in the late twenties had caused dividend rates on stocks to fall almost to the level of long-term interest rates. This threatened to reverse the relationship between dividends and interest rates that had held since data began to be collected in the nineteenth century and presented a warning signal that could not be ignored by adherents to traditional norms of stock valuation. If stocks were riskier than bonds, they must yield more than bonds to compensate investors for that risk. By definition, if dividend rates fell below bond yields, stocks must be overvalued.

Even the normally reticent secretary of the treasury, Andrew Mellon, took note of the low dividend rates. In March 1929 he publicly urged "prudent investors" to buy bonds, implying that relatively low dividend rates made stocks unattractive compared with bonds.[2] Mellon may have been urged to make this comment by President Hoover, whom he had met with at length before speaking to the press. Whatever the case, for the secretary of the treasury to render such advice was quite unusual, and Mellon's statement attracted a great deal of attention. But he was certainly not the only person to express concern about high stock prices and low dividends.

The burgeoning use of "leverage" in the stock market was another source of alarm for skeptics of the bull market. Derived from the physics associated with the use of a lever to magnify a force, the term "leverage" in the financial markets referred to the use of borrowed money to "magnify" potential gains in investment results. If an investor expected his stocks to appreciate at least 20% per year (seemingly not an unrealistic appraisal in the late 1920s), why not borrow money at the going rate on broker loans of between 5% and 12% to buy more stocks, using the stocks themselves as collateral? By mid-1929, the dollar amount of margin loans used to finance stocks totaled more than three times the amount that had been outstanding at the beginning of 1927. The risk, as seen by critics who frequently cited these figures, was that a serious decline in the stock market would imperil the value of the collateral, forcing the margin investors to sell out their stocks to repay the loans. This forced selling would exacerbate the market drop, potentially causing a crash.

Leverage was also employed by popular new investment vehicles that had begun to appear after 1921, called investment trusts. In theory, these entities served a purpose similar to that of the mutual funds of the second half of the twentieth century. Individual investors would buy shares in the trusts, which would then reinvest the money in a portfolio of stocks. The investor who could not afford to hire a professional investment manager, or did not have the resources to buy a diversified portfolio of stocks, could achieve both professional management and diversification by means of the trust.

Most mutual funds, however, do not employ leverage, whereas most investment trusts did. In essence, the trusts borrowed money to supplement the funds raised from selling stock to investors, with the intent of enhancing the fund's overall rate of return. This was no different in principle from the investor who bought stock "on margin." Like the margin investor, the leveraged investment trust was willing to take more risk (buying stocks with borrowed money) in order to reap greater rewards if stock prices rose.

The impact of leverage can be seen through the following example, that of a hypothetical investment trust organized in early 1929. (New investment trusts were created at a furious pace throughout most of 1929, with a new trust appearing approximately every business day.) The hypothetical new trust would be capitalized at perhaps $150 million, of which $50 million would be raised from the sale of common stock, and $100 million from the sale of fixed-income securities, such as bonds and preferred stock. Since the holders of the bonds and preferred stock expected only to receive a fixed return, all the gains (if any) beyond the amount necessary to pay the fixed-income investors would go to the common holders.

Say the value of the stocks in which the trust had invested rose by 50%. The value of the trust's assets (before interest, preferred-stock dividends, and expenses) would increase from the original $150 million to

$225 million. Since the holders of the bonds and preferred stock had a claim on only $100 million, the common shares of the trust would now be worth $125 million, or 150% more than at the creation of the trust. In effect, "leverage" had magnified a 50% gain in the market into a 150% gain in the value of the trust's common shares.

This leverage could be further increased if the hypothetical investment trust invested in the shares of other leveraged trusts, to the point where a relatively small gain in the overall stock market could be magnified into large gains for the shareholders in the trust. Unfortunately, leverage worked in reverse as well. A relatively small decline in the market, when magnified by a chain of leveraged investments, could completely wipe out the trust shareholder. This possibility was discounted by trust investors, who were convinced that the professional investment managers who ran the trusts were sufficiently insightful to prevent such an eventuality. The reputation of many trust managements was enhanced by the presence of noted members of the academic community as directors or advisers; it was not uncommon for leading economists and finance professors from major universities to be associated with investment trusts. (Not until the appearance of large multinational "hedge funds" in the 1980s and 1990s would such a premium again be placed on academic advice.) With or without the learned professors, however, leveraged investment trusts were feared by critics to be ticking time bombs that would eventually explode, destroying trust investors and perhaps bringing down the entire market as well.

The high level of stock prices and the increasing use of leverage in the stock market were the two factors most frequently pointed to in early 1929 by those who saw disaster looming. These concerns penetrated the inner sanctum of the Federal Reserve Board. Unable to address the issue of high stock prices directly, or to influence the financial structures of the investments trusts, the central bank took action to arrest the growth in broker loans that made investing on margin possible. On February 2, in a step that initiated one of the most curious chains of events in the history of the Federal Reserve System, the board sent a letter to member banks advising them not to borrow from the Federal Reserve "either for the purpose of making speculative loans or for the purpose of maintaining speculative loans." There was no doubt that the term "speculative loans" referred to loans made to finance stocks bought on margin.

A storm of controversy ensued, not just between the Federal Reserve and its critics, but also between the Federal Reserve Board and one of its own regional branches—the Federal Reserve Bank of New York. The directors of the New York bank, which by virtue of its location was the most affected by the new policy, did not agree with the idea of attempting to restrict certain kinds of loans. Instead they preferred to increase the discount rate for all loans as a means of checking speculative activity. They in fact did so on February 14, unilaterally increasing the New York bank's discount rate from 5% to 6%. The Federal Reserve's board of governors in Washington, facing political pressure from business borrowers who opposed general interest rate increases, stepped in to quash the New York rate increase. But this was only the beginning.

One of the most influential directors of the Federal Reserve Bank of New York was Charles E. Mitchell, chairman of the board of National City Bank, who was himself heavily involved in stock market speculation. Mitchell was a handsome, broad-shouldered extrovert with a booming voice and a flair for publicity; he was not about to knuckle under to what he thought was misguided policy implemented by Washington bureaucrats. Although the Federal Reserve Bank of New York was forced to rescind its discount rate increase, Mitchell was to be heard from again.

The stock market initially sold off after the Federal Reserve letter was made public, but it soon righted itself. Departing President Calvin Coolidge, not noted for possessing particular insight on either the stock market or the economy, blithely remarked to reporters that the economy was "absolutely sound" and that stocks were "cheap at current prices." For perhaps this or other reasons, stock prices rallied in early March. The Federal Reserve watched, waited, and did nothing.

Then in late March a flurry of activity was reported. The Federal Reserve's board of governors met daily in Washington, in secret, even including a highly unusual Saturday session. Rumors abounded that the Fed would take some sort of decisive action to quell speculation. By Tuesday, March 26, the pressure of uncertainty was unbearable; stocks dropped in a near–free fall on record volume that would total over eight million shares.

Charles Mitchell stepped in to rescue the market. In spite of his position as a director of the Federal Reserve Bank of New York, ostensibly answering to the board of governors, Mitchell would not wait for the board to announce a decision. He instead took unilateral action, undercutting any attempt the Fed might make to control speculation. Mitchell announced that his National City Bank would provide money to the broker loan market to prevent forced liquidation of stocks. He stated bluntly, "We feel that we have an obligation which is paramount to any Federal Reserve warning, or anything else, to avert any dangerous crisis in the money market."[3]

The stock market promptly rallied on Mitchell's statement. More important, the Federal Reserve's board of governors did nothing to contradict him. Even so, the board came in for harsh criticism from proponents of the boom on Wall Street. One observer remarked that the Fed "should mind its own business."[4] *Barron's* questioned whether the Fed "was adequately interpreting the times," because of its apparent inability to recognize the obvious fact that high stock prices were amply justified by the dynamic, unprecedented growth taking place in the economy. Professor Joseph S. Lawrence of Princeton went so far as to complain that Wall Street had been the target of "blatant bigotry and turbulent provincialism" and declared the Street to be "innocent."[5] He chastised the Federal Reserve, charging that the central bank had "aroused the enmity of an honest, intelligent and public spirited community."[6] (Jesse Livermore and his fellow operators must have been surprised to realize that the "community" referred to by Lawrence included them.)

Charles Mitchell did not escape criticism, especially from those in Congress who had been denouncing speculation for years. Senator Carter Glass called for Mitchell's resignation as a director of the Federal Reserve Bank of New York, denouncing his "contempt" for the board. When informed of Glass's statement, Mitchell declined comment. He later defended his action by arguing that since his National City Bank was not in debt to the Federal Reserve at the time, it was not restricted by the board's directive against making speculative loans.[7]

Whatever the case, Mitchell was widely perceived as having defied the Federal Reserve and won. The stock market roared ahead. The central bank's inaction was now reassuring; when the Federal Reserve Board took no steps against Mitchell, it was clear to all that the central bank would do little to arrest the stock market boom.

It is always easy, with the benefit of hindsight, to spot decisive turning points in the stock market. Unfortunately, it is much more difficult to recognize such instances as they are occurring. September 3, 1929, would prove to be the crest of the great bull market of the 1920s; from that point on the trend was down, although interrupted from time to time by rallies of varying strength. But there was nothing particularly unusual about September 3 (or even many of the days that would follow in the next few weeks). There were occasional voices of caution, such as the *New York Times* commentary on September 9 that warned, "It is a well-known characteristic of 'boom-times' that the idea of their being terminated in the old, unpleasant way is rarely recognized as possible." But such opinions had often been expressed before (particularly by *The New York Times*). They were nothing new.

The disturbing downward trend in the market accelerated in October; by the middle of the month prices were significantly below their September highs. This slide was met with ever more vigorous incantations by the apostles of the bull market, as if their words alone could reverse the direction of stock prices. Charles Mitchell announced that the "industrial condition of the United States is absolutely sound" and predicted that "nothing can arrest the upward movement."[8] Big-time speculators like Arthur Cutten continued to voice confidence in the economy, and the market, to anyone who would listen. But the remark that received the most attention came from Professor Irving Fischer of Yale. Fischer proclaimed on October 15 that "stocks have reached what looks like a permanently high plateau."[9] A few days later stocks fell off Professor Fischer's plateau with a resounding crash.

Thursday, October 24, 1929, is the first of the days most often associated with the crash of '29. The market opened on heavy volume, and prices quickly began to fall. The stock ticker, which transmitted information on prices to brokerage offices around the country, soon fell behind the pace of transactions, adding to the uncertainty of worried investors who found they had no means of knowing just how bad the situation was. By 11:30 the market was in a free fall; all semblance of order was lost as the floor of the Exchange was swept by a frenzied panic.

Outside the Exchange building an unearthly roar was audible. A crowd began to gather, and the New York City police commissioner dispatched a squad of policemen to keep the peace. Rumors swirled through the crowd, heightening the sense of anxiety. When a workman appeared atop a nearby building, people assumed he was a likely suicide and waited expectantly for him to jump. An observer thought that people's expressions showed "not so much suffering as a sort of horrified incredulity."[10]

Where were the big operators, and the Wall Street bankers who seemingly had so much at stake in the market and presumably could not afford to let it fall? The press searched out the leading figures for comment and soon discovered that a meeting was to convene at the offices of J. P. Morgan & Company at noon to discuss an organized effort to stabilize the market. Charles Mitchell of National City Bank and the chief executive officers of other leading New York banks were to attend, hosted by the senior Morgan partner, Thomas Lamont. The elder J. P. Morgan had almost single-handedly stopped the panic of 1907; his successors were now equally determined to do the same.

A decision was quickly reached by those assembled at the Morgan offices to pool resources to support the market. Thomas Lamont, speaking for the group, came out to talk to reporters. In what Frederick Lewis Allen later termed one of the most remarkable understatements of all time, Lamont said, "There has been a little distress selling on the stock exchange."[11] He went on to say that the weakness was "due to a technical condition of the market" and was "susceptible to betterment."[12]

At approximately 1:30, the debonair Richard Whitney, acting president of the New York Stock Exchange and closely connected with J. P. Morgan & Company (his brother was a Morgan partner), crossed the floor to the post where U.S. Steel traded. He bid 205, the price of the last preceding trade, for ten thousand shares. He then proceeded self-confidently around the floor to the trading posts of other leading stocks, entering similar bids. The market reacted instantaneously. Prices shot upward in a move almost as violent as the downdraft that had occurred that morning. Miraculously, by the close most of the day's losses had been recovered. A phenomenal 12.9 million shares traded, nearly half again more than the previous record volume.

For the moment, the bankers were heroes. They, like the legendary J. P. Morgan, Sr., had quelled the panic and prevented a catastrophe. Wall Street, reported *The New York Times*, was now "secure in the knowledge the most powerful banks in the country stood ready to prevent a recurrence [of the collapse]." Even President Hoover was induced to say that "the fundamental business of the country . . . is on a sound and prosperous basis." Reportedly, President Hoover was also asked to say something positive about the stock market but declined.[13]

The bankers' glory was short-lived. On Monday, October 28, the decline began again with a vengeance. This time nothing could stem the collapse. Shortly after one o'clock Charles Mitchell was observed entering the Morgan offices, and rumors flashed that another bankers' pool was forming. But no organized buying materialized. In fact it is likely that Mitchell, far from approaching J. P. Morgan & Company to organize support for the market, was instead seeking a personal loan made necessary by his own speculative losses. The decline on the Exchange accelerated, with a crushing 3 million shares trading in the last hour alone.

That evening, by coincidence, Bernard Baruch hosted a dinner party for Winston Churchill, who was then visiting the United States. Attending were several members of the ill-fated bankers' pool. Charles Mitchell, seemingly taking his setbacks in stride, offered a facetious toast to "my fellow former millionaires."[14] Overall, Baruch's dinner guests were cautiously optimistic, the consensus opinion being that the worst was over. They were soon to be disabused of that notion.

Tuesday, October 29 (Black Tuesday), was a disaster: 16.5 million shares traded in a collapsing market that wiped out all of the gains of the preceding year. The members of the bankers' pool met again but did nothing. Thomas Lamont somewhat lamely claimed that it had never been the purpose of the pool to maintain a particular level of stock prices. Worse, he was forced to deny rumors that the bankers had actually been selling stocks (conducting a bear raid) rather than buying. (It would later be revealed that Albert Wiggins, the chairman of Chase National Bank and a member of the pool, was personally short several million dollars' worth of stock at the time the bankers sought to organize support for stock prices.)

The market in fact had demonstrated, with awesome ferocity, that it was not to be controlled by a few bankers or big operators. But what of the Federal Reserve System, which had been created in part to deal with crises like the 1929 crash? When the market broke in late October, the Federal Reserve Open Market Committee had been operating under a rule that allowed the purchase of only $25 million in government securities per week. The Federal Reserve Bank of New York immediately discarded this rule and quickly bought $160 million in short-term government notes in the marketplace in an effort to inject funds into the banking system. By the end of November, the New York bank had purchased a total of $370 million in government securities. The bank's governor, George Harrison, responding to criticism that he had exceeded his powers, said, "It is not at all unlikely that had we not bought governments so freely, thus supplementing the reserves built up by large additional discounts, the stock exchange might have had to yield to the tremendous pressure brought to bear on it to close on some of those very bad days in the last part of October."[15]

During the next two weeks, tens of thousands of margin calls went out to investors whose stockholdings had declined in value to the point where they no longer provided sufficient collateral to cover the investors' margin loans. Nonbank lenders cut their broker's loans by $1.4 billion in the last two weeks of October, and non–New York banks recalled $800 million during this same period. The big New York commercial banks stepped into the breach, making $1 billion in additional loans available. The funds necessary to do this were raised partly from borrowings from the Federal Reserve and partly from selling government securities. This process was aided immeasurably by the liquidity provided by the Federal Reserve Bank of New York. Overall, in the two months of October and November 1929, $4.5 billion in broker's loans were liquidated, in a remarkably orderly process that caused not a single major bank or brokerage failure.

The Federal Reserve Board in Washington acted on November 14, dropping its discount rate from 5% to 4½%. But George Harrison's timely actions in New York undoubtedly prevented an even worse crisis. Previous market crashes had invariably been accompanied by financial sector bankruptcies. That such a chain of collapses did not take place in 1929 can be attributed in large part to the actions of the Federal Reserve Bank of New York. Harrison may well be the unacknowledged hero of 1929.

To some observers, the crash, painful as it was, served the useful purpose of purging speculative excess from the markets. Treasury Secretary Andrew Mellon, commenting after the crash, said bluntly, "Let the slump liquidate itself. Liquidate labor, liquidate stocks, liquidate the farmers, liquidate real estate . . . it will purge the rottenness out of the system. High costs of living and high living will come down. People will work harder, live a more moral life. Values will be adjusted, and enterprising people will pick up the wrecks from less competent people."[16]

The press sought out those presumed to be responsible for the debacle. Not surprisingly, Jesse Livermore, the King of the Bears, received the most attention. Eclipsed by perennial bulls like Arthur Cutten during the rising market of the late 1920s, Livermore was rediscovered by the press when the market crashed. A clash between Livermore and his presumed nemesis Cutten was highlighted, with one newspaper declaring, "Livermore, formerly one of the country's biggest speculators, is the leader of the bear clique against Arthur Cutten, leader of the bulls . . ."[17]

The New York Times marveled that "the ascendancy of Livermore to the position he once held as a leading market operator on the bear-side after years of eclipse is one of the most intriguing developments of the market." Other papers openly speculated that Livermore was leading a bear raid on the market. *The Wall Street Journal,* while not specifically identifying Livermore, complained that there had been "a lot of selling to make the market look bad." Livermore exulted in the publicity, playing to the galleries with his customary élan.

The stories were untrue. None of the major market operators possessed the wherewithal to have caused the crash, even if they had desired to do so. While Livermore made about $6 million from his shorts during the crash, he apparently lost about the same amount on stocks he owned. Financially, he was no better off than before. In any case, the magnitude of his trading was nowhere near large enough to have had a significant impact on the overall market.

Bernard Baruch is another trader who emerged from the crash with an enhanced reputation unjustified by the facts. On June 29, 1929, he said that "the economic condition of the world seems on the verge of a great forward movement." He went on to note that market bears did not have houses on Fifth Avenue.[18] In his memoirs, Baruch claims that he then suddenly turned bearish while visiting Scotland in late August, and immediately returned to New York to position himself for a market decline. But his brokerage records and other evidence do not support this assertion.[19] Like most speculators caught up in the boom psychology of the 1920s, Baruch was slow to recognize changed circumstances. It was his inherent conservatism (especially his reluctance to speculate with borrowed money), not his astute market judgment, that enabled him to weather the storm.

Others would not be so lucky. By November 15, 1929, Arthur Cutten had lost more than $50 million. He would spend many of the remaining years of his life battling with government tax and regulatory authorities. Charles Mitchell was arrested in 1933 on charges of income tax evasion and forced to resign his position at National City Bank. He won an acquittal on the criminal charges but later lost a judgment for $1.1 million in a civil procedure, finally settling with the government in 1938.

After the crash, the aura of omnipotent genius attached to leading market operators and New York bankers disintegrated almost as fast as stock prices had fallen. Rarely has press coverage and public perception changed more abruptly, with deference and respect quickly replaced by hostility and ridicule. Men who had been assumed only weeks earlier to be veritable titans of finance were suddenly denounced as ineffectual at best, mendacious at worst.

Even more abasing was the treatment meted out to the academic advocates of the New Era, and no prominent member of the academic community suffered as much as Professor Irving Fischer of Yale. Fischer's unfortunate utterance a few days before the crash—that stocks were on a "permanently high plateau"—would come back to haunt him again and again. Struggling to salvage his reputation, Fischer wrote a book defending his viewpoint, published in 1930 under the title *The Stock Market Crash— and After*. There he reiterated the arguments of the New Era advocates— that the systematic application of science to industry, and continued consolidations leading to economies of scale, had increased corporate profits and fully justified the 1920s stock market boom. He pointed out that corporate earnings had grown at an annual rate of 9% from 1922 through 1927, while dividends had increased at a rate of 6.8%. After 1927, the rate of increase in earnings was even faster; comparing the first nine months of 1929 with the comparable period in 1928, Fischer found an increase in earnings of 20%. According to Fischer, "This record is eloquent in justification of a heightened level of common stock prices during 1929."[20]

Fischer tried to explain what had gone wrong with the market. He attributed the decline to "the psychology of panic. It was mob psychology, and it was not, primarily, that the price level was unsoundly high . . . the fall in the market was largely due to the psychology by which it went down because it went down."

The Commercial and Financial Chronicle observed acidly, "The learned professor is wrong as he usually is when he talks about the stock market." According to the Chronicle, the "mob" didn't sell—it got sold out. Speculators owning stock on margin were forced to sell when the value of the shares collateralizing their loans declined; this selling in turn sent prices lower, which forced other margined speculators to sell, and so on.

Fischer agreed that excessive leverage exacerbated the crash; there was too much margin debt employed by speculators, and there were too many leveraged vehicles like the investment trusts. But Fischer resolutely refused to concede that stocks in general were overvalued in 1929. Instead, he said, the problem was to be found in the "unsound financing of sound prospects."

Fischer has repeatedly been denigrated by critics of presumed "over-speculation." While these critics freely admit that leverage played an important role in the market collapse, they view that leverage as simply another symptom of the speculative excess of the time. Much was made of the fact that Fischer lost most of his personal wealth as a result of his speculative activities, and rumors abounded that the Yale endowment fund, to which Fischer was an adviser, was badly hurt by the crash. (This was not true; apparently the Yale endowment fund pursued a fairly conservative investment strategy in 1929.)

But what of Fischer's basic argument—that enhanced productivity and the rapid growth of corporate profits justified the high level of stock prices in 1929? Since his reasoning is very similar to that frequently heard in the booming years at the turn of the twenty-first century, it bears closer examination. Such is the mystique associated with the 1929 crash that even today scholars still debate its causes, and the question of whether or not the market was badly overvalued before the collapse. While the results of the ongoing debate are not definitive (and probably never will be), Fischer and his fellow New Era advocates fare much better in retrospect than they did in their own time.

The "revisionist" (pro–New Era advocates) interpretation of the 1929 crash did not begin to gain credence until several decades after the crash. Writing in the *Business History Review* in 1975, Gerald Sirkin cited data going back to 1800, from which he identified a major change in the nature of the growth process in the American economy beginning early in the twentieth century. According to Sirkin, before 1900 most growth in the economy was generated by providing more capital to business, but after 1900 much of the economy's growth resulted from increases in productivity, which enhanced the return on capital earned by business and accelerated the rate of increase in corporate earnings. This evidence provides statistical justification for the arguments of New Era proponents like Irving Fischer.

Specifically analyzing market valuations in 1929, Sirkin concluded the market P/E ratios were justified by the growth of earnings in the late 1920s. While some stocks were overvalued, he found that the overvaluation was concentrated in only approximately 20% of stocks, leaving the overall market fairly priced. Sirkin writes that the data do not present a picture of "speculative orgy" in "a time of madness." Instead, in his words, most stocks were "cold sober," although a few did show signs of "overindulgence." His conclusion: "not much of an orgy."

The most recent book published on the 1929 crash is *The Causes of the 1929 Stock Market Crash*, written by Harold Bierman, Jr., a professor at Cornell University. Bierman applies modern standards of market valuation to analyze 1929 stock prices. First, he calculates that the market P/E ratio in 1929 was 16.3 to 1. Then, using the discounted cash-flow model developed many years after the 1929 crash (which will be discussed in detail in later chapters; see definition on page 156), he finds that an annual rate of dividend increase of 3.6% would have been sufficient, by later standards, to support the 1929 market P/E. In fact, the rate of dividend increases throughout the 1920s was significantly higher than 3.6%, and even conservative estimates of future dividend growth were at least as great. Bierman does admit that certain segments of the market appear to have been overvalued in 1929; he specifically cites electric utilities, which were among the speculative growth vehicles of the late 1920s. But, like Sirkin, Bierman argues that this overvaluation was confined to limited sectors and did not infect the market as a whole.

Bierman's reasoning seems quite convincing. It is hard to argue, by modern standards, that the stock market as a whole was overvalued in 1929. But of course modern standards were not used (and many of the models now employed to evaluate stocks didn't even exist) in the late 1920s. This is the essence of the problem. If 1929 is judged by standards previously prevailing, stock prices were too high. But if the bull market of the 1920s is instead seen as part of a transition from traditional, conservative standards to the modern approaches used today, it does not appear that prices were far out of line.

The close association of the 1929 crash with the subsequent Depression invariably taints efforts to analyze the crash itself. It is commonly believed that the crash somehow "predicted" the onset of the Depression. In fact, the economy began to turn down in August 1929, two months before the crash. Such was the state of economic statistics at the time, however, that no one could have been certain a serious recession, let alone a depression, was developing until many months later. To argue that the collective action of market participants in October 1929 anticipated the Depression of subsequent years is to impute an omniscience to stock traders that is simply not credible.

While the crash could not have "predicted" the Great Depression, could not the precipitous market collapse have caused, or at least exacerbated, the economic contraction of the 1930s? John Kenneth Galbraith implies that the answer to this question is yes. His argument is based on what economists would now call the "wealth effect," whereby a sharp drop in the stock market suddenly reduces the wealth of investors, causing them to feel less prosperous and to therefore spend less. Declining consumer spending slows the economy, perhaps resulting in a recession. If simultaneously affected by other contractionary economic forces, the recession could very well slip into a depression.

In 1929 one-third of all individual income in the United States was received by the top 5% of the population. According to Galbraith, this unequal distribution of income made the economy very susceptible to a stock market "shock" that would disproportionately affect the high-income individuals who were most involved in the market. If those people suddenly cut back on their spending, the economy could be adversely affected. Galbraith reasons that something like this may very well have happened in 1929.

Problems with this line of reasoning are immediately evident. First, the 1929 crash, severe as it was, erased only a part of the gains registered by the 1920s bull market. Stock prices at the end of 1929 were still significantly higher than they had been as recently as early 1928. Given the fact that most long-term investors were still substantially ahead in late 1929, is it reasonable to assume that they would have drastically altered their consumption patterns because of the crash?

Second, changes in the pace of economic activity do not track well with changes in stock prices during and after the crash. The economic slowdown began in August 1929, while the stock market was still rising. The decline in economic activity was quite gradual during the crash itself, in October and November. The slowdown then became more severe in early 1930, but this was during a period when the stock market rallied substantially. While the economy may have responded to the "wealth effect" with a lag, it is hard to credibly match changes in stock prices with changes in the economy.

Any analysis of a possible wealth effect leads to another question. Exactly how many people were actually invested in the stock market in 1929? If the number was very large, clearly the wealth effect argument might have some validity. And if many of the investors owned stocks on margin (thereby likely suffering proportionately greater losses in the crash), the impact of the wealth effect could be powerful indeed.

Anecdotal accounts of the period often portray a general public consumed with little else than stock market speculation. A British correspondent in the United States wrote how the stock market invariably dominated conversations at social affairs he attended: "You could talk about Prohibition or Hemingway, or air conditioning, or music, or horses, but in the end you had to talk about the stock market, and that was when the conversation became serious."[21] A familiar story, variously attributed to Joseph Kennedy and Bernard Baruch, describes how even shoe-shine boys were dispensing tips on the market in the summer of 1929. John Brooks, in *Once in Golconda*, describes scenes of brokerage offices packed with amateur speculators who had quit their jobs to devote themselves full-time to the market.

Unfortunately, this popular "myth" of 1929 does not conform to observable reality. In 1929 there were approximately 1.5 million active brokerage accounts in the country, out of a population of 120 million, consisting of between 29 and 30 million households. Of these 1.5 million accounts, 600,000 were margin accounts, in which borrowed money was used to buy stocks. Since some investors maintained more than one bro-kerage account, the total number of people holding accounts was undoubt-edly significantly less than 1.5 million, and the total number of individuals maintaining margin accounts less than 600,000.

From these data, it appears that only 3% to 4% of American house-holds were actively engaged in stock trading in 1929, with less than half that number investing on margin. Given that the crash brought stock prices down only to where they had been in 1928, and given the relatively small number of Americans actively involved in trading stocks, it is hard to see how the wealth effect associated with the crash could have been sufficient to cause a serious downturn in economic activity.

It is important to note that although the number of Americans actively playing the stock market in the late 1920s was relatively small, the number who owned stocks in one form or another was substantially greater. Adolph Berle and Gardiner Means estimated that at the beginning of 1928, between 4 million and 6 million Americans were shareholders, a figure much larger than the number of brokerage accounts would suggest. But most of this discrepancy can be explained by allowing for the effect of cus-tomer and employee stock purchase plans that became popular in the 1920s.[22]

Partly because of the tax-induced reluctance of high-income people to buy stocks in the period during and immediately after World War I, some companies, particularly public utilities, began to actively solicit their cus-tomers to buy shares. In 1925, the peak year for these plans, utilities sold 23% of all newly issued stock directly to their customers. By 1928, a total of nearly 1.9 million sales had been made. While this number inevitably in-cluded some customers who made more than one purchase, it is estimated that over 1 million people, most of whom never owned stock before, be-came shareholders through this process. But these holdings individually were quite small, and by the end of the decade stock acquired through cus-tomer purchase arrangements accounted for only 1.5% of all stock out-standing.

Likewise, employee stock purchase plans grew rapidly in the 1920s.

(These plans should not be confused with the employer-operated pension and retirement plans that would become quite common, and vastly more significant, in the second half of the twentieth century.) By 1928, more than 800,000 people had purchased stock through these employee stock plans. Again, the typical holdings were very small, totaling only 1% of all stock outstanding.

Together, customer and employee purchase plans created nearly 2 million small shareholders in the 1920s, with the stock purchases occurring through mechanisms other than standard brokerage accounts. While these people were technically stockholders, they were certainly not active participants in the stock market. There were many other small shareholders as well; an examination of the shareholder records kept by major corporations of the period suggests that many of their stockholders owned trivial numbers of shares. (For example, in the mid-twenties, 37% of AT&T shareholders owned five shares or less and received less than $46 in dividends annually from the company.) All these small holders, taken together, add up to millions of people. But their tiny holdings could not have been significant enough to have caused them to drastically alter their consumption patterns after the crash. Their actions are not likely to have induced a wealth-effect economic slowdown.

If the 1929 crash did not either predict or cause the subsequent depression, what, then, is its significance? In reality, probably much less than has been made of it over the years. Stocks fell more than 40% from the September 3 high to the mid-November low, undeniably a substantial decline, but not much different in magnitude from what had occurred in several nineteenth-century panics, 1907, or the bear market of 1919–1921. Declines of similar magnitude would later occur in 1937, 1969–1970, and 1973–1974. On one day (October 19, 1987) the market would drop twice as much, in percentage terms, as it did on the single worst day of the 1929 crash. Seen from this perspective, the 1929 crash, while obviously severe, was not by any means unique.

Beginning in mid-November 1929 a subdued but steady recovery developed that stretched into April 1930. During the recovery, prices recouped nearly half the losses sustained in the crash. An observer of the market in April 1930 could be forgiven if he simply viewed the crash as having been another of the many market breaks that had occurred throughout history. It was only after the Great Depression of the 1930s set in that the crash was imbued with the ominous import so often attached to it since.

All sorts of explanations have been advanced to explain why the crash occurred, citing various events in the fall of 1929 that could conceivably have had an adverse effect on investor psychology. None of these explanations is particularly convincing, in that similar incidents had occurred before and had not led to market collapses. Galbraith says simply that the market was "shattered by a spontaneous decision to get out," and that anything could have caused it. He goes on to write, "What first stirred these doubts we do not know, but neither is it very important to know."

In a way, Galbraith is probably correct, although perhaps for the wrong reasons. Stocks had advanced to unprecedented levels in 1929. As has been seen, while Galbraith paints a picture of unrestrained speculative excess in 1929, there were in fact many voices sounding notes of caution, not the least of which was the Federal Reserve Board. Even if high stock prices would ultimately appear to be justified by modern analytical techniques, there is no question that the rapid rise in the late 1920s, and constant warnings about overspeculation, made many people uneasy. It would not have taken much to convert this sense of unease into fear, and then panic.

In spite of its notable failure to face down Charles Mitchell and his fellow New Era advocates over the specific issue of broker loans in early 1929, the Federal Reserve had been pursuing a tight money policy for some time, a policy that in large part reflected concern about overspeculation in the stock market. Milton Friedman and Anna Schwartz state quite succinctly, "There is no doubt that the desire to curb the stock market boom was a major if not dominating factor in Reserve actions in 1928 and 1929."[23] The tight money policy may well have induced the economic slowdown that began in August 1929. Although the eventual magnitude and duration of that downturn could not have been evident in October, the first inklings may have been enough to tip the precarious psychological balance in the market.

According to this reasoning, the Federal Reserve, in its efforts to restrain speculation, pursued a policy that stalled the economy. The stock market, bounding ahead on the optimistic assumption that high rates of economic growth would continue unabated, stumbled over early hints of an economic slowdown. The initial decline in stock prices forced selling by heavily leveraged margin investors, accelerating the market correction into a rout. Evidence to support this hypothesis was presented in a study completed in 1961, in which economic data from the late 1920s were analyzed. The study concluded, "The US authorities precipitated the crisis by the crusade against speculation, instead of leaving stock prices to their fate and supporting the expansion of economic activity."[24] In effect, this argument is the exact opposite of Galbraith's. While Galbraith believes that unrestrained speculation created a bubble that inevitably burst, the "revisionist" interpretation is that efforts by authorities (notably the Federal Reserve) to restrain speculation unintentionally slowed the economy, which in turn brought the bull market of the 1920s to an abrupt halt.

Economic historians will likely never fully agree on the precise causes of the 1929 crash. Perhaps, as Galbraith suggests, an exact determination of the causative factors may not really be all that important anyway. Several conclusions about the crash, however, should be quite clear. First, by the standards of valuation that would prevail for most of the remainder of the twentieth century, stocks were not badly overvalued in the fall of 1929. The bull market of the 1920s, far from being a period of speculative excess, was instead simply part of a process in which stock valuations adjusted upward from the low levels of earlier years, toward the higher levels that would routinely prevail in the future. Second, the crash could not in any realistic way have "predicted" the Great Depression that followed. There was no hard evidence in October 1929 that a serious downturn in economic activity was in the offing, and thus it is not reasonable to assume that the collective action of market participants anticipated an economic collapse. Third, the crash could not have caused the Depression. Given the small number of people actually involved in stock speculation, and the fact that the crash merely returned stock prices to levels they had been at in 1928, the wealth effect of the market decline could not have been of sufficient magnitude to severely dislocate the economy. And finally, if the crash is viewed independently from the Depression that came later, it was not really all that much different from other panics that had occurred in the past.

Market declines of similar duration and magnitude had occurred before, and would occur later; 1929 was not in any way unique.

Such is the mythology that surrounds the crash of 1929 that these conclusions may seem almost heretical. Conventional wisdom has it that the crash of 1929 was a calamity of extraordinary significance that forever altered the lives of tens of millions of people and foreshadowed the Great Depression. The facts indicate otherwise.

Dow Jones Industrial Average, 1930–1939

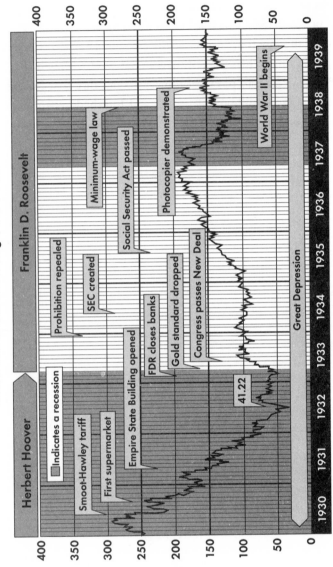

Herbert Hoover

Franklin D. Roosevelt

■ Indicates a recession

Smoot-Hawley tariff

First supermarket

Empire State Building opened

FDR closes banks

Prohibition repealed

SEC created

Gold standard dropped

Congress passes New Deal

Social Security Act passed

Minimum-wage law

Photocopier demonstrated

World War II begins

Great Depression

41.22

400 350 300 250 200 150 100 50 0

1930 1931 1932 1933 1934 1935 1936 1937 1938 1939

7

REVOLUTION

RICHARD WHITNEY WAS born to lead. The son of a Boston bank president and nephew of a former J. P. Morgan & Company partner, Whitney was the scion of a family that had come to America on the ship that followed the *Mayflower*. Tall, with an athletic build and handsome features, he had been captain of the baseball team and acting captain of the football squad at Groton, before matriculating at Harvard. His elder brother, George, married the daughter of a Morgan partner and subsequently obtained a Morgan partnership himself. Richard formed his own Wall Street brokerage firm, Richard Whitney & Company, with funds provided by his family. Suave, urbane, and ever conscious of his class, he had a formally proper manner of dealing with people he considered to be his social inferiors. He was proud of his breeding, and made certain everyone knew it.

In the depths of the Great Depression in 1932, Whitney lived on a grand scale in an impressive town house in Manhattan and on a 500-acre estate in Far Hills, New Jersey. He raised champion Ayrshire cattle on the New Jersey property, maintaining a staff of twelve "outside hands"—including herdsmen, grooms, and a jockey—in addition to a full complement of servants who worked inside the main house.[1] Whitney was best known to the public as the president of the New York Stock Exchange who, as acting president during the 1929 crash, had been the point man on the floor of the Exchange for the ill-fated bankers' pool that had briefly attempted to stabilize the market. Shortly after the crash, the Governing Committee of the Exchange passed a resolution "in appreciation of Whitney's efficient and conscientious" efforts during the crisis. "It is an old saying," the resolution continued, "that great emergencies produce the men who are competent to deal with them . . ."[2] To many outside the Exchange, however, Whitney's efforts were the object of derision rather than praise. He epitomized the blue-blooded bankers and brokers who had amply demonstrated their impotence, if not their outright complicity, in the disastrous events of October 1929.

By 1932 Whitney, and the "old guard" he represented, were frequently assailed by politicians of all persuasions who blamed the Wall Street community for the crash and subsequent Depression. In January, President Herbert Hoover summoned Whitney to the White House; in his memoirs Hoover wrote that he "warned Richard Whitney . . . that unless they took measures to clean their own house I would ask Congress to investigate the Stock Exchange with a view to Federal control legislation." In April 1932, Republicans, who controlled the Senate, moved formally to investigate the stock market, particularly focusing on allegations that organized bear raids were forcing prices down. One Republican senator, Frederic C. Wolcott of Connecticut, expressed fears that Democratic market operatives were planning bear raids on the market before the 1932 elections to embarrass President Hoover. Wolcott was not the only prominent Republican to suspect a sinister purpose behind the long market slide that had commenced in April 1930. The chairman of the Republican Party had said: "Persons high in Republican circles are beginning to believe that there is some concerted effort on foot to utilize the stock market as a method of discrediting the Administration. Every time an Administration official gives out an optimistic statement about business conditions, the market immediately drops."

Hearings of the Senate Banking and Currency Committee, chaired by Republican senator Peter Norbeck of South Dakota, got under way in April 1932. Richard Whitney, in his capacity as president of the New York Stock Exchange, was the first witness. He confronted a scene of disorder; the hearings had been convened in haste, and the committee room was crowded with spectators, some sitting on filing boxes while others actually leaned against the back of the chair in which Whitney sat. The senators themselves were unprepared and often clearly did not understand the complexities of the subject matter they were dealing with. Whitney did not give an inch, and at times seemed to be lecturing the panel on basic economics. Finally Senator Norbeck fumed in frustration, "You don't grant that anything in the market is illegal. You don't grant anything. You're hopeless."[3]

While the investigation did not uncover evidence of the politically motivated machinations the Republicans feared, it did bring to light an unseemly array of pools and other manipulative activity. These disclosures further tarnished the image of the Stock Exchange and reinforced the widely held belief that the market was basically crooked. After the Democrats, and Franklin Roosevelt, handily won the election of 1932, the Senate hearings that the Republicans had organized took on a different character. Wall Street brokers and bankers now feared an inquisition, not just an investigation.

It is difficult, looking back from the perspective of prosperous times many years later, to fully appreciate the climate of fear and foreboding that pervaded Wall Street in early 1933. The rally in stock prices that had developed immediately after the crash and extended into April 1930 had been snuffed out in one of the most painfully protracted bear markets in history. When the stock market finally hit bottom in July 1932, the Dow Jones Industrial Average had dropped 89% from its September 1929 high to a mere 41.22. Stocks of the country's most substantial corporations showed shocking declines: U.S. Steel dropped from 262 to 22, General Motors from 73 to 8, and AT&T from 304 to 73. RCA, the speculative darling of the late twenties, fell 98% from its 1929 peak. Once mighty Anaconda Copper dropped to $4 per share; *The Commercial and Financial Chronicle* observed, "The copper shares are so low that their fluctuations are of little consequence."

The market had been dragged down by one of the most severe economic depressions in the nation's history. By mid-1932, the gross national product had fallen by one-third from 1929 levels, industrial production was at only 12% of capacity, and unemployment stood at nearly 25%. Economists today still debate the causes of the Great Depression; a detailed examination of this question is beyond the scope of this book. Suffice it to say that, like all macroeconomic phenomena, a confluence of several factors was likely responsible, including a weak banking system, unduly contractionary Federal Reserve monetary policies, and protectionist legislation that stifled international trade. All these (and probably other) factors accelerated a cyclical economic downturn into a severe depression.

Much of the public and many government officials blamed Wall Street for the economic collapse. The "excess speculation" explanation for the crash of 1929 had already become conventional wisdom; even leading Wall Street authorities subscribed to it. As early as 1930, Richard Whitney's predecessor as head of the New York Stock Exchange, E.H.H. Simmons said, "It is obvious . . . that the high level of share prices last August rendered the stock market vulnerable to a considerable price decline . . . Every serious break in the stock market is always attributed to over-speculation . . ."[4] Not only was the crash seen as the result of "overspeculation," but, more ominously, it was commonly believed to have been a precursor of the Depression. Thus it did not require a great leap of logic to attribute at least part of the severity of the Depression to the irresponsible actions of Wall Street bankers, brokers, and speculators. The Street would inevitably be a target of the New Deal reformers.

By early 1933 the nation's banking system was on the verge of collapse. To deal with the crisis, newly inaugurated President Franklin Roosevelt declared a "Bank Holiday"; as part of the "holiday," all stock exchanges were closed from March 6 to March 14. Many bankers and brokers spoke openly of the possibility of revolution. Joseph P. Kennedy, himself one of the leading market operators, wrote three years later that "I am not ashamed to record that in those days I felt and said I would be willing to part with half of what I had if I could be sure of keeping, under law and order, the other half."[5]

It was under these conditions that Richard Whitney was again called to give testimony before the Senate committee, this time controlled by Democrats. He was not a good witness. Whitney appeared very condescending when explaining the intricacies of the market, as if the senators on the committee were incapable of understanding them. He placed the entire blame for the Depression on government and suggested that the greatest contribution the senators could make would be to balance the federal budget. To achieve this, he recommended cutting the pensions and benefits of veterans who had no service-connected disability, and all government salaries. Asked the amount of his own salary, Whitney demurred, describing it as "very little." When pressed, Whitney said his salary was currently "only" $60,000, a princely sum to most Americans, ten times the annual salary of members of the Senate.[6]

Perhaps the most memorable exchanges came when Whitney allowed himself to be drawn into a discussion of the nature of markets and the economy with Senator Smith W. Brookhart of Iowa. Brookhart had for years been a leading critic of "gambling" on Wall Street, describing the New York Stock Exchange as a "great gambling hell" that should be closed down and "padlocked." In defending the Exchange and its role in the economy, Whitney went so far as to describe the Exchange as a "perfect" institution.[7] Needless to say, Brookhart and most of his fellow senators were unconvinced.

President Roosevelt moved quickly, proposing a law to regulate new underwritings of securities. Roosevelt asked that the law be based on "the ancient truth that those who manage banks, corporations and other agencies handling other people's money are trustees acting for others."[8] Wall Street had always operated on the basis of caveat emptor; Roosevelt proposed that "the burden of telling the whole truth [be placed] on the seller."[9] In response, Congress passed the Securities Act of 1933, granting the federal government the power to oblige underwriters to observe certain guidelines in their solicitations, and also requiring that most new issues be registered with the government before being sold to the public.

Shortly thereafter, the Banking Act of 1933, to become better known as the Glass-Steagall Act, gave the Federal Reserve more control over member banks' speculative activities and drew a distinct line between the activities of commercial and investment banks by requiring that commercial banks divest themselves of investment affiliates. The legislation also created the Federal Deposit Insurance Corporation to insure bank deposits, an extremely important innovation that would virtually eliminate bank runs in the future. Neither the Securities Act of 1933 nor Glass-Steagall met strong resistance from the Wall Street community, which recognized that some form of new regulation was inevitable and found these first pieces of New Deal legislation to be at least tolerable.

Overt regulation of the market, however, was a different matter. It was commonly assumed that abusive behavior by stock market operators had at least in part caused the crash, and thus the Depression. Even so, efforts to ban market manipulation engendered great controversy. The next piece of regulatory legislation proposed by the Roosevelt administration was designed to do just that, and was bitterly opposed by Whitney and his supporters. Whitney warned that "the nation's securities markets would dry up" if the legislation was enacted.[10]

His objections were swept aside. Congress enacted the Securities and Exchange Act of 1934, which outlawed specific practices such as trading on "material non-public information" (insider trading), pools designed to influence stock prices, and the deliberate dissemination of false information. The Federal Reserve Board was empowered to set limits on how much investor-speculators could borrow to finance stock transactions (margin requirements). To enforce these rules, the Act created the Securities and Exchange Commission. The SEC, as it came to be known, was described as having powers "so sweeping . . . that there is scarcely a single aspect of the operations of a securities exchange which is beyond the commission's reach."[11]

It was generally assumed that President Roosevelt would select a strong advocate of reform to be the first head of the SEC, but Roosevelt surprised both supporters and foes alike when he instead picked notorious stock market operator Joseph Kennedy for the job. Kennedy had been an active supporter of Roosevelt, and his appointment was rationalized by many Roosevelt backers as payback for that support. Even so, the move sparked strong criticism from proponents of market reform who felt betrayed. But it reassured many Wall Street brokers and bankers, who had feared far worse.

Ironically, Kennedy had recently been investigated by a congressional committee looking into his role in the well-publicized manipulation of the stock of Libbey-Owens-Ford Glass in 1932. The stock had run up sharply before the presidential election, under the presumption that a Democratic victory would presage the repeal of Prohibition and a resultant increase in the demand for bottles. The investigation did not find Kennedy guilty of any specific crimes, but disclosures were made that called into doubt the morality of his actions. It was widely—and correctly—assumed that Kennedy's machinations in the Libbey-Owens-Ford case were not atypical.

Kennedy was one of the few stock market operators of the 1920s who survived the 1929 crash and subsequent bear market with their fortunes intact. By his own account, he had grown nervous about the state of the market in 1928 and 1929 and liquidated most of his stockholdings. Stories circulated that he was actually short stocks at the time of the collapse, but these accounts could not be confirmed. Kennedy publicly denied selling short but occasionally, according to *The New York Post*, "hinted broadly that the stories were true." Like Jesse Livermore, Kennedy was not averse to a little publicity highlighting his presumed market acumen.

After the crash, Kennedy reputedly teamed up with notorious bear raider Bernard "Sell 'em Ben" Smith. Smith had acquired the nickname Sell 'em Ben in an incident that is said to have occurred during the worst moments of the 1929 crash, when he rushed into his broker's office screaming, "Sell 'em all! They're not worth anything!" Kennedy and Smith organized raids targeted at speculators who found themselves in precarious financial positions. The two men would allegedly identify individuals with large loans collateralized by inactively traded stocks; Kennedy and Smith would then sell the stocks short, driving the price down and reducing the value of the collateral until the unfortunate victim was forced to sell out, enabling the bear raiders to "cover" their shorts at a profit.

By the time his appointment to head the SEC was announced, however, Kennedy had divested himself of his stockholdings and placed all his liquid wealth in government bonds. He moved expeditiously to enforce the new securities laws, which made illegal many of the very maneuvers he had often employed. Kennedy was no doubt aided by his personal experience; it was said that he could watch the market action as reported on a stock ticker and notice immediately when a pool or some other form of now-illegal activity was present. The SEC, under his guidance, created a body of rules to eliminate manipulation from the market. One of the most important new rules was a requirement that short sales on a stock exchange be permitted only on an "uptick," defined as a price greater than the last preceding different price at which that stock had traded. More than anything else, this rule would stymie potential bear raiders, who could no longer aggressively sell short at progressively lower prices to force stocks down.

Kennedy's tenure at the SEC lasted only one year, but during that period his moderation in the use of the agency's powers did a great deal to reassure Wall Street. In 1934 and early 1935 there was much talk of a "capital strike," with investment bankers and investors allegedly unwilling to underwrite and invest in new securities issues because of the uncertainty created by government regulation. The new-issue market finally reopened in the spring of 1935 when Swift & Company was able to successfully sell $43 million worth of bonds, the largest offering since 1929. Other new issues followed, as investment bankers regained confidence in the markets. The capital strike, if it ever really existed, proved to be short-lived, and the return to normal markets was undoubtedly hastened by the manner in which Kennedy handled his sensitive job at the SEC.

All talk of a capital strike aside, the stock market actually performed very well in the first Roosevelt administration. Between March 1933 (after the "Bank Holiday") and July, the market more than doubled, the most rapid rise in percentage terms in its history. Another sustained rally began in the spring of 1935, roughly at the time the so-called capital strike ended, and continued until January 1937, when the Dow Jones Industrial Average stood nearly 200% higher than it had on the day Roosevelt was inaugurated. Had this rise not begun from such a low base, it would be viewed as one of the most impressive bull markets in history.

But by comparison with the lofty levels of the late 1920s, stock prices in the mid-1930s, even after rebounding from the abysmal lows of 1932, were still very depressed. Trading volume on the New York Stock Exchange was lethargic; during the 1933 "bull market" an average of 2.5 million shares per day were transacted, well below the average of 4.2 million shares per day in 1929. Volume in 1934 was only half the 1933 level, and while trading activity picked up a bit in subsequent years, it would not be until 1955 that even the relatively low volume levels of 1933 were surpassed.

In early 1935 the ever-diligent Richard Whitney and his New York Stock Exchange colleagues set out to reverse this distressing trend, inaugurating a marketing campaign designed to revive interest in the stock market. Whitney embarked on a speaking tour of the country, and advertisements were placed in newspapers and magazines. Unfortunately, the campaign was met with derision and quickly became the butt of jokes. Comedian Eddie Cantor opined that conditions in the market did seem to be getting better—all the brokers who planned to jump out of windows had already done so. Another comedian volunteered that he might consider buying stocks again, if the broker who had put him into stocks in 1929 would take back those shares, which were presently serving as wallpaper in his bathroom.

The crash and the prolonged bear market that followed not only turned the public against Wall Street but also left an indelible imprint on academia. The New Era advocates had been thoroughly routed; "traditionalists" were back in control. The tenor of the times was captured in 1931 by a book written by Lawrence Chamberlain and William Hay entitled *Investment and Speculation*. Implicitly attacking Edgar Smith's 1924 work *Common Stocks as Long Term Investments*, which had provided an intellectual basis for the 1920s boom, Chamberlain and Hay stated bluntly, "Common stocks, as such, are not superior to bonds as long-term investments, because primarily they are not investments at all. They are speculations."

What would prove to be one of the most influential books ever written on the subject of investing, entitled *Security Analysis*, was published in 1934 by Benjamin Graham and David Dodd. Ben Graham would, over the years, become something of a legendary figure among Wall Street investors. He is generally thought of as the father of modern security analysis, defined as a rigorous, quantitative approach to calculating the true value of a given stock. Graham had been born Benjamin Grossbaum but had changed his Germanic-sounding surname to Graham during World War I. Short, with intense blue eyes and large lips that resembled those of a fish, he was described by a friend as "a funny little guy, sort of ugly."[12] A student of Latin and Greek classics and Spanish poetry, Graham was offered teaching positions at Columbia after graduating in 1914, but turned them down to work on Wall Street.

Graham soon recognized that Wall Street lacked adequate information on most of the stocks that were traded there, and set out to remedy the situation. His approach was to identify hidden value—usually a company that possessed assets that were not fully reflected in its stock price. The market was rife with such opportunities in Graham's early years; stock prices were low, and he faced little competition from others attempting to ferret out "value." However, after much initial success, Graham was hit hard by the post-1929 bear market. He bought stocks aggressively after the crash, believing that they were undervalued, only to see prices slide much lower in the dismal years that followed.

In spite of this experience, Graham did not subscribe to the Chamberlain-Hay view that stock investing was inherently speculative. Instead he and his coauthor, David Dodd, believed that the systematic application of sound analytical techniques to stock selection would enable investors to achieve solid returns with reasonable risk, even in bad market environments. They conceded that the period from 1927 to 1932 had been very difficult for stock market analysts but argued that the experience was atypical, calling it "unprecedented." In their view, it should not be used as a basis for evaluating the true long-term potential of stocks held by conservative investors.

Graham and Dodd believed that the so-called New Era that began in 1927 had in fact represented a departure from traditional standards and the abandonment of a rigorous analytical approach to valuing stocks. They wrote, "While emphasis was still seemingly placed on facts and figures, these were manipulated by a sort of pseudo-analysis to support the delusions of the period. The market collapse of October 1929 was no surprise to such analysts as had kept their heads, but the extent of the business collapse that later developed, with its devastating effects on established earning power, again threw their calculations out of gear. Hence the ultimate result was that serious analysis suffered a double discrediting: the first— prior to the crash—due to the persistence of imaginary values, and the second—after the crash—due to the disappearance of real values." In the Graham and Dodd view, the serious student of the market was whipsawed, first by a speculative mania that made no sense, and then by an economic depression that could not have been anticipated.

Graham and Dodd argued that a securities analyst should seek to determine the "intrinsic value" of a given stock, which was often very different from the current market price of that stock. However, they specifically rejected the concept of "intrinsic value" commonly employed in the early years of the century, defined as the book value of a company's shares (assets per share minus liabilities per share), admitting that time had shown that book value had no connection to corporate earnings or stock prices. To Graham and Dodd, a stock's "intrinsic value" was "that value that was justified by the facts, e.g., the assets, earnings, dividends [and] definitive prospects" of a company, "not capitalization of entirely conjectural future profits."

The term "definitive prospects" is key. Graham and Dodd sought out stocks whose stable patterns of revenues and earnings could be safely used to anticipate future results, and whose market price seemed cheap when analyzed on this basis. They explicitly recognized that their methodology would not work well in periods of great uncertainty or those that were subject to radical change. To Graham and Dodd it was "manifest . . . that future changes are largely unpredictable, and that security analysis must proceed on the assumption that the past record affords at least a rough guide to the future."

Much of what would later be known as "value" investing is based on the Graham and Dodd approach. Benjamin Graham went on to lecture and write extensively on the subject of investment analysis. Perhaps the best pupil in the courses he taught over the years was a baby-faced 20-year-old from Omaha, Nebraska, named Warren Buffet. Buffet would become the most famous, and probably most successful, adherent of the "value" school of investing. He would carry the torch long after Graham had passed from the scene.

Writing as they did in the depths of the Great Depression, Graham and Dodd were obviously influenced by the overspeculation explanation of the 1929 crash. But in reality their approach represented something of a compromise between traditionalists who denounced any attempt to estimate future profits as "speculation" and New Era proponents who allegedly placed too much emphasis on forecasted earnings. Graham and Dodd were willing to anticipate the future, but only as it could be seen to be predictable based on past results.

A counterpoint to the Graham and Dodd "value" approach to investing was provided a few years later by a man who had been an avid student of the stock market throughout his adult life, T. Rowe Price, Jr. Fearful of inflation, Price believed that the only way an investor could safely protect himself was to invest in what he called growth stocks. In a series of articles in *Barron's*, Price defined growth stocks as "shares in business enterprises which have demonstrated favorable underlying long-term growth in earnings and which, after careful research study, give indications of continuing secular growth in the future." The best way to determine whether a particular stock met these criteria was to measure the growth of the company's unit sales and to examine the trend in earnings.

Even though he was defining an approach to investing that would be widely embraced in future market booms, Price, like Graham and Dodd, was still deeply influenced by the Great Depression. He argued that corporations, much like individuals, pass through life cycles, which he identified as growth, maturity, and decadence. Price said that the greatest opportunities came in the growth phase, and that investors should actively seek out companies in that category. Unfortunately, Price believed (clearly influenced by the Depression) that American industry in the late 1930s was mature, having already experienced its greatest growth. Thus it was necessary for astute investors to work even harder to find growth stocks in a sea of mature or decadent companies. Only then could the investor fully protect himself against future inflation.

Price's essential argument—that investors should purchase growth stocks to beat inflation—proved to be of far more lasting significance than his characterization of American industry in the 1930s as mature. It may seem incongruous that Price was worried about potential inflation during the 1930s, which were in fact years marked by substantial deflation. However, fears of inflation were actually quite common among those who were uncomfortable with New Deal policies that had devalued the dollar and substantially increased government spending. T. Rowe Price, Jr., was certainly not alone when he argued that future inflation was the greatest risk to be borne by long-term investors.

It is ironic that two approaches to stock market investing that would be widely accepted in the prosperous second half of the twentieth century—Graham and Dodd's "value" investing and T. Rowe Price's "growth" investing—were spawned within a few years of each other during the depressed 1930s. Neither Graham and Dodd nor Price anticipated the long boom that would finally get under way in the 1940s. But the analytical approaches they developed, even though profoundly colored by the searing experience of the Great Depression, proved to be very durable, providing systematic methodologies for investing that would be successfully employed under very different conditions in the future.

At the same time Benjamin Graham and David Dodd were writing *Se-*

curity Analysis, another student of the market, Alfred Cowles, was collecting data in an effort to answer a basic question that intrigued him. Seeking sound investment advice, Cowles had become confused by the bewildering array of investment newsletters published in the 1920s. He finally decided in 1928 to conduct a test in which he would monitor 24 of the most widely circulated publications to determine which was actually the best. The results of his efforts proved quite disappointing; none of the services correctly anticipated the 1929 crash or the subsequent bear market, and most of the advice offered proved to be quite poor.

It was then Cowles asked the question that he would spend years attempting to answer: Can anyone really consistently predict stock prices? Using his inherited wealth to fund research on the subject, Cowles assembled a great deal of data and eventually reached a tentative answer to his question. Summed up in three words, the answer was "It is doubtful."[13]

Cowles found that only slightly more than a third of the investment newsletters he monitored had performed well and that he could not prove definitely that the results of even the best of them were attributable to anything other than luck. He also took on the proponents of the Dow theory, exhaustively examining the predictions of William Hamilton, the *Wall Street Journal* editor who succeeded Charles Dow. For more than 25 years, Hamilton had been publishing market prognostications based on Dow's ideas. Hamilton died in 1929, shortly after issuing, only days before the crash, his most famous prediction: that the bull market of the 1920s had come to an end. He received a great deal of posthumous credit for his timely market call from observers who forgot that he had made similar calls in 1927 and, twice, in 1928. Cowles did not overlook the previous faux pas; his analysis concluded that although a Hamilton portfolio would have grown by a factor of 19 during Hamilton's years as editor of the *Journal* (1903–1929), an investor who simply bought into the market and held his stocks over that same period would have done twice as well.

Cowles, although not a trained academic expert, compiled an impressive array of information that would be used decades later by scholars seeking to examine the same questions that had interested him. (Much of the data used in this book to compute price-earnings ratios and dividend rates for the nineteenth and early twentieth centuries comes from Cowles's work.) Cowles founded the Cowles Center for Economic Research in Colorado Springs; the facility was moved to the University of Chicago in 1939 and would over time support the work of many Nobel Prize–winning economists. But in the 1930s, Cowles's insights were understandably unpopular with professional investment advisers, most of whom preferred to ignore his conclusions.

What must have been most galling was a simple point Cowles often made that was never answered effectively by the investment advice practitioners. As Cowles put it, "Market advice for a fee is a paradox. Anybody who really knew just wouldn't share his knowledge. Why should he? In five years, he could be the richest man in the world. Why pass the word on?"[14]

In spite of the conclusions he reached, Cowles never doubted that investors would keep buying newsletters. As he put it, "Even if I did my negative surveys every five years, or others continued them when I'm gone, it wouldn't matter. People are still going to subscribe to these services. They want to believe that somebody really knows. A world in which nobody really knows can be frightening."[15]

The recovery of stock prices in the mid-1930s stalled in 1937. From August on, prices slid lower in the face of slumping economic activity; the substantial economic recovery that had occurred between 1933 and 1937 (in which GNP rose from $56 billion to $82 billion, and corporate pretax profits from $200 million to $5.7 billion) had come to an end. But critics of the SEC, and government regulation, seized on the market drop as evidence that government regulation was destroying the market. Richard Whitney declared that the decline "confirmed my worst fears" about government regulation.[16]

More likely, the rapidly developing recession was responsible for the market drop. The business slump was probably caused in part by the Roosevelt administration's attempt to balance the budget by cutting spending. (The federal deficit dropped from $3.5 billion in 1936 to $200 million in 1937.) As the economic news worsened, the decline in stock prices continued; by the end of 1937 the market had given back half the gains it had registered since 1934.

In the meantime, Richard Whitney had other problems. For many years his firm, Richard Whitney & Company, had been at best only marginally profitable, generating earnings insufficient to support his way of life. The firm was a staid, conservative bond dealer; Whitney seemed to prefer a gentlemanly pace of business, transacting primarily with wealthy friends and acquaintances, not the general public. Not possessing any inherited wealth independent of his family, Whitney, for more than a decade, had sought out speculative investments in an effort to provide the wealth necessary for financial independence. Unable to provide the funds himself, Whitney financed these purchases with loans from his brother George, who was a rising star at J. P. Morgan & Company, and by borrowing from friends. By the end of 1929 he owed his brother over $1 million, and friends at least $250,000.

The rapidly developing depression of the 1930s was not kind to Whitney's investments, or to his firm. On June 30, 1931 (based on calculations made later), Richard Whitney & Company actually had a net worth of only $36,000, even though it regularly handled transactions valued in the millions of dollars. At that time, J. P. Morgan & Company loaned Whitney $500,000 to pay off a bank loan. In reviewing a financial statement Whitney submitted in connection with the loan, the Morgan partners were shocked to find the value of his investments—in which he had sunk $1.5 million—to be virtually nothing. Ultimately George Whitney pledged personal assets to collateralize his brother's loan; by the end of 1931, Richard Whitney owed $2 million he could not possibly repay.

In 1935 he was forced to borrow from Exchange members, having run out of friends who could provide him with more cash. His status and reputation on the Exchange served him well; some of the members he casually approached felt "honored" to be asked for loans. Never once did his haughty manner and bearing betray the extent of his predicament; if a loan request was refused (and it rarely was), he would shrug it off as if it were a matter of little consequence.

As his investments continued to sour, Whitney, in desperation, resorted to an action that under ordinary circumstances would have been unthinkable. As treasurer of the New York Yacht Club, of which he was an active member, he had custody of securities belonging to the club. On February 14, 1936, he took $150,000 in the Yacht Club's bonds and pledged them as collateral for a personal loan. He had stepped over the line, both legally and ethically. And he had set in motion a chain of events that would lead to his doom.

Whitney would ultimately make improper use of other securities entrusted to him, by the New York Stock Exchange Gratuity Fund and by clients of his firm. But the extent of his transgressions was not immediately evident; meanwhile the pace of his borrowing accelerated. He eventually even approached notorious market operator Bernard "Sell 'em Ben" Smith. Smith later described the meeting with Whitney this way: "He came up to see me and said he would like to get this over quickly, and he told me he would like to borrow $250,000 on his face. I remarked he was putting a very high value on his face, so he said . . . his back was to the wall and he had to have $250,000. I told him he had a lot of nerve to ask me for $250,000 when he didn't even bid me the time of day. I told him I frankly didn't like him—that I wouldn't loan him a dime."[17]

A routine investigation of the affairs of Richard Whitney & Company by the New York Stock Exchange (an investigation required, ironically, by the very same reforms Whitney had so ferociously opposed) finally uncovered Whitney's misdeeds in early 1938. The denouement came swiftly. On March 8, Richard Whitney & Company filed for bankruptcy. On March 10, District Attorney Thomas Dewey issued a warrant for Whitney's arrest. On March 17, he was expelled from the New York Stock Exchange. Whitney refused to enter a plea in his own defense and was eventually sentenced to five to ten years in prison.

It was later revealed that over the four years preceding his failure, Whitney had negotiated 111 loans for more than $27 million, loans that were often turned over to pay off other loans. *The Nation* magazine said, "Wall Street could hardly have been more embarrassed if J. P. Morgan had been caught helping himself from the collection plate at the Cathedral of St. John the Divine." Whitney's bankruptcy petition provided further evidence of his almost pathetic penchant for untried, speculative investments; a listing of his business interests included patent rights to a process for spraying metal to repair rust, and a patented air-pressure bearing that was described as "almost revolutionary in its possibilities."[18] Years later, Whitney's parole officer wrote, "Contributing factors to his delinquency are pride, obstinacy, unshakable belief in his own financial judgment, and a gambling instinct . . ." But the officer also admitted that Whitney "possesses a certain gentlemanly code of honor . . ."[19]

The Whitney affair ended Wall Street opposition to government regulatory reforms; at the same time, however, the growing threat of war in Europe and Asia soon caused the Roosevelt administration to shift its focus elsewhere. A time of grave national peril was not conducive to tinkering with the economy. As 1938 passed into 1939, the New Deal passed ineluctably into history. But the New Deal regulatory regime remained, and was accepted as a given by the Wall Street community. As early as 1940, many brokers and bankers actually began to speak positively of the new regulations, recognizing that they were an indispensable first step to restoring public confidence in the stock market.

That confidence was still sorely lacking as the 1930s came to a close. In May 1939 the SEC published the results of a survey that found that in the month of April, 21% of all trading on the New York Stock Exchange was done by members acting for their own accounts. The problem was not so much that private trading was increasing but that trading by the public had diminished so dramatically. Only 20 million shares traded in the entire month of April 1939 on the New York Stock Exchange; in the same month in 1930, 111 million shares had changed hands.

Once again, as in 1935, the Exchange embarked on an advertising campaign to generate new business, but with an important difference. For the first time, member firms were allowed to advertise individually. This move was controversial; it was generally considered inappropriate for professionals—such as lawyers, doctors, and brokers—to actively solicit new business. But the Exchange desperately needed more activity. It encouraged its member firms to advertise, but to do so "tastefully." The first advertisements were run in major newspapers on May 4, 1939, by the brokerage firm Fenner & Beane and were designed ostensibly to "educate" investors.

On May 3 several commission houses announced a "novel" way for small investors to participate in the stock market. The firms proposed to offer "baby portfolios," consisting of a package of dividend-paying blue-chip stocks. Ranging in price from a few hundred to a few thousand dollars, the baby portfolios would be sold at reduced commission rates that barely covered costs in an effort to interest first-time investors in the market.[20] Some observers were not impressed. *The New York Herald Tribune* wrote, "It seems that the scheme is more a frantic effort to aid brokers in keeping body and soul together than an invention that is likely to revolutionize investment practice." The idea was soon dropped.

Somewhat surprisingly, the Exchange marketing efforts ran into criticism from SEC chairman William O. Douglas. Douglas said that he supported attempts to improve the working of the capital markets but that he was skeptical of schemes that smacked of attempts "to bring investors back on a 1929 basis."[21] The aversion to the presumed speculative "excess" of 1929 was still very strong. No marketing plan by the Stock Exchange, or by individual brokerage firms, could realistically hope to reverse it.

In 1939 average trading volume on the New York Stock Exchange fell below 1 million shares per day for the first time in sixteen years; even the outbreak of war in Europe in September failed to spark a sustained increase in activity. In 1929, 125,000 people had been employed in the securities industry; by the end of the 1930s the number had fallen below 40,000. In 1928, 17% of all Harvard Business School graduates entered the investment business; in 1940, only 4.4% did.[22] Many observers began to believe that the stock market would never again be as important to the economy as it had been before 1929. On September 2, 1939, *The Christian Science Monitor* wrote, "A fair case can be made for the thesis that stock exchanges in general are permanently shrunken in economic performance in the last decade."

The stock market bust of the 1930s took many victims, destroying men who in the 1920s had been seen as titans of finance. But perhaps the fate of one man—Jesse Livermore—symbolized the drastically altered environment of the 1930s better than that of any other. Livermore, probably the most famous stock market trader of all time, had been crowned the King of the Bears by a worshipful press corps. If any market operator should have survived and prospered in the difficult markets of the 1930s, Livermore, by all rights, should have been that man. But it was not to be.

In spite of his reputation as Wall Street's leading bear, Livermore had been forced in March 1934 to declare bankruptcy for the second time in his life. His financial statement at the time revealed $2,259,212 in debt, offset by only $184,000 in dubious assets. By all appearances undaunted, Livermore confidently predicted to the press that he would "come back." After all, he had done so many times before.

According to his friend Bernie Chapman, Livermore made use of some very unconventional means to try to recoup his fortune. Perhaps the strangest of all was a stray black cat Chapman had adopted. The cat was quite promiscuous, frequently becoming pregnant. Each time the animal gave birth, Livermore would reverse his position in the market. "Invariably," Chapman stated, "he made money every time I wired him that the cat had kittens. And when I one day wired him that the cat was dead, he fainted!"[23]

Unfortunately, such feline prognostication was not sufficient to restore Livermore to wealth. The newly regulated environment was not conducive to his brand of manipulative speculation. Livermore found it much more difficult to succeed when he had to play by a set of clearly defined and enforced rules.

Then, in 1939, he hit upon a new idea. If he could not make money speculating in the heavily regulated markets, why not make money instead by writing a book about his trading strategies? He still had something of a reputation in the press (albeit somewhat tarnished by his bankruptcy filing in 1934). Could he not capitalize on that reputation by writing a book?

Livermore's nemesis, Arthur Cutten, had once said, "Anybody who really makes money in the market won't go around telling anybody else how he did it."[24] Livermore probably, for once, agreed with Cutten's sentiments. But he also had a low opinion of the investing public he had so often bamboozled in the past. He was certain the public would pay good money for a formula promising investment success. And he, Jesse Livermore, would provide it.

The problem was that he didn't really have any such formula and would thus have to invent one. A strategy based on now-illegal manipulative ploys was obviously not viable, nor was a scheme based on signals given by a black cat. But Livermore was not to be deterred. With a great deal of fanfare, he rented out an expensive office suite in which he placed several large blackboards constantly monitored by boys hired to mark them up with colored lines and numbers. Visitors, particularly members of the press, were given the impression that important calculations were being made. Eventually this process produced what Livermore called the Livermore Key, which depended on signals provided by the market actions of two stocks in each of four representative groups. By early 1940 his book was completed, and in March it was published.

The book flopped. The public, remembering well the crash and its aftermath, was in no mood to rush back into stock market speculation, and had little interest in a book by a failed speculator purporting to tell them how to do just that. Once again, success had eluded Livermore. The game on Wall Street would go on, but it would go on without players like him.

On the afternoon of November 28, 1940, Jesse Livermore shot himself to death in the cloakroom of a bar at the Sherry-Netherland Hotel in New York City. He left behind debts totaling $365,000, not a large sum by the standards of his earlier speculations, but large enough. A suicide note written to his wife rambled on for eight pages, with one phrase recurring repeatedly: "My life has been a failure."

The New York Times obituary of Livermore aptly summed up his downfall, and the times. "He lived in a time when the speculating he did came to seem like that of boys pitching pennies . . . The 'Street' in which he operated is not what it used to be. His death punctuated the end of an era."

8
PEOPLE'S CAPITALISM

A S HE BOARDED a train in New York bound for Chicago in late 1939, 54-year-old Charles Merrill recognized that he faced a crucial turning point in his career, and his life. He would shortly be meeting with Winthrop Smith, an old friend and business associate who now managed the Chicago office of E. A. Pierce & Company, a brokerage firm in which Merrill had personally invested $1.9 million nearly ten years earlier. The hard years of the 1930s had ravaged Pierce & Company; by the end of the decade, Merrill's investment in the firm had lost nearly 85% of its original value.[1] Merrill himself was quite secure financially, with a fortune estimated at more than $30 million from his own brokerage business and shrewd investments in grocery store chains. But he knew Smith had no such personal wealth and would lose everything if E. A. Pierce & Company failed. And failure certainly loomed large as a possibility

Smith, like Merrill before him, had attended Amherst College; he came to Merrill's attention upon his graduation in 1916. Merrill soon hired him as a runner and office boy for his young firm of Merrill Lynch. Smith rose through the ranks and eventually made partner in 1929, an inauspicious year in the brokerage business. After the crash, fearful of a depressed business environment, Merrill and senior partner Edmund Lynch decided to dispose of their firm's brokerage operations, to concentrate instead on investment banking. The brokerage business was transferred lock, stock, and barrel to E. A. Pierce & Company, and Win Smith with it.

Dow Jones Industrial Average, 1940–1949

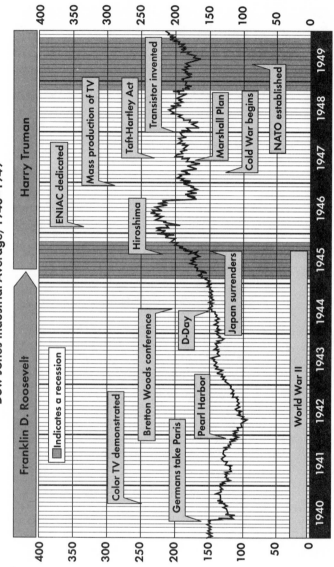

Franklin D. Roosevelt

Harry Truman

■ Indicates a recession

Color TV demonstrated

Bretton Woods conference

Germans take Paris

Pearl Harbor

D-Day

Japan surrenders

ENIAC dedicated

Mass production of TV

Hiroshima

Taft-Hartley Act

Transistor invented

Marshall Plan

Cold War begins

NATO established

World War II

© *Dow Jones & Company Inc.*

Now Smith wanted Merrill back, to provide Pierce & Company with a desperately needed infusion of new capital and management talent. Merrill was not certain he wanted to take on the responsibility; after all, he had plenty of money and had just been married for the third time, to a woman who expected him to lead a life of leisurely semiretirement. It was not an easy decision.

Merrill was fully aware that the business climate was grim. His firm quietly commissioned a poll to measure the true depth of the public's antipathy toward Wall Street. The survey found that the public greatly distrusted brokers, believing that they deliberately tried to lure investors into speculative stocks because commissions were higher on those shares. Suspicion of Wall Street was such that many people were unwilling to even leave their securities on deposit with brokerage firms. The poll also revealed that the public was appallingly ignorant; at least half of the respondents did not know the difference between a stock and a bond, and a majority believed that stock exchanges themselves actually sold the stocks the public bought, thus making money when stock prices declined.[2]

But Charles Merrill had a vision, which was gradually to take shape as he negotiated the fate of Pierce & Company. His own experience in the brokerage business had taught him important lessons, as had his involvement in retail grocery chains. He believed that innovative marketing and management techniques, like those employed by chain stores, could be adapted to brokerage houses. In early 1940 he made his decision: he would merge Merrill Lynch with Pierce & Company and put his radical ideas to the test.

The year 1940 would be trying, both for the new firm and for the entire market. Stock prices slid steadily lower in spite of renewed vigor in the economy. All the prerequisites for a sustained bull market seemed to be in place, but the market ignored them. Credit was easy, and by late summer the money supply was 66% higher than it had been two years earlier. Industrial production at the end of 1940 exceeded the 1929 peak by 16%; corporate profits before taxes nearly reached 1929 levels ($9.3 billion versus $9.6 billion), and would substantially exceed 1929 figures the following year (rising to $17 billion). Unfortunately, the good news was not reflected in stock prices.

Part of the reason was undoubtedly uncertainty over the war in Europe. When the conflict broke out in September 1939, the New York Stock Exchange authorities, not wanting to overreact as in 1914, when the Exchange had suspended operations, allowed trading to continue. The market at first rallied, perhaps anticipating another war boom, but then subsided back into the doldrums. German victories in Europe created uneasiness that tempered the optimistic outlook for the domestic economy. Trading was lethargic; the turnover rate for stocks listed on the Exchange in 1940 was only 12%, the lowest of the twentieth century. The historian Robert Sobel describes conditions this way:

> The [New York Stock Exchange] floor was a quiet place, with only a fraction of the specialists* and representatives there at any given moment. Most would remain in their offices, reading newspapers, making telephone calls, or simply passing the time of day. Others would lounge outside the building, in the smoking room, or pay a visit to the local saloon, while their clerks remained at their posts to take messages. If a buy or sell for 100 shares came down, the clerk would rush to fill the order then return outside to celebrate. It was a period during which active issues would trade fewer than 8,000 shares on most days, when a specialist could spend an entire session on the Street and fill only a dozen or so orders.[3]

Help-wanted advertisements indicated that unskilled workers in defense plants could earn as much as New York Stock Exchange specialists. The environment was so bad that many brokers, specialists, and private traders could not afford to dine at the Exchange's Luncheon Club. As a result the Luncheon Club was forced to open its doors to outsiders.

---

*A "specialist" was (and still is) an Exchange member who is designated by the Exchange to handle trading in a particular stock. The specialist's function is to coordinate all the buy and sell orders in that stock so as to create an orderly market, using his own capital when necessary to make up the difference when temporary imbalances between buyers and sellers occur. The specialist system was created by accident around 1900, when a broker with a broken leg was forced to remain in a fixed position on the Exchange floor; other brokers began to give him orders to execute in stocks trading at nearby posts. Over time, the arrangement was formalized into the modern specialist system.

An SEC study of shareholders in 1941 estimated that there were approximately 4½ million shareholders nationally. Brokerage firms reported that they were servicing 394,000 accounts, down from 1.5 million in 1929, and that many of these accounts were inactive. The number of brokerage accounts had declined every year since 1936. The average P/E ratio for the Standard & Poor's Industrials in 1940 stood at 10.2 to 1, having seemingly reverted to the tried-and-true 10 to 1 ratio prevalent at the turn of the century. War or no war, the crash of 1929 and subsequent Depression had left a stultifying legacy.

"Charlie" Merrill would attempt to change all this. Shortly after completing the merger with E. A. Pierce & Company, he attacked the problem with missionary zeal. Merrill saw a vast potential market of middle-class investors who could radically reshape Wall Street if only they could be persuaded to invest a portion of their savings in stocks, instead of confining themselves to government bonds, savings accounts, and life insurance policies. Old-line Wall Street firms like J. P. Morgan & Company had traditionally assisted an already wealthy clientele that wished to invest conservatively to preserve capital. Merrill instead sought out middle-class people who wanted to accumulate wealth for retirement and other long-term considerations.

To reach these potential investors, Merrill knew he had to overcome the pervasive popular distrust of Wall Street. He was perhaps the perfect salesman for the task; the son of a Florida doctor, Merrill was a handsome man who exuded southern charm and possessed an easy informality with persons of all social classes. But substance was required as well as style. Tangible reform in the way Wall Street did business was essential if his ambitious efforts were to succeed.

The first change Merrill made was quite controversial; in order to shed the image of hucksterism that plagued stockbrokers, Merrill abolished commissions and instead paid his brokers a fixed annual salary. Then he aggressively advertised the new compensation system, hoping that skeptical investors would no longer fear "churning" of their accounts by brokers seeking to earn commissions from unnecessary trades. (The approach was somewhat disingenuous, in that high-producing brokers were paid subjective bonuses in addition to their fixed salaries, with the bonuses based in part on the business they generated. But for whatever reason, this system did not seem as objectionable to the public as the straight commission plan did.) Merrill's ostentatious move to eliminate commissions initially met derision from the Wall Street community, but, as would often be the case with his reforms, was grudgingly adopted over time by many other firms.

In another reform that shook up the Street, Merrill announced that his firm would begin publishing comprehensive annual reports, explicitly detailing its financial position. He was correct in assuming that these reports would attract publicity when they were issued. In fact, their release elicited accolades from the press. *The New York World Telegram* effused that since the firm "deals with the public, the public has a right to know something about its financial affairs . . . Merrill is to be congratulated for recognizing this fact." The release of annual reports occasioned much grumbling from competitors, who had no desire to make public information that had customarily been a closely kept secret. The New York Stock Exchange had long-standing rules against membership by corporations; Merrill Lynch, although a partnership, proposed to act like a publicly held company. Again, many other firms were forced to reluctantly follow Merrill's lead.

But Charlie Merrill wasn't finished. He greatly loosened restrictions on the dissemination of the firm's research. Traditionally, stock market research conducted by in-house analysts had been made available by brokerage firms only to good clients; Merrill now allowed journalists and even competitors to gain access to it. Once more, he was correct in assuming that the advertising benefits of the new openness would be greater than any damage done by the loss of proprietary material. The firm coined the slogan that customers should be encouraged to "investigate, then invest"; Merrill Lynch research was to be an important tool in this process.[4]

By any measurement, Merrill's strategy was an outstanding success. In the first nine months of 1940, the firm's base of accounts grew by one-third, to 50,000. The growth would continue; by the end of the war, in 1945, Merrill Lynch had 250,000 customer accounts and was by far the largest brokerage firm in the country. But much more important than the individual success of one Wall Street firm was the fact that Merrill's new approach helped remake the image of Wall Street.

Nowhere was this more evident than in the response to an unorthodox advertising campaign Merrill Lynch introduced later in the decade. Even Merrill Lynch officials initially had doubts about the strategy, which called for running full-page advertisements in major newspapers, each consisting of six thousand words of dry, tightly spaced text entitled "What Everybody Ought to Know About This Stock and Bond Business." The material was purely explanatory, in no way touting Merrill Lynch or its products. The only reference to the firm was a small note at the bottom of the page inviting readers to contact Merrill Lynch for a reprint if they were interested. Initially reluctant to pay the steep $5,000 per page charged by *The New York Times*, Merrill Lynch first placed the advertisement in *The Cleveland Plain Dealer* to test the reaction. Only then, when the results seemed encouraging, was the material run in the *Times*.

The response was overwhelming. The firm received thousands of requests for reprints. One Merrill official said, "What was most amazing was that we got hundreds and hundreds of long and thoughtful letters." One person wrote: "God bless Merrill Lynch . . . I have been wanting to know this all my life . . . I owned stocks and bonds and I never really knew what I owned."[5] The reaction confirmed Charlie Merrill's belief that there was a vast pool of interest in the stock market that could be tapped if the public could be assured that the market was fair and open. Merrill himself went a long way toward creating that assurance. Often referred to as people's capitalism, the reforms Merrill implemented, which were eventually copied by most of the brokerage industry, did far more to dispel public antipathy toward Wall Street than the various ineffectual New York Stock Exchange advertising campaigns. Even though it took many years for his efforts to fully bear fruit, Charlie Merrill, more than any other individual, brought Wall Street to Main Street and laid the groundwork for the explosion of public interest in the stock market in the second half of the century.

The market itself did not turn decisively higher until the Allied victories of 1943. But even after the 1943 recovery, stocks (as measured by the Dow Jones Industrial Average) were still down by more than 60% from the 1929 peak, despite the fact that the gross national product had almost doubled and corporate profits before taxes were two and one half times 1929 levels. The performance of stocks appeared quite perverse; one explanation is that investors feared heavy wartime taxes and controls would strip corporations of their profits, as had occurred to a more limited degree in World War I. These concerns were not unjustified. In October 1942, Congress passed the Revenue Act of 1942, which President Roosevelt called the greatest tax bill in history.[6] The Act established a 90% excess profits tax, raised the top corporate tax rate from 31% to 40%, and created a 5% "victory tax" surcharge, to be refunded after the war. Additional revenue measures were enacted in 1943 and 1944.

By 1945 the war effort was consuming 57% of national income, compared with 25% in 1918. In 1918 there had been selective curbs on civilian production; by 1944 the same industries were almost completely government-controlled. High taxes gushed revenue, with net federal budget receipts for 1939–1945 totaling $338 billion, compared with only $45.6 billion for the previous seven years. Over the course of the war, taxes covered 43% of all war-related spending, compared with approximately 32% during 1917–1918.

Wage and price controls and rationing greatly limited the consumer sector of the economy, but in spite of the efforts of Charles Merrill, most surplus cash created by the "war boom" did not immediately find its way into the stock market. Whether because of high tax rates, or distrust of stocks, or both, most people put their savings in banks or government bonds, or used the money to pay off debt. Stocks languished; by the time Japan surrendered in 1945, the Dow Jones Industrial Average, even after a substantial rally, still stood at less than half its 1929 peak.

An undertaking as massive as the war effort inevitably had some serendipitous consequences. Perhaps the most important was the tax-induced creation of employee pension funds that occurred during the war years. Searching for means of providing tax-deductible employee compensation not subject to wage controls, many corporations began to offer pension plans. These innovations at first had no real impact on the stock market, in that they were usually "defined benefit"* plans funded by corporate investments in fixed-income assets, not equities. Few pension fund managers considered stocks to be prudent investments. Over time, however, this would change, and pension and retirement funds would become

---

*"Defined benefit" pension plans required employers to provide a specific annual dollar benefit to retirees; since the payouts were set in advance, the plans could be funded with fixed-income securities like bonds and preferred stocks rather than common stocks.

the single most important engine driving the bull markets of the later twentieth century.

Other changes, gradual yet perceptible, were also occurring. The pounding that conservative members of the Wall Street establishment had taken during the New Deal, particularly after the Whitney scandal broke, was reflected in the evolving character of the New York Stock Exchange. The clubby atmosphere was slowly dissolving as the Exchange (and the Wall Street community) became more like the rest of the country. Absent were the legendary figures like J. P. Morgan, Bernard Baruch, and Jesse Livermore, who had been presumed to tower over the market in an earlier age. Not fully recognizing the altered circumstances, the press searched for a new generation of market operators. They eventually found a candidate in the mysterious person of Serge Rubenstein.

The story of Rubenstein's life reads like a Hollywood script, replete with glamour and intrigue. Serge was born in tsarist Russia in 1908, the son of a Jewish financier named Dimitri Rubenstein, who skillfully made use of calculated alliances with members of the Russian aristocracy to advance himself in a society infected with virulent anti-Semitism. (Serge later claimed that his father had been financial adviser to the mystic Russian monk Rasputin, but this assertion, like so much of what Rubenstein said, appears to have been significantly embellished.) Eventually the Rubenstein family was forced to flee Russia. Secreted in Serge's clothing was a large emerald later sold for $20,000.

Dimitri served as finance minister for one of the White Russian armies contesting the Bolsheviks' seizure of power during the Russian Revolution; reportedly, when he realized that the cause was lost, he absconded with much of the army's treasury. Moving to Vienna, he became involved in several questionable banking schemes during the turbulent postwar era. Young Serge was placed in a private school, but proved to be an indifferent pupil. At age 15 he suffered bouts of depression that concerned his mother, who sent him to a psychologist. After examining him, the doctor said, "You will be driven by ambitions and desires all your life, forever reaching out for bigger things . . . This is your way of compensating for your inferiority complex."[7]

Serge recovered from his depression and enrolled in Trinity College,

Cambridge, where he became embittered by the ingrained anti-Semitism of the British upper classes. He ultimately passed his finals but never formally took his degree. He did make one important contact at Cambridge, however; one of his professors was the noted economist John Maynard Keynes, who reputedly told him, "You will be one of the world's top financial figures."[8] Keynes endorsed Serge's research project, which involved tracking down owners of dormant Swiss bank accounts. In one instance, Serge earned a substantial finder's fee from the grateful owners of one such "lost" account. Whatever Rubenstein's sources of income, his fellow Cambridge students observed that he never seemed short of cash.[9]

After Cambridge, Rubenstein moved on to Paris, where he entered into financial machinations involving Korean mining ventures. At one point Rubenstein traveled to highly xenophobic prewar Japan (which controlled Korea) to dissuade the Japanese government from expropriating the properties. He summed up his dealing with the Japanese in one succinct sentence: "Bribery is the best investment."[10] Rubenstein would later tell the story of how he met Emperor Hirohito. According to his account, the emperor was an insomniac but was cured by deep-breathing exercises Rubenstein personally demonstrated for him.

Using money smuggled into America from Japan, Rubenstein established himself on Wall Street in 1938. Even though the now heavily regulated American markets were very different from those of Europe or Asia, Rubenstein seemed unconcerned. He boldly announced his presence with frequent press releases and lavish parties. Several times he loudly proclaimed, "I'm going to run the world. I'm going to own Wall Street"[11] He donated money to the 1940 reelection campaign of Franklin Roosevelt and made ostentatious contributions to some of Eleanor Roosevelt's favorite charities. (The relationship with the First Lady soon soured, however, when she publicly accused Rubenstein of the unauthorized use of letters written by her.)

Press reports began to refer to Rubenstein as the Boy Wonder of Wall Street. There were occasional voices of dissent; *New York Times* financial writer Burton Crane unearthed unsavory details from Rubenstein's past, but in general critical comments were few and far between. By 1940, Rubenstein seemed to have firmly established himself as a "player" on Wall

Street. His prominence was in no small part due to his self-promoting activities and to the fact that in the post-Depression era there were so few other market operators like him.

Rubenstein moved quickly, bribing officials to gain access to inside information and, like Jesse Livermore, making skillful use of the press to plant stories about stocks in which he had an interest. He scored his greatest coup in a New York Stock Exchange–listed stock—Panhandle Refining Company of Texas—eventually running it up from $2 per share to over $13, where he sold out. In spite of making profits of several million dollars from this and other blatantly illegal schemes, Rubenstein was not immediately targeted by the SEC.

Rubenstein did run afoul of government authorities, but for reasons entirely unrelated to his stock market operations. During the war, in an apparent attempt to evade the draft, he had purchased an interest in a small defense contractor and then claimed that his activities were essential to the war effort. Once he tried to bribe draft board officials to secure an exemption, but his efforts at draft evasion were less effective than his market machinations, and Rubenstein was convicted of draft law violations in 1946 and jailed for two years.

Public sentiment turned against him; at one point a group of veterans refused to participate in a parade down Fifth Avenue because the route passed in front of Rubenstein's town house. The negative publicity apparently prodded the SEC to action. When Rubenstein was released from jail on the draft conviction, he was immediately rearrested, this time for stock manipulation related to the Panhandle transactions. After a complicated trial, Rubenstein was found not guilty on all counts. His battles with the government were far from over, however. He would spend the next years battling attempts by the Immigration Service to deport him. The matter was abruptly brought to a close in January 1955, when Rubenstein was found strangled in his apartment, gagged, with his arms and legs bound. The murder was never solved.

How significant was Serge Rubenstein's Wall Street career? The fact that he was able to engage in obviously illegal manipulative activities without being caught brought into question the efficacy of the new government regulatory regime. If Rubenstein, who received a great deal of attention from a press corps still accustomed to the flamboyant market manipulators of the past, could escape effective SEC action, how could the public be certain that other unscrupulous market operators were not also active? But in reality Rubenstein's machinations were confined to small, peripheral companies and had little impact on the overall market. The well-publicized pools of the 1920s, active in big-capitalization stocks like RCA, were nowhere to be seen in the 1940s. Rubenstein was, at best, a small-time operator; while he may temporarily have slipped through the regulatory cracks, his brief career as a player on Wall Street did not by any means mark a return to the rollicking, anything-goes environment of the 1920s.

The stock market moved erratically in mid-1946, then broke sharply lower in early September. Corporate earnings were strong; again, the market seemed to be moving contrary to the economy. As had often happened in the past, some people became suspicious. An Illinois congressman demanded that the SEC investigate, claiming that the market was being manipulated to influence the upcoming congressional elections. Of course no such manipulation was found, but the incident served notice that Washington would react quickly to sharp, adverse moves in stock prices. Political considerations notwithstanding, the market continued to lag behind the economy in 1947, with the P/E ratio for New York Stock Exchange–listed stocks languishing below 10 to 1.

In the late 1930s many market observers (such as T. Rowe Price) had expressed a premature concern about inflation, fearing that New Deal policies were inherently inflationary. While the New Deal itself did not generate inflationary pressures, the massive government war effort that followed certainly did. The Federal Reserve, as it had done in World War I, pumped up the money supply to provide funds for the Treasury's unprecedented borrowing needs. This policy continued even after the war. Federal Reserve chairman Thomas McCabe said, "I am convinced that we could not have abandoned our support position during this period without damaging repercussions on our entire financial mechanism as well as serious effects on the economy generally."[12]

But Marriner Eccles, who resigned from the Federal Reserve over the issue, disagreed. "In making a cheap money policy for the Treasury," Eccles argued, "we cannot avoid making it for everybody. All monetary and credit restrictions are gone under such conditions; the Federal Reserve became simply an engine of inflation."[13] In effect, the central bank pegged Treasury bonds at high prices (low interest rates) by aggressively buying government securities in the open market. Combined with the elimination of price controls after the war, which released pent-up pricing pressures in the economy, this aggressive expansion of the money supply inevitably produced a virulent inflation.

By year-end 1948, the wholesale price index had risen 70% since the war. Consumer prices increased by 34% over the same period. The severe inflation was disquieting, and stories on the subject frequently appeared in the press. *The New York Herald Tribune* wrote, "The purchasing power of the dollar . . . is at the lowest point in recent history." *The New York Post* described investors' fears "that the value of cash in the bank and in U.S. bonds will dwindle even more . . ." Many analysts believed that the root cause of the inflation was not just the war-induced easy money policy of the Federal Reserve but the nature of the New Deal welfare state itself. An editorial in *Barron's* in the fall of 1949 stated this view succinctly: "The state is growing omnipotent, and it is doing so through use of the money power. The policies of the welfare state create inflation, feed on inflation, and necessitate inflation." Later that fall, the president of the Federal Reserve Bank of Philadelphia predicted that the United States faced a prolonged period of inflation, caused by the government's emphasis on full employment and constantly rising wage rates.

Inflation of this magnitude had been unknown since the World War I years. But there was an important difference between the two periods, at least as far as the stock market was concerned. After the Second World War, a theory of investing existed (enunciated by T. Rowe Price and others) that explicitly viewed stocks as a means of protecting investors from inflation. Stocks in corporations with real assets and real earnings would presumably rise with inflation, unlike fixed-income investments such as bonds and savings accounts. Thus when Truman administration officials conceded in late 1949 that they would be unable to balance the federal budget, *Barron's* immediately pointed out the potentially inflationary impact and declared that "the implication to equity owners of so momentous a declaration of national budget policies should be obvious."

That same month, another prominent article in *Barron's* raised a related issue that would take on great significance in the coming years. Commenting on the recent agreement between steel producers and unions, which mandated pension benefits for steelworkers, *Barron's* made the case for investing the new funds in stocks. Noting the rapid growth in pension funds since the beginning of the war, and observing that 90% of the accumulated monies had been invested in fixed-income securities, *Barron's* complained that the excessive conservatism of fund managers in an inflationary environment was hurting the very workers they were supposed to represent, as well as starving the economy of needed equity capital. The editors published an analysis of stock returns for the ten years from 1939 to 1949, showing that stocks had performed much better than bonds after adjusting for inflation. Decrying the "legal lists" of conservative securities that some states restricted pension fund fiduciaries to, *Barron's* editorialized that it was high time to abandon the "ultraconservative packages which bankers and insurance experts consider acceptable" for pension fund investments.

One important retirement fund that accepted *Barron's* argument was the Teacher's Insurance and Annuity Fund, otherwise known as TIAA. TIAA moved to create a separate affiliated entity—the College Retirement Equity Fund (CREF)—to invest in stocks. The reasoning behind the move was explained by William Greenburgh, a consultant for TIAA, who wrote, "An effort should be made to provide more income when [consumer] prices are high, even though this means taking risk that income will be less when prices are low." Greenburgh observed that many economists believed the economy had a "built-in inflationary bias" due to heavy defense spending, a progressive tax structure, wage escalator clauses, budget deficits, easy money, an emphasis on full employment, and a disinclination to return to the gold standard. Thus it was unwise to commit retirement fund assets exclusively to traditional fixed-income investments.[14]

What would become one of the biggest bull markets in history began inconspicuously in June 1949. Like the market top of September 1929, the bottom in 1949 appeared unremarkable at the time. Activity was sluggish, with no extraordinary occurrences. The prime rate that banks charged their best customers was 2%, and home mortgages could be obtained for about 4%. The Federal Reserve discount rate, reflecting the Federal Reserve's easy money policies, stood at 1½%.

The gap between stock dividends and bond interest rates, which had nearly disappeared at the 1929 market peak, reached one of its widest margins ever in 1949. Long-term government bonds paid 2½%, whereas stocks, as measured by the Moody's Industrials, paid dividends averaging 6.82%. There were many solid companies, which had not missed dividend payments even during the Depression, that in 1949 paid dividend yields above 7%. High dividends, and inflation-induced acceptance of a "growth" stock investment strategy, enticed buyers. Stock prices rose steadily from June 1949; in every one of the ensuing twelve months, the market showed gains. As analyst Leslie Gould said, "The stock market is sounding the warning bell on inflation."[15]

The nascent bull market soon began to throw up a new breed of growth companies, eventually to be referred to as glamour stocks. The first examples appeared in 1950, when firms producing television sets suddenly took off. The stock of one of the leading manufacturers, Motorola, doubled in a few months, and continued to rise thereafter. Motorola's revenues in 1950 came to $35.5 million, with per share profits of $3.50, as opposed to $15.2 million and $1.14 in 1949, respectively. The company paid an annual dividend of $1.50 per share. Zenith, Admiral, and Emerson recorded similar increases in earnings and stock price, as did RCA, the largest firm in the industry. However, the sharp share price rises in 1950 inevitably caused dividend rates to fall, to between 3% and 4%, well below what was available elsewhere in the market.

Business Week took note of the problem, warning that future dividend increases in the group would not keep pace with the jump in stock prices. "When you are growing as fast as TV," *Business Week* stated, "you have to conserve cash to take care of expansion costs and needs for new working capital. It is doubtful if the industry will be able to pay out in dividends more than a small part of earnings for a long time."[16] Perversely (at least by today's standards), rapid growth financed by retained earnings was seen as a mixed blessing at best; the focus of traditional analysis on current dividend payouts was still quite evident, in spite of a growing acceptance of "growth" stocks. As a result, most of the television manufacturers did increase their dividends, despite the need for capital to finance growth, in an effort to satisfy analysts' concerns. The need to conform to Wall Street's time-honored standards could not be ignored.

Those conservative standards crimped growing companies with exciting new technologies. A good example was Eckert-Mauchly Computer Corporation, one of the few manufacturers of computers in the immediate postwar period. The company seemingly had a promising future, but heavy start-up costs meant that earnings would be skimpy in the early years, and dividends would be nonexistent. Because of this, the equity capital markets were closed to Eckert-Mauchly; investment bankers would not underwrite shares in such a "speculative" company, and the public would not buy. Commercial bank financing was likewise unavailable. Like many small, fast-growing companies, Eckert-Mauchly was finally forced into a merger in March 1950 with Remington Rand to form Univac. At the time, a merger with a larger, deep-pocketed firm was often the only way for a promising small company to secure the financing necessary to expand.[17]

The great bull market that began at midcentury was in large part based on the growing acceptance of a new model of investing—the idea that "growth" stocks would protect investors from inflation. But traditional standards that required a proven record of earnings and high current dividend payments had not been abandoned by any means. The growth stocks that investors sought out were usually established firms, not speculative start-ups. Even companies in fast-growing new industries like television and computers could not totally free themselves from constraints imposed by traditional standards.

But a trend had begun that would become ever more important in the upcoming years. Concern over inflation was forcing individual investors and the managers of rapidly growing pension and retirement funds to embrace equity investments. In the 1930s the Depression had smothered interest in the stock market and discredited stocks as investments in the eyes of a generation of Americans. In the late 1940s a bout of sustained inflation, as well as the implementation of much-needed reforms, finally began to reverse these attitudes. It was now that the truly explosive growth of the American stock market could begin.

9

THOSE DAYS ARE
GONE FOREVER

A S HARRY MARKOWITZ entered the University of Chicago conference
room to defend his Ph.D. dissertation, he bucked up his confidence
by telling himself, "I know this deal cold. Not even Milton Friedman can
give me a hard time."[1] Friedman, a senior economist on the faculty, was already a star in academia, and could be quite intimidating to students. But
Markowitz thought he was prepared for anything Friedman could throw at
him.

He was in for a rude surprise. Only minutes into Markowitz's presentation, Friedman interrupted, saying, "Harry, I don't see anything wrong
with the math here, but I have a problem. This isn't a dissertation in economics, and we can't give you a Ph.D. in economics for a dissertation that's
not economics. It's not math, it's not economics, it's not even business administration."[2] Markowitz was stunned. For the next 90 minutes he was
grilled by the panel, with most of the questioning focusing on the same
complaint. He left the examining room badly shaken, worrying that his
academic career was in jeopardy.

Markowitz tensely awaited the verdict. It wasn't long in coming; five
minutes later his academic mentor emerged from the room. "Congratula-
tions, Dr. Markowitz," the professor said with a wry smile. Markowitz
could only heave a sigh of relief.

Markowitz's Ph.D. thesis expanded on concepts he had earlier developed in a short article in the *Journal of Finance* in 1952. Although it re-

Dow Jones Industrial Average, 1950–1959

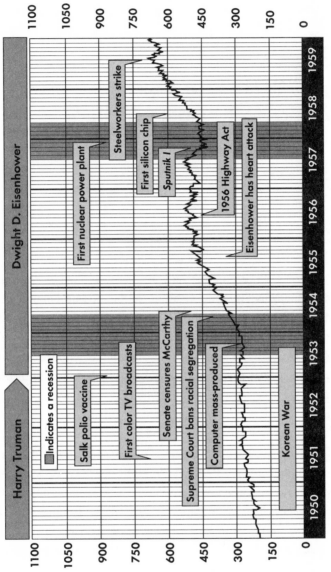

Harry Truman

Dwight D. Eisenhower

Indicates a recession

Salk polio vaccine

First color TV broadcasts

Senate censures McCarthy

Supreme Court bans racial segregation

Computer mass-produced

Korean War

First nuclear power plant

Steelworkers strike

First silicon chip

Sputnik I

1956 Highway Act

Eisenhower has heart attack

© *Dow Jones & Company Inc.*

ceived little attention at the time, economic consultant Peter Bernstein would later term Markowitz's work "the most famous insight in the history of modern finance . . ." The ideas expressed would finally win Markowitz a Nobel Prize nearly four decades later; unfortunately, the paper was to languish for years after its initial publication, receiving virtually no attention from the academic community, or from Wall Street.

The 1952 paper was short—only 14 pages in length, consisting mostly of mathematics—published in a journal that was itself relatively new, having only been in existence for seven years. Entitled "Portfolio Selection," the paper explored the seemingly arcane question of how to select a portfolio of stocks. The stock market was not generally considered to be an area of respectable academic inquiry; what little theoretical work had been done had invariably concentrated on techniques for valuing individual stocks. Ironically, Markowitz was only incidentally interested in the stock market when he wrote the article. What had led him to the issue was the broader question of how to make decisions involving trade-offs.

A tall, sandy-haired young man in his mid-20s who had been an only child in a middle-class Chicago household, Harry Markowitz admitted that as a boy he could have been classified as a nerd. In high school he read voraciously, played chess and the violin, and joined a national club for amateur cryptographers. He never tried out for sports. The summer he turned 14 he read Darwin's *Origin of Species* and was greatly impressed. Markowitz's "hero" was the English philosopher David Hume, who died in 1776. When he applied for admission to the University of Chicago, Markowitz was able to overcome objections to his mediocre high school grades by impressing the admissions officers with what he had learned from his own reading.[3]

Markowitz decided to major in economics because it was the only social science with a mathematical bent. A big attraction at the University of Chicago was the Cowles Center for Research in Economics, founded by Alfred Cowles in the 1930s; Markowitz eventually went on to do graduate work at the Cowles Center. Once, while waiting to consult with his academic adviser, he had a chance meeting with a stockbroker who urged him to apply techniques of economic analysis to the stock market. The idea intrigued both Markowitz and his adviser, but neither was knowledgeable enough about the market to know where to start. Markowitz was forced to go to the dean of the Business School for suggestions.

The dean referred him to what was then the authoritative work on the valuation of financial assets—a thesis written by a Harvard Ph.D. student in 1937 entitled *The Theory of Investment Value*. The author, John Burr Williams, had developed a three-step model for valuing individual stocks. First, a long-term projection of the company's future dividend payments would be made. Next, an estimation of the accuracy of the dividend estimates would be attached; for example, forecasts for an industrial stock whose earnings varied substantially over time would be less accurate than forecasts for a utility that had a much more stable pattern of earnings. Finally, projected future dividends would be "discounted" back to the present to determine the "present value"* of the dividend stream. Williams called his creation the Dividend Discount Model and used it to estimate what he called the intrinsic value of a stock. (Williams explicitly insisted that dividends, not earnings, be used in the calculations. He argued that any earnings not immediately paid out to shareholders as dividends would either be used to generate additional earnings that would provide future dividends, or would be wasted; either way, by measuring dividends, his model would capture the full value of what the shareholder ultimately received.)

One implication of Williams's work bothered Markowitz. Williams seemed to be saying that an investor should select the single stock that had the highest expected return and invest everything in that one stock. But this appeared to Markowitz to represent a very risky strategy; unfortunately, there was nothing in Williams's paper to account for risk. As Markowitz put it, "That afternoon in the library, I was struck with the notion that you should be interested in risk as well as return."[4]

---

*The concept of "present value" provides a means of comparing dollars to be received in the future with dollars received in the present. Since it is assumed that a dollar received now can be invested to generate income, a dollar received in the present is worth more than a dollar to be received in the future by the amount the "present" dollar would earn until the "future" dollar is received. Put another way, that value of the dollar to be received in the future is "discounted" back to the present using an interest rate that reflects what the present dollar could earn over that time.

Markowitz had stumbled on a question that had been largely neglected: the tension between risk and return in investments. Typically, Wall Street had focused purely on the maximization of return. Markowitz's paper in 1952 developed the notion of a trade-off between risk and return that seems intuitively obvious today. He then went on to develop the concept of a "portfolio" of securities, which represented a radical departure from the way Wall Street professionals traditionally selected investments.

Markowitz's insight was that the risk inherent in a portfolio of securities depended on the covariance of the securities in the portfolio (in other words, the degree to which the prices of those securities moved together) rather than the riskiness of each individual security. Thus it might be possible to construct a portfolio of relatively risky securities that would itself not be unacceptably risky, if the securities making up the portfolio had low covariances (did not tend to move together). Diversification was the means to minimize risk and maximize return, but it had to be the right kind of diversification. The securities selected should be in different industries and consist of different types of companies. As Markowitz put it, "It is necessary to avoid investing in securities with high covariances among themselves."[5]

Markowitz's ideas, when they finally received the attention they deserved, turned traditional concepts of investment management upside down. Until that point, persons with fiduciary responsibility for managing investments had been guided by the Prudent Man Rule, first formulated by Justice Samuel Putnam of the Commonwealth of Massachusetts in an 1830 ruling. The case involved the estate of a John McLean of Boston, who had died in 1823, leaving a will that provided his wife with the income from a $50,000 trust. Upon the wife's death, the estate was to be divided equally between Harvard College and Massachusetts General Hospital. Unfortunately, by the time Mrs. McLean passed away in 1828, the value of the estate had shrunk to $29,450. Harvard and Massachusetts General sued the trustees, seeking to hold them liable for the loss.

Justice Putnam ruled against the plaintiffs, finding that the trustees could not be held responsible for a loss of capital that was not "owing to their willful default," reasoning, "If that were otherwise, who would undertake such hazardous responsibility?" Putnam then defined what came to be known as the Prudent Man Rule:

Do what you will, the capital is at hazard . . . All that can be required of a trustee to invest, is . . . to observe how men of prudence, discretion and intelligence manage their own affairs, not in regard to speculation, but in regard to the permanent disposition of their funds, considering the probable income, as well the probable safety, of the capital to be invested.[6]

Putnam's "rule" guided investment managers for well over a century. In essence, the Prudent Man standard dictated that *each* investment purchased by a person acting with fiduciary responsibility be "prudent," which was interpreted to rule out "speculative" securities. Thus for many years conservative investment managers often refused to consider common stocks, purchasing bonds or preferred stocks instead. Even if they did occasionally add common stocks to the portfolios they managed, they invariably chose only the most stable, dividend-paying shares, which often had less growth potential than stocks that might be defined as speculative. It was this approach that Markowitz attacked broadside. He showed that a diversified portfolio of stocks, even one that included more "speculative" shares, could actually be no more risky than some of the "prudent" portfolios, if the stocks included in the diversified portfolio were carefully selected to minimize covariance. He even found that some portfolios of so-called safe securities could actually be quite risky because the securities had high covariances, meaning that they could move together adversely under certain circumstances. (A good example would be a portfolio that consisted exclusively of long-term high-quality bonds. Such a portfolio of "safe" securities could fall dramatically in value if interest rates rose sharply.)

Markowitz eventually developed the concept of an "efficient" portfolio, which maximized expected return for a given level of risk. Careful diversification was the key. Markowitz declared, "Diversification is both observed and sensible; a rule of behavior which does not imply the superiority of diversification must be rejected both as a hypothesis and as a maxim."[7] While this line of reasoning may seem unremarkable today, it ran contrary to accepted wisdom at the time Markowitz did his research.

Andrew Carnegie had defined a much different approach decades earlier when he advised, "Put all your eggs in one basket and watch the basket very carefully." Gerald Loeb, in his 1935 classic, *Battle for Investment Survival*, stated bluntly, "Once you obtain confidence, diversification is undesirable. Diversification [is] an admission of not knowing what to do and striking an average . . . The intelligent and safe way to handle capital is to concentrate. If things are not clear, do nothing. When something comes up, follow it *to the limit* . . . If it's not worth following to the limit, it is not worth following at all." The noted economist John Maynard Keynes expressed similar sentiments, writing, "I am in favor of having as large a unit as market conditions will allow . . . To suppose that safety-first consists in having a small gamble in a large number of different [companies] where I have no information to reach a good judgment, as compared with a substantial stake in a company where one's information is adequate, strikes me as a travesty of investment policy."[8]

Ultimately, the greatest impact of Markowitz's work was on investment managers in mutual funds, pension funds, and insurance companies, who were acting as fiduciaries for others. By freeing portfolio managers from the Prudent Man Rule, which required that *each* security purchased in a portfolio be "prudent," it made possible the rush to stocks by institutional investors that would characterize the second half of the twentieth century.

One man who would be instrumental in this process, although for different reasons, was Edward Crosby Johnson II. A quiet, intense young man from a prominent Boston family, Johnson was educated at the prestigious Milton Academy and at Harvard College. In deference to his father's wishes, he studied law and worked for more than a decade as a lawyer specializing in mergers and corporate reorganizations. But Johnson also became fascinated by the stock market; his interest was first piqued when he read a biography of Jesse Livermore in 1924. That the Livermore book was a carefully sanitized version of reality was not evident to Johnson or to the thousands of other Americans who eagerly read its pages. Instead the book provided what seemed to be an insider's insight into the great game on Wall Street. Years later Johnson would say, "I'll never forget the thrill. Here was a picture of a world in which it was every man for himself, no favors asked or given."[9] Livermore "operating in the market," Johnson exclaimed, "was like Drake sitting on the poop of his vessel during a cannonade. Glorious."[10]

Using proceeds from the sale of his father's dry goods business, Johnson in 1943 acquired the little-known Fidelity Funds. Three years later, he fired the funds' investment adviser and took over the management of the portfolio himself. Well before Harry Markowitz first published his ideas (and certainly well before those ideas gained broad acceptance), Johnson had come to question the application of the Prudent Man Rule to the management of equity mutual funds. He believed that such a conservative approach to investing caused portfolio managers to underperform in a surging economy; in such an environment, "prudence" was in fact imprudent.

Johnson described his approach as laissez faire without chaos.[11] He believed in diversification, but he also sought to beat the market by aggressive stock selection. Johnson's approach at Fidelity was unorthodox; he would trade stocks actively, instead of adopting the traditional conservative "buy and hold" strategy. "We didn't want to feel we were married to a stock when we bought into it . . . ," he commented. "Possibly now and again we liked to have a 'liaison'—or even, very occasionally, a couple of nights together."[12] Johnson's track record was good; his marketing strategy was even better. By the time he finally turned Fidelity Funds over to his son in 1972, the funds' assets under management had grown from $3 million to $3 billion.

Much of the increased public participation in the market in the 1950s was channeled through mutual funds like Fidelity. Unlike the notorious investment trusts of the 1920s, the modern funds were usually "open ended," meaning that they stood ready to sell new shares or redeem outstanding shares at all times, at a price equal to the current market value of the funds' assets. Also unlike the investment trusts, the new mutual funds typically did not employ leverage. They were marketed to small investors as a means by which those investors could acquire a diversified portfolio of stocks selected by professional managers.

In 1950 there were slightly fewer than 1 million mutual fund shareholders, with the value of fund assets totaling approximately $2.5 billion. Ten years later, there would be 3.5 million mutual fund shareholders, and the funds would own assets valued in excess of $17 billion. The rapid growth was the product of aggressive sales efforts by an army of part-time salespeople working on commission. One writer described a conversation with two friends on the subject. The first friend reported, "I live in a big apartment building uptown. I think that half of the tenants are selling mutual funds. Within the past year five or six of my neighbors knocked on my door and asked if I wanted to buy." The other friend retorted, "That's nothing. Out where I live, my gas station attendant sells mutual funds to his gas customers while that automatic thing is filling up the tank."[13] Many fund organizations preferred to use part-time rather than full-time salespeople because "the more salesmen, the more friends and relatives" who could be solicited to buy shares.

The amateur salesmen were paid commissions based on the amount of money invested by their customers; the standard payouts were frequently as much as 8.5%. This amount, known as a sales "load," was generally subtracted upfront, meaning that an investor who put up $1,000 would actually receive fund shares valued at only $915 ($1,000 − $85). Thus the typical fund investor would start off behind by a healthy amount. A significant rise in the market would be required just to get back to even.

To make matters worse, in spite of claims advertising the benefits of "professional management," the performance record of most mutual funds was not impressive. A report in *Forbes* magazine in 1953 showed that while the Standard & Poor's Ninety stock index rose by 151.2% from 1946 to 1952, the 41 largest mutual funds gained only 146.5% over that period. A *Business Week* survey comparing 45 large funds to the Standard & Poor's Industrial Index over the first ten months of 1955 showed that while the market as measured by the index rose by 15%, the funds gained only 6.3%. In 1958, Congress requested that the SEC investigate the mutual fund industry; the SEC responded by commissioning a comprehensive study by the Wharton School of Business. After an exhaustive inquiry, the Wharton study concluded, "On the average [mutual fund performance] did not differ appreciably from what would have been achieved by an unmanaged portfolio . . ."[14] And this was before taking into account the drag on returns imposed by the heavy sales loads.

Defenders of the mutual fund industry pointed out that despite the funds' poor performance relative to market averages, the typical fund investor in the 1950s did much better than he would have had he invested in traditional vehicles like savings accounts or government bonds. And they argued that the high sales loads were necessary to market the new product to a public that was inherently suspicious of the stock market. In fact, a handful of "no load" (no sales commission) funds did exist, where investors could buy shares directly from the fund without paying a salesman. But these funds failed to attract much attention, never making up more than 5% of industry assets in the 1950s. It did seem that funds had to be "sold" to investors; few people actively sought out such investments on their own. In spite of poor performance and high sales commissions, mutual funds introduced millions of new investors to the stock market. Their combined buying power undoubtedly helped fuel the impressive market gains of the decade.

At the beginning of the 1950s, however, the market was still driven by individuals, not institutions. In 1951, 61% of all transactions on the New York Stock Exchange were made by individual investors. Stock market wealth was quite concentrated, with 2.1% of shareholders owning 58% of all common stock. The Exchange released a stockholder census in 1952, published by the Brookings Institution, which revealed that there were slightly fewer than 6.5 million shareholders in the United States, and that one-third of these had purchased stock for the first time in the previous three years. The average age of shareholders was 51, and the median annual income was $7,100. Even though interest on the part of the public was growing significantly, Exchange president G. Keith Funston pointed out that there were still over 41.5 million people between the ages of 30 and 49 who owned no shares at all.

In 1951, William McChesney Martin, a former president of the New York Stock Exchange, became chairman of the Federal Reserve System. He quickly established himself as an enemy of inflation, questioning the Fed's long-standing policy of holding down interest rates by pumping money into the economy. Under Martin's direction the Fed discontinued the practice of pegging government bond prices, preferring instead to strictly control the money supply. Martin is credited with the oft-repeated remark that it is the Fed's job "to be the chaperone at the party who must take away the punch bowl just as the party gets going."[15] Martin didn't share the view that enthusiasm for stocks represented a vote of confidence in America. Instead, he worried that broad public participation in the stock market signaled a return to the boom-and-bust cycles of the 1920s.

The Fed's tight money policy likely contributed to the mild recession that occurred in 1953, the first year of the Eisenhower administration. Eisenhower supporters referred to the slump as a rolling readjustment, while Democrats called it a prelude to depression. The stock market was briefly affected, but after a mild dip in 1953 stock prices roared ahead in 1954, spiking upward by a phenomenal 50% (as measured by the Dow Jones Industrial Average). Whatever Martin's qualms, public interest in the market was clearly increasing. One of the best anecdotal indicators of the new attitude was the influential radio commentator Walter Winchell's decision in early 1954 to begin offering stock tips on his Sunday evening broadcasts. Winchell was always on the lookout for new material that would attract listeners; he had earlier offered tips on horse racing. Most of the Winchell stock picks were low-priced, thinly traded issues that jumped sharply on the buying that inevitably followed his recommendations. In January 1955, Winchell claimed that an investor who had bought round lots (100 shares) of each of his selections would have made $250,000. This was not true; most stocks spiked initially, then fell back. Over the longer term, the performance of his picks was mediocre at best.[16] Financial columnist Sylvia Porter observed that investors could have done just as well by purchasing any one of hundreds of stocks that rose in the bull market. (Winchell retaliated by reporting in his newspaper column that an unnamed "female financial genius" had dropped a bundle in a silver stock.[17]) Such recriminations aside, Winchell's broadcasts drew many new people into the market. They were far more effective than the fruitless New York Stock Exchange advertising schemes of previous years.

On March 5, 1954, the Dow Jones Industrial Average broke through 300; the last time the Dow had been that high was on October 26, 1929, immediately before the worst of the '29 crash. The secretary of commerce hailed what he called the Eisenhower prosperity, and went on to say, "I believe the stock market is still one of the best barometers of business this country has."[18] But the truly momentous milestone was reached on November 17, when the Dow finally exceeded the September 1929 high of 381.37. This event made front-page news; the 1929 mark still had tremendous psychological significance. It had taken the market twenty-five long years to recover from the crash and Depression. Inevitably the question was asked, "Is it for real?"

A committee of the United States Senate was convened to investigate whether the presumed "excess speculation" of 1929 was again infecting the market. The panel was chaired by Arkansas Democrat J. William Fulbright. The inquiry did not attract a great deal of attention, except for an appearance by Harvard economist John Kenneth Galbraith, then completing his book on the events of 1929 entitled *The Great Crash*. Galbraith testified that he believed it was possible such a calamity could occur again. He steadfastly refused to be drawn into any specific predictions, offering little advice other than suggesting margin requirements be raised. But the market reacted swiftly (and quite unexpectedly) to his words; the afternoon he testified, stock prices fell 1.5%, a large move at the time.

The next day newspaper headlines proclaimed EGGHEAD SCRAMBLES MARKET.[19] But stocks recovered quickly, and it soon became clear that nothing of consequence would come out of the Senate hearings, Galbraith's remarks notwithstanding. *Business Week* later editorialized that "1954 will go down as the year when we conquered the depression phobia." These remarks were premature, however. For many years to come, bearish market analysts would continue to cite "parallels" with 1929 when making cautionary statements about the market.

The strong market of the 1950s brought with it a resurrection of sorts of what had come to be called technical market analysis, which had its roots in the original Dow theory, developed by Charles Dow at the turn of the century. Some of the most influential market analysts of the 1950s were "technicians," believing as Dow had that since stock prices at any point in time represented the best accumulated knowledge of all market participants, any additional analysis of business fundamentals was pointless. In the technicians' opinion, the only way to predict stock price moves was to watch the action of the market itself. Technicians relied on seemingly esoteric devices such as point-and-figure charts, odd-lot indexes, short-interest ratios, confidence indexes, overbought-oversold indicators, and volume momentum charts. All these tools in one way or another were designed to measure the dynamics of the market, irrespective of traditional business fundamentals like earnings, revenues, asset values, etc.

James Dines, one of the leading technicians of the 1950s, described the difference between technical and fundamental stock market analysis. He wrote, "Technicians, using deductive logic, compute from what *is*, back to what might be happening in the company. The theory is that the price of the stock is already the sum of every positive and negative factor anyone in a position to act knows about." On the other hand, Dines said, "Fundamentalists (using inductive logic) compute *from* earnings, dividends and quality what the price of a stock *should* be. If this conclusion varies from the current price, the stock is then deemed to be either under- or over-priced."[20]

Many technicians diligently sought to avoid being influenced by "fundamentals." One prominent analyst, John MaGee, refused to read newspapers until they were two weeks old, and boarded up all the windows in his office so he could not see outside while he studied his stock charts. MaGee was in his mid-fifties, with a heavily lined face under bushy brows and slightly protruding ears that gave him a pleasantly unassuming appearance. He coauthored a book entitled *Technical Analysis of Stock Trends* and published a twice-weekly advisory letter. He was often quoted as flippantly saying, "Don't confuse me with the facts."[21]

In describing why fundamental analysis would not work for most investors, MaGee drew an analogy to Bernard Baruch. Baruch could succeed by examining fundamentals, MaGee explained, because he had a staff of assistants to examine financial data and go out into the field seeking information. Baruch thus had sources most investors could not gain access to. The only hope for the typical investor was to attempt to follow knowledgeable investors like Baruch by watching for signs of their actions in the market.

MaGee admired Jesse Livermore, whom he called the great technician and anti-fundamentalist trader of the early part of this century. According to MaGee, "Livermore wouldn't have been caught dead studying a profit-and-loss statement." Admitting that most technicians (presumably including Livermore) didn't fully understand why their theories worked, MaGee still insisted that charting was "a science, or at least a quasi science." He continued, "The chartist regards the development of stock-chart formations as a natural phenomenon, the way a botanist regards the development of plants."[22]

MaGee recognized that "nowadays the Dow Theory is often derided, on the ground that it gives its signals too late to do any good, or gives downright wrong signals." He conceded that "the 'theory' certainly isn't perfect . . ." but claimed that it had served to "introduce the technical approach." MaGee described his own methods as post-Dow.[23] When questioned about his results, MaGee claimed that his recommendations for his clients had been quite successful but that his trading for his personal account had been somewhat less so. MaGee attributed the lackluster performance to "emotions," believing that with his own money at stake he was less able to impartially interpret the technical signals his methods produced.

Unwittingly, MaGee seemed to give credence to a statement made years earlier by Fred Schwed, Jr., author of the popular critique of Wall Street, *Where Are the Customer's Yachts?* As Schwed put it, "A busted chart reader . . . is never apologetic about his method—he is, if anything, more enthusiastic . . . If you have the bad taste to ask him how it happens that he is broke, he tells you quite ingeniously that he made the all too human error of not believing his own charts." It was to be a refrain that would be repeated many times over the years by market technicians.

Unknown to most market participants, a body of academic research was slowly accumulating that would dramatically undermine the key assumption of technical analysis—that past market activity could be used to predict the future. The research was performed by statisticians and mathematicians who had little direct knowledge of or contact with the financial markets. Much as Alfred Cowles's studies demonstrating the poor performance of investment advisory newsletters had been generally ignored in the 1930s, little attention was at first paid to the new data. Academia and Wall Street seemed to operate independently of each other, on entirely separate planes.

In 1934, one year after Cowles published his research, a paper by Stanford University professor Holbrook Working appeared in the *Journal of the American Statistical Association*. Working was unfamiliar with Cowles and had had little prior interest in the financial markets. As later described by economist Paul Samuelson, Working was "a dry stick . . . not a sparkling expositor." He was extremely thin and "old looking." Samuelson believed that Working's research would have received more attention had he been associated with Harvard or the University of Chicago; as Samuelson put it, Stanford at the time was considered to be "in the boondocks."[24]

Working's article carried a title only a statistician could love: "A Random Difference Series for Use in the Analysis of Time Series." He collected voluminous quantities of data on commodity prices and then plotted the data on graphs; he observed what appeared to be identifiable and repetitive patterns rather than "a completely hit or miss character." This confirmed what professional commodity traders told him; the traders all believed that prices followed certain rhythms and trends. But when Working went on to plot price changes from one transaction to the next, he made a startling discovery. While price *levels* did not seem to follow random patterns, individual price *changes* did tend to be "largely random." To test the results, he then prepared two sets of charts—one based on actual price movements, and the other based on randomly generated numbers. When he showed the charts to the professional traders, they were unable to distinguish between the real charts and the random ones.[25]

Working's findings had revolutionary implications, but as a statistician not involved in the Wall Street community, he failed to recognize them. Nothing much further was done with the subject until a professor of statistics at the London School of Economics published a paper in the *Journal of the Royal Statistical Society* in 1953. Maurice Kendall's "The Analysis of Economic Time Series" posed a straightforward question: How could short-term "ripples" in such series be distinguished from long-term results? Kendall examined British stock prices and American wheat and cotton prices, and confirmed Working's conclusion that there was no structure of any sort in successive price changes. As Kendall put it, "The patterns of events in the price series [were] much less systematic than is generally believed."[26]

Describing one particular set of data, Kendall said, "The series looked like a 'wandering' one, almost as if once a week the Demon of Chance drew a random number from a symmetrical population of fixed dispersion and added it to the current price to determine next week's price." Commenting on stock prices, he added, "Investors can, perhaps, make money on the Stock Exchange, but not, apparently, by watching price movements and coming in on what looks like a good thing . . . But it is unlikely that anything I say or demonstrate will destroy the illusion that the outside investor can make money by playing the markets, so let us leave him to his own devices." Kendall's paper, and its pointed conclusions, caused an uproar when presented to the Royal Statistical Society.

In essence, both Working and Kendall demonstrated that successive price *changes* in markets were random, implying, as statisticians put it, that they are independent of each other. But if this was true, what was the intellectual basis of technical analysis? Market technicians assume that past market data can be used to predict future results. But if future results are statistically independent of past results, by definition there can be no predictive value. Working and Kendall drove a very sharp stake through the heart of market technicians.

As might be suspected, papers presented before the Royal Statistical Society in London did not have a wide audience on Wall Street. In March 1959, Harry Roberts, a statistician at the University of Chicago, sought to carry the matter directly to the financial community. Writing in the *Journal of Finance*, Roberts documented the empirical data and showed why they refuted the basic assumption underlying technical analysis. Roberts stated that he wanted to bring to the attention of analysts evidence "that seems to have been ignored in the past, for whatever reason." His targets were so-called chartists and proponents of the Dow theory. Roberts, like Working, used a series of random numbers from which he succeeded in generating patterns that looked like typical stock charts. He concluded that the chart formations technicians claimed to be significant could be (and probably were) generated by pure chance.

But Roberts's efforts failed to appreciably diminish the technicians' appeal. In fact, when a new book by Nicholas Darvas, a ballet dancer who claimed to have made $2 million in the market using charts, was published the following year, it met with an overwhelmingly enthusiastic response. Subsequent books on the subject of technical analysis were also well received. Even though the intellectual basis of technical theory was dubious at best, there is no question that the technicians attracted new investors to the market. Much like Walter Winchell's stock touting in 1954, the well-publicized claims of Darvas and others reinforced the trend toward increased public participation in the stock market.

That momentum had originated in the late 1940s in large part due to fear of inflation. Surprisingly, even though by later standards the low, single-digit inflation rates of the 1950s appear relatively benign, inflation continued to be a major topic of concern throughout the decade. Except for short bursts of rising prices associated with wars, inflation had been largely absent throughout American history. Thus a persistent upward bias in prices, even if slight, was quite unsettling.

To combat inflation, the Federal Reserve pursued a fairly consistent tight money policy, after abandoning earlier attempts to hold down interest rates. This policy dovetailed with the Eisenhower administration's anti-inflation program, which involved efforts to restrain the growth of federal spending. Administration officials consistently stressed the need to balance the budget and cut spending. Treasury Secretary George Humphrey warned that if the nation didn't stick to fiscal responsibility, "I will predict that you will have a depression that will curl your hair."[27] This remark was misquoted, so that some people thought Humphrey was actually predicting a depression. Former President Hoover replied that he doubted a depression was in the offing. "[My hair] has already been curled once," Hoover commented, "and I think I can detect the signs."[28]

Although no depression developed, the tight fiscal and monetary policies of the period probably contributed to the inconsistent growth of the 1950s. There were three recessions during the Eisenhower administration. Even so, concern about inflation did not abate. Investors continued to flock to stocks as a means of hedging themselves against future increases in the consumer price level. Stock prices (as measured by the Dow Jones Industrials) fell each year the economy slid into recession (roughly 4% in 1953, 17% in 1957, and 10% in 1960) but immediately rebounded by much larger amounts as the recessions abated (50% in 1954, 38% in 1958, and 24% in 1961). By the end of the decade, acceptance of the "growth stock" model had seemingly become ubiquitous.

Two actions taken by the quintessential conservative "blue chip," American Telephone and Telegraph, symbolized the triumph of the new thinking. First, the stodgy AT&T pension fund finally began to purchase common stocks in 1958, instead of restricting itself to the traditional portfolio of bonds and preferred stocks. Then, later that year, the company announced it was splitting its shares 3 for 1 and increasing its dividend by 10%. AT&T's common stock dividend had been fixed as long as most investors could remember; the company had taken pride in maintaining a consistent payout year in and year out. But now, as *Business Week* put it in late December, "Telephone" had transformed itself into a growth stock.

Analysts suddenly discovered exciting growth possibilities in such AT&T subsidiaries as Western Electric and Bell Labs. As *Business Week* saw it, if AT&T was seen as an appealing investment for "growth-oriented" investors, it could compete much more effectively for the large amounts of equity capital it would need to raise in the future.

New York Stock Exchange volume in 1959 was the second highest in history, exceeded only by that of 1929. Electronics and technology stocks led the advance, often carrying unheard-of valuations. Some Wall Streeters joked that the market was discounting not only the future, but the hereafter as well.[29] Texas Instruments, one of the leading technology issues, rose from 16 in 1957 to 193½ in 1959, during which time earnings per share increased from $1.11 to $3.59. Stocks of companies like Texas Instruments routinely carried P/E ratios of 50 to 1 and more.

Exchange officials issued the familiar warnings against excess speculation, but did nothing. The dilemma they faced was summarized succinctly by Charles Schwarz, senior partner at Bache & Company. Schwarz said, "It is stupid, after years of a publicity campaign to get people to buy stocks, to come out now and blow the whistle."[30]

Most disturbing of all to adherents of traditional standards of valua-

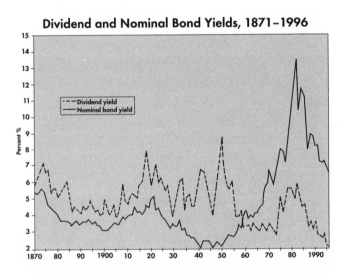

Dividend and Nominal Bond Yields, 1871–1996

From Stocks for the Long Run (1994) *by J. Siegel. Reprinted with the permission of The McGraw-Hill Companies.*

tion was an epochal event that occurred in 1958. For the first time in history, stock dividend yields fell below long-term government bond interest rates. This threatened the bedrock assumption of traditional standards of valuation—that stocks should yield more than bonds because they are riskier than bonds. *Business Week* raised the matter in an August 1958 article that warned, "An Evil Omen Returns." The magazine noted that whenever in the past yields on stocks had fallen near those of bonds (such as in 1929), a major decline in the stock market invariably followed. In September 1958 the magazine revisited the issue, seeking to explain why many investors seemed unconcerned about the classic stock-bond yield relationship. *Business Week* wrote, "The relationship between stock and bond yields was clearly posting a warning signal, but investors still believe inflation is inevitable and stocks are the only hedge against it." Finally, in its year-end 1959 issue, *Business Week* reported, "To some Wall Street veterans, the cult of equities has some ugly parallels to the New Era of the late 1920's. They are worried by the fact that stock yields have dipped below the level available on high-grade bonds. And they feel that the abandonment of historical price-earnings ratios means that the future is being discounted too far. If the economy does not have an inflationary binge, they warn, many of today's stocks are much too high." The editor of the *Financial Analysts Journal* stated the matter much more succinctly, observing that "some financial analysts called [the reversal of the traditional stock-bond yield relationship] a financial revolution . . ."

But the stock market continued to gain ground even after the "great yield reversal" occurred. In fact, stock dividends would never again rise above long-term government bond interest rates. Fears of inflation were not only pushing investors to buy stocks but were also causing bond buyers to demand higher yields. (If bonds were to be paid back with cheaper, "inflated" dollars in the future, anyone holding bonds would need to receive higher interest rates as compensation.) A "revolution" had truly occurred, with "inflation psychology" overwhelming the markets. Adherents to traditional standards of valuation were left in the dust.

Unfortunately, at least as far as some market bulls were concerned, one very important institution, the Federal Reserve System, seemed to be intractably committed to the old standards. In March 1959 the central bank raised its discount rate to 3%, signaling a move toward tighter money. The move was widely seen as a reaction to the rapid rise in stock prices and was much criticized. *The New York Times* declared the rate increase to be "completely uncalled for," and *The Wall Street Journal* labeled the move "unnecessary." *Business Week* noted that the "nation's productive capacity is still not fully utilized . . ." and warned that "in making this decision, we strongly suspect, the Fed has been influenced too much by what has been going on in the stock market, and not enough by what has been going on in business as a whole." The dilemma the Fed had first faced (and badly mishandled) in the 1920s seemed to be recurring: Given the increasing importance of the stock market to the broader economy, could (or should) the central bank attempt to restrain what was perceived as market excess?

The average dividend yield on New York Stock Exchange–listed stocks had fallen from more than 6.5% in 1950 to under 3.25% in 1959. Over the same period, the P/E ratio for NYSE-listed stocks rose from approximately 7 to 1 to 17 to 1. Stock prices had advanced approximately 250% faster than earnings. Obviously this sharp upward revaluation reflected at least in part a rebound from the abnormally depressed valuations of the late 1940s. But just as obviously, the market seemed to have moved beyond a normal recovery into entirely new territory, a state of affairs that made many observers nervous.

The March 1959 edition of *Fortune* attempted to provide a comprehensive explanation of what was happening. The article quoted unnamed financial columnists who saw the market's rise as a sign of "quiet desperation" about the "coming inflation." But *Fortune* also found other reasons for the market's strong performance.

One obvious source of buying came from rapidly growing institutional participation in the market. *Fortune* reported that in 1957 mutual funds accounted for $2.3 billion, or 62% of the net buying of stocks, with pension funds responsible for $1 billion more, or 27% of total net buying. Together these institutional purchases represented 89% of all net buying. As of January 1, 1959, *Fortune* estimated that open-end mutual funds had assets of $13 billion, up $4.5 billion from the previous year. Likewise, the magazine estimated that by 1959 pension funds had 30% of their assets invested in stocks, up from 10% in 1950. Although mutual funds and pension funds still held only about 10% of all stocks, their share of the market was obviously rising rapidly, and their purchases were inevitably driving share prices higher.

Fortune also cited specific reasons investors found stocks attractive. These included the consistent growth of corporate earnings, a 25% tax rate for long-term capital gains (considerably below the tax rate applied to bond interest income), and built-in stabilizers in government, such as Social Security and unemployment insurance, which, combined with contracyclical monetary and fiscal policies, had presumably made severe economic downturns less likely (and stocks less risky).

Fortune did present cautionary opinions. A young economic consultant named Alan Greenspan of Townsend-Greenspan Financial Advisors, Inc., warned that the booming stock market itself could ultimately be the cause of economic dislocations. He said that the Fed's ability to pursue contracyclical monetary policies to restrain speculative excess in the market was limited by the fact that the tight money required would have the side effect of paralyzing legitimate business. But if not restrained, Greenspan predicted, stock prices in boom periods would tend to rise to levels that could not be justified by any logical methodology. At that point, stocks would be bought simply to sell to someone else at a still higher price. Eventually the "bubble" would collapse, resulting in a panic that would not easily be offset by "built-in stabilizers" and easy money policies. In this way, Greenspan warned, "*over exuberance*" in the stock market could ultimately do a great deal of damage to the broader economy. It would not be the only time Greenspan expressed concern about such "exuberance."

But it was left to the "dean" of security analysis, Benjamin Graham, coauthor of the classic book *Security Analysis* and foremost proponent of the "value" school of investing, to provide a comprehensive critique of the "new thinking" of the late 1950s. Looking back over his forty-four-year Wall Street career, Graham observed that the nature of speculation had changed. Formerly, he said, elements of speculation had most frequently arisen from uncertainties surrounding an individual company. But over time these uncertainties had been lessened, by virtue of improved accounting standards, disclosure requirements, and better, more professional corporate management. What Graham defined as the traditional "three M's" that once fed the fires of speculation—mystery, manipulation, and (thin) margins*—were largely things of the past. Speculation had now shifted, he argued, to ever more frantic attempts to anticipate future earnings.[31]

Graham cited as an example the case of International Business Machines (IBM), which had recently become one of the small group of companies generating over $1 billion in annual sales. Graham had first come into contact with IBM's predecessor company, the Computing-Tabulating-Recording Company, in 1915, when he was a college student working part-time on a job that required him to use the company's Hollerith calculating machines. He became interested in C-T-R and presented an analysis of the stock to his boss. The shares were selling in the mid-40s, with earnings of $6.50 per share. The company had just initiated an annual dividend of $3 per share.

As Graham described it, his boss looked at him with a "pitying" expression and said, "Never mention that company to me again . . . I would not touch it with a ten-foot pole." The 6% bonds were selling in the 80s and were "no good," so how could the stock be good? Graham's superior concluded with the derisive comment that "everybody knows there is nothing behind it but water."[32]

Graham, recounting this story in the late 1950s, felt obliged to provide his audience with a definition of what was meant by the term "water." Graham's boss in 1915 gave no thought whatsoever to future earnings growth; thus any excess in the stock price beyond what was justified by the assets of the company and a record of stable dividends was "water." But the notion of water in the financial structure of a company had, by the late 1950s, become an anachronism. That Graham needed to explain the term is a telling indicator of just how much valuation standards had changed.

Graham admitted that he had been so impressed by his boss's condemnation of Computer-Tabulating-Recording that he had never bought a share, even when the company's name changed to IBM in 1926. By that time, the earnings had increased from $691,000 to $3.7 million, the stock

---

*The phrase "thin margins" referred to the pre-1930s practice where investors could put up only a small amount of money (margin) when they bought stocks, borrowing the rest.

had split 3.6 for one, and a dividend of $3 had been set on the new stock. At an average price of $45 in 1926, IBM was selling at a P/E of 7 to 1, with a dividend rate of 6.7%. Graham noted that even after the rapid increase in earnings of the previous ten years, these P/E and dividend yield numbers were virtually identical to those of 1915. The market's valuation of the stock seemed to be unaffected by the impressive record of growth.

To Graham, this example illustrated how traditional valuation standards persisted into the mid-twenties, at which point things began to change. By 1946, Graham records, when earnings had increased five times over 1926 levels, IBM's P/E ratio had grown to 17.5 to 1. Earnings growth then accelerated further; by 1956, the company's earnings were four times higher than 1946, and the P/E ratio had expanded to 32.5 to 1. As Graham saw it, the contemporary buyer of IBM shares was paying not only for the established earnings power and good name of the company but for the assumption that these factors would inevitably produce higher profits in the future.

Graham was particularly disdainful of what he called the new mathematical approach to valuing stocks, saying that in his 44 years of experience he had never seen dependable calculations of stock values that went beyond simple arithmetic or basic algebra. "Whenever calculus is brought in," he argued, "you could take it as a warning signal that the operator was trying to substitute theory for experience, and usually also to give speculation the deceptive guise of investment." Graham warned that mathematical models of future growth combined precise mathematical techniques with very imprecise estimates of future earnings. Thus the final estimation of value, although in fact of dubious accuracy, was given the imprimatur of hard science by the use of higher math.[33]

Mathematics notwithstanding, the real question was future growth, and how the prospects of such growth should be reflected in stock prices. To return to Graham's IBM example, by the 1950s IBM's earnings were growing 20% per year consistently. Given that growth rate, an IBM share price that created a P/E ratio of 32.5 to 1 in 1956 would, if unchanged, represent only a 13 to 1 P/E ratio five years later. IBM occupied a dominant position in an exciting, rapidly growing industry. How much was too much to pay for the company's obvious potential?

Graham looked back with admitted nostalgia to the early days of the century, when stock investors "paid only for the present and got the future for nothing." He conceded, however, that "those days are gone forever." Perhaps better than anyone else, Graham described the evolution of the stock market over his lifetime. In earlier years, when the market lacked integrity and transparency, stocks were valued by very simple, unsophisticated standards allowing investors to get something (the future) for nothing. By the late 1950s this was no longer true.

Generally accepted accounting standards and better reporting requirements had removed much of the mystery from financial reporting, allowing for more transparency. Government regulation, and the sheer size of the modern market, had relegated market manipulators like Serge Rubenstein to small, fringe stocks rather than established, large-capitalization issues. (In 1959, more than 6 billion shares were listed on the New York Stock Exchange, compared with 1 billion in 1929; the market was simply too large for a single individual or group of individuals to manipulate.) More sophisticated means of valuing future earnings streams, and managing portfolios, were gaining acceptance. It is not surprising that stock valuations would rise as the market adjusted to these changed conditions. In fact, it would have been quite surprising if they had not.

Old standards, such as the traditional stock-bond yield relationship, now fell by the wayside. Something similar had happened in the 1920s, as new valuation methodologies based on future growth first began to be accepted. But that trend had been brutally aborted, and thoroughly discredited, by the 1929 crash and subsequent Great Depression. Now, in the late 1950s, the market was again moving onto uncharted ground armed with new theories of valuation. Would the result be the same?

10

THE KENNEDY MARKET

JOHN FITZGERALD KENNEDY seemed ideally suited to a stock market increasingly dominated by "growth" psychology. A young, vibrant man whose father, Joseph P. Kennedy, had been a legendary market operator, Kennedy espoused an economic philosophy that was explicitly critical of the conservative fiscal and monetary policies of the Eisenhower administration. After his narrow election victory, the new President assembled a staff of economic advisers whose stated objective was to "get the economy moving again." The sluggish growth during the preceding eight years (marked by GNP increases averaging 2.5% per year) was grossly inadequate; Kennedy and his advisers believed they could do much better. A target of 5% annual GNP growth was set, which, if attained, would manifestly increase personal incomes, reduce poverty and unemployment, and generate billions of dollars of new wealth.

This ambitious objective was to be achieved primarily by the use of tax incentives for business, including an investment tax credit (a direct tax subsidy for capital spending), liberalized depreciation rules (quicker tax write-offs for new plant and equipment), and eventually a general tax cut. Critics accused Kennedy of "growthmanship"—the notion that all the country's problems could be solved simply by increasing the pace of economic expansion. In effect, Kennedy's economic plan had much in common with what would later be called "supply side" economics, although that term had not yet been invented. But to the President's conservative critics, the

Dow Jones Industrial Average, 1960–1963

Eisenhower | John F. Kennedy

1200 | 1200

Indicates a recession

Telstar communications satellite

First weather satellite

1050 | 1050

U.S. escalates aid to Vietnam

900 | 900

Nobel Prize for DNA discovery

John Glenn orbits Earth

750 | 750

JFK assassinated

600

Bay of Pigs

Kennedy confronts steel industry | Cuban Missile Crisis

1960   1961   1962   1963

© *Dow Jones & Company Inc.*

strategy had one potentially fatal flaw: the rapid growth the President envisaged could easily unleash inflation.

The Kennedy administration proposed to deal with the problem of inflation by means of "moral suasion," whereby the President would use the prestige and authority of his office to pressure labor and business to hold down wages and prices. Many observers were dubious about the efficacy of this approach, but their concerns did not much trouble the stock market. After all, investors bought stocks in large part because they feared future inflation; a high-growth policy that risked inflation was not at all bad for stocks. The market responded to the Kennedy victory with an impressive postelection rally; by February the Dow Jones Industrial Average was 15% above its October 1960 low. But "moral suasion" had yet to be tested. When it was, the results would stun Wall Street. The new policy would precipitate an ugly confrontation with big business and be blamed for causing the worst stock market crash since 1929.

None of this was evident in 1961, as the "Kennedy market" bounded ahead. Many mainstream economists went so far as to argue that modern economic theory, as applied by sophisticated government policy makers, would make the business cycle "obsolete." Recessions would be relics of the past. As might be expected, established growth stocks did quite well in this environment, but concern was expressed by some analysts that there weren't enough growth shares around to meet demand. Mutual funds and pension funds now accounted for more than 20% of all stockholdings, and were continuing to grow rapidly. In addition, individual investors were flocking to the market. The New York Stock Exchange estimated that by 1961, 15 million Americans owned stocks, compared with 6.5 million in 1952. Proven growth companies (such as IBM, Polaroid, and Xerox) were so profitable that they could usually finance their expansion out of retained earnings, making it unnecessary for them to issue more stock. In fact, they sometimes actually bought back outstanding stock in the marketplace. In 1960, for example, the net positive differential between new stock issued and stock repurchased was smaller than in any year in the 1950s.[1]

The "shortage" of good growth stocks caused analysts to search for emerging growth companies—in effect, to seek out "the next IBM." Much of the action was found in smaller firms not listed on the New York Stock Exchange; shares of these companies usually traded on the American Stock

Exchange, or in the Over-the-Counter (OTC) market. In stark contrast to earlier eras, when entrepreneurs struggled to secure financing for young companies with new technologies, the 1961 market was very receptive to small start-ups with intriguing concepts. In the second half of 1961, 70% of new securities were issued by companies that had never sold securities to the public before.[2]

In the spring of 1961, New York Stock Exchange president G. Keith Funston, taking note of the scramble to buy shares in unproven companies (most of which were not listed on the NYSE), began to warn of the dangers of ill-conceived speculation. Citing "disquieting evidence that some people have not discovered that it is impossible to get something for nothing," Funston worried that "would-be investors are attempting to purchase shares of companies whose names they cannot identify, whose products are unknown to them, and whose prospects are, at best, uncertain."[3] In May he returned to the same theme, declaring, "There still seems to be a preoccupation with low price shares because they are low-priced, and an unhealthy appetite for new issues of unseasoned companies merely because they are new . . ."[4]

Funston's warnings notwithstanding, "speculation" became more widespread as 1961 progressed. In April total margin debt surpassed $5 billion for the first time in 20 years; the significance of this event was downplayed, inasmuch as the Federal Reserve margin requirements, then set at 70%,* seemed sufficiently stringent to prevent forced selling by margined investors in the event of a market turndown. But concern about the hot market was expressed in Congress, and the inevitable investigation mandated, this time to be conducted by the SEC. Was excess speculation again imperiling the market, and presumably the broader economy? Had the mania for "growth" gone too far too fast? The year 1962 was certainly not the first time (nor would it be the last) that concerns about high earnings multiples would be expressed. More often than not, such concerns

---

*A 70% margin requirement means that investors are required to put up at least 70% of the value of the stocks they purchase. They can then borrow any part of the remaining 30%, using the stock itself as collateral for the loan.

were shrugged off and the market continued to move higher. But the spring of 1962 would be very different.

Beginning in January, a series of events occurred that *Fortune* magazine declared "would reverberate for years to come through the political and economic life of the US." On January 23, President Kennedy and Labor Secretary Arthur Goldberg met secretly with U.S. Steel chairman Roger Blough and United Steelworkers Union president David McDonald. The administration's objective was twofold—first, to avert a disruptive steel strike, and second, to ensure that the resulting wage settlement would not force up steel prices. Both Blough and McDonald resisted administration pressure; McDonald needed to negotiate a good deal for his members, and Blough felt that price increases would be required if the industry was to generate the capital necessary to modernize facilities.

As negotiations continued over the next several weeks, administration officials stepped up the pressure on McDonald, provoking a rebuke from AFL-CIO president George Meany. When Goldberg made a speech in March asking for compliance with government guidelines, Meany stormed, "He is infringing on the right of free people and free society." Goldberg responded that it was the government's responsibility to "provide guidelines . . . to insure that the settlements reached are the right settlements."[5] Meany was particularly indignant about Goldberg's role in the negotiations; Goldberg had formerly been counsel to the AFL-CIO and was seen by some union officials as a turncoat.

In the end, McDonald agreed to a pact that was within Kennedy's guidelines. The first of a series of contracts with producers was signed on March 31; Kennedy congratulated everyone involved for their "statesmanship." The President assumed that with a noninflationary wage settlement, the steel companies would not raise prices. He was wrong.

On Tuesday, April 10, only days after the last labor contract was signed, the U.S. Steel board of directors voted to increase prices an average of $6 per ton. Roger Blough telephoned the White House to request a meeting with the President, to personally inform Kennedy of the board's decision before it was made public. Since Blough was also chairman of the Business Council, a group of businessmen who served as informal advisers to the administration, it was not unusual for him to meet with the President. Yet this particular request puzzled Kennedy and his staff. As far as Kennedy was concerned, the steel wage-price matter was resolved; he could not imagine why Blough wanted to see him.

Roger Blough was a tall, outwardly affable man who, according to one popular characterization, was "like a warm, likable IBM machine" who could turn on the charm at will.[6] A Yale-educated lawyer who had been with U.S. Steel for years, he was a quintessential organization man and an adept corporate politician. Unfortunately, Blough was not nearly as experienced in the national political arena. Over the next few days his actions would be likened by one columnist to those of a "country boy too far from home."[7]

When Blough was ushered in to meet Kennedy on the evening of April 10, he brought along a copy of a press release announcing a 3.5% steel price increase. Kennedy was shocked; he had been under the impression that the steel companies would hold the line on prices. The President coldly told Blough he was "making a terrible mistake" and then called in Arthur Goldberg. Goldberg lambasted Blough, stating that his (Goldberg's) credibility with the unions would be destroyed by this action, inasmuch he had pressured labor to agree to a noninflationary settlement with the understanding that the industry would not increase prices.

Blough denied that he had ever agreed to hold down prices in return for a moderate labor settlement and cited figures showing declining steel profit margins. Kennedy was unmoved; after Blough left, he exploded, reportedly making a statement he would later come to regret. "My father always told me that all businessmen were sons of bitches," he fumed, "but I never believed it until now."[8]

U.S. Steel stock opened on Wednesday at 70¾, up 2¾, but fell back to 68½ after Kennedy issued a blistering statement questioning the patriotism of "a tiny handful of steel execs whose pursuit of private power and profit exceeds their sense of public responsibility."[9] Behind the scenes, the administration moved quickly to mobilize the massive machinery of government to quash the price rise. As other steel producers followed U.S. Steel's lead and increased prices by similar amounts, the Justice Department reviewed the possibility of antitrust action against the industry. The Federal Trade Commission commenced an investigation as to whether a 1951 consent decree agreed to by the industry had been violated, and the Defense Department was instructed to seek means by which foreign steel could be purchased to meet procurement needs.

More ominously, other measures allegedly taken by the administration took on the characteristics of a bare-knuckled brawl. *The Wall Street Journal* reported that the Internal Revenue Service had been ordered to make a check on the U.S. Steel stock option plan, which benefited top executives, and that tax inspectors had begun audits of the steel executives' personal returns. This was denied by the Treasury, the White House, and the IRS itself but was widely believed to be true.[10] Then, in the early-morning hours of April 12, FBI agents awakened two reporters (one with the Associated Press and the other with *The Wall Street Journal*), seeking their notes from a press conference held by the president of Bethlehem Steel the day before. The agents' immediate objective was to determine whether statements made at the press briefing provided evidence of collusion between the major steel companies. But the image of law enforcement agents rousting reporters from their beds in the middle of the night was chilling, to say the least. One anonymous White House official was quoted by *The Wall Street Journal* as saying, "Kennedy can be a hater, and right now I don't think there's any doubt he hates U.S. Steel."

The stock market slid lower on Thursday, continuing the downtrend that had been in evidence since January, falling to the lowest level since mid-1961. U.S. Steel fell 1⅛ to 67⅜. Attention focused on the few steel producers that had not yet joined in the price increase. What would they do? Industry observers believed that if any major company held out, competitive market conditions would force U.S. Steel to back down. The question was answered on Friday morning, April 13. Joseph Block, president of Inland Steel, was quoted from Tokyo as saying, "Even though steel profits are not adequate, we do not feel that an advance in steel prices at this time would be in the national interest."[11] Block's statement jolted Wall Street, and the other steel producers. Inland's stock jumped two points in Friday trading, while U.S. Steel shares continued to slide.

Hours after Block's statement was reported, Bethlehem Steel rescinded its price increase. It was now obvious the battle was over; when U.S. Steel finally backed down later that day, the announcement was anticlimatic. Kennedy had won. But would it prove a Pyrrhic victory?

The business press lambasted Kennedy, and his administration. *The*

Wall Street Journal wrote, "We never saw anything like it. One of the country's companies announced it was going to try to get more money for its product and all hell broke loose." On May 5, *Business Week* reported, "The market also reflects a wide-spread belief that the Kennedy Administration is anti-business, that business will become the scapegoat when it becomes inevitably necessary to shake out the economy . . . In this view, the steel uproar typifies the anti-business attitude. The episode didn't cause the downfall in stock prices, but it accelerated the trend."

The "trend" *Business Week* referred to continued in the coming weeks, with stocks falling almost daily during May. On Wednesday, May 23, Kennedy was asked about the market during his regular press conference. He said simply, "I believe that the stock market will move when—in accordance with the movement of the economy as a general rule."[12] Burton Crane of *The New York Times* observed that conditions were generally bad when reporters ran around "asking important people for their opinions on the market and the economy." In any case, Kennedy's remarks failed to stem the decline; on Friday, May 25, the Dow Jones Industrials dropped 38.83 points, or 4.2%. The ticker that reported NYSE transactions ran 32 minutes late at the closing bell, on very heavy trading volume of 6.3 million shares.

Burton Crane summarized the week: "Stocks went down for five days in a row last week, five days that carried the market averages back to the levels at the end of 1960, and 15 million shareholders suffered from unusual demands to their minds." The sharp decline was an unfamiliar, and very unpleasant, experience for the many new investors who had never witnessed a severe break in prices. Frequent references were made to the fact that the decline of May 20 to May 25 was the "worst since 1929." Crane offered no advice, but thought that "the professional would say, 'get out.' " On Monday many of his readers would try to do just that.

As trading opened for the week on May 28, prices immediately began to fall. The ticker again fell hopelessly behind the frenzied pace of transactions, and at 10:20 the Exchange began to send out current "flash" prices on selected stocks. By noon even these were abandoned; no one outside the Exchange had any idea where prices really were. Many orders were lost or left unfilled in the confusion. One broker said later, "It was as though some great natural calamity had occurred to some far-distant people, and we watched with horror and fascination . . ."[13] By the time the market closed, the Exchange floor was in chaos, and the Over-the-Counter market was in shambles. It took hours before accurate closing prices became available. Once the damage was tallied up, it was determined that the Dow Jones Industrials finished with a 5.7% loss, an extremely large move at the time, on the highest trading volume in nearly thirty years.

The New York Times reported, "Something resembling an earthquake hit the stock market." On Tuesday morning, May 29, the decline resumed with a vengeance, again on very heavy volume. The reported prices for the Dow Industrials dropped another 2% in the first hour of trading, with the ticker quickly falling behind the frenetic pace of trading. But the situation was actually far worse because many major stocks (such as IBM) did not begin trading when the Exchange opened; the imbalance of sell versus buy orders was so great that traders on the Exchange floor were unable to find a price that matched supply and demand. Then, just when it appeared that the market would disintegrate, something quite remarkable, and inexplicable, occurred. The market reversed itself, for no apparent reason, and shot upward. By 1:30, a rally stronger than any that had occurred since World War II was thrusting prices higher. Because of the late ticker, most people were unaware of the sudden reversal until late in the session, but by the close the Dow Industrials were actually up 4.7% on the day, having traded through a range (from the intraday low to the intraday high) of an astounding 10%.

Even though prices drifted lower again in June, the decisive turnaround on May 29 marked the end of the panic of 1962. Why did the market break occur? Almost immediately after the 1962 debacle, many opinions were offered, invariably expressed with great confidence, and quite often contradicting one another.

New York Stock Exchange president Funston blamed the decline squarely on the federal government. He alleged, "There has been a growing disquiet among investors because of President Kennedy's steel action."[14] *Fortune* magazine blamed the "Kennedy crash" on Kennedy himself, whose "double-barreled blast hit the expectations of the average investor and business alike." Undersecretary of Commerce Edward Gudemen heard an earful from his former business colleagues. "You son of a bitch," one of them reportedly screamed. "You guys down there are to blame for the market collapse."[15]

Eleanor Roosevelt, never noted for taking a particular interest in the stock market, declared that the "crash" was the result of a "conspiracy" on the part of big business to embarrass President Kennedy. From Moscow, *Izvestia* alleged that "certain circles in the US are trying to use the market situation as a pretext for a new onslaught on the rights of the working class."[16] Former President Dwight Eisenhower blamed the "reckless spending programs of the Kennedy Administration" and called for the end of the "planned economy."[17] Perhaps the most straightforward explanation came from Treasury Secretary Douglas Dillon, who told a Senate committee that the crash occurred because "finally the investing public just decided the prices were too high."[18]

The argument that Kennedy's heavy-handed handling of the steel crisis so undermined business confidence that it precipitated the stock market crash is appealing but, upon close examination, has obvious flaws. Most important, the market began trending lower in January, well before the steel crisis erupted in April. And the worst of the decline did not take place until late May, more than one month after the steel price issue had been resolved. This chronology suggests that there were other factors at work; while the administration's acts may have created unease on Wall Street, they alone cannot fully explain the January–May bear market.

Another explanation of the market action is that the steel crisis accentuated a bear market that had already developed for other reasons. Many analysts suggested that the 1962 market break occurred because prices had been "too high." They pointed to the fact that by the spring of 1962 there were disturbing indications that corporate profits were not increasing as fast as anticipated. Commentators had begun to speak of a "profit squeeze," with Burton Crane writing about "a growing belief that the rates of earnings growth for some of the glamour stocks were no longer justifying the price-earnings multipliers conferred by the markets of the past." From 1958 through 1961, while the gross national product increased nearly 20%, corporate profits had risen only a meager 3.3%.[19] The large P/E multiples of the popular "growth" stocks *assumed* that future earnings would increase rapidly; any indication that growth was slowing had ominous implications. By this reasoning, high stock prices were susceptible to a tumble for reasons entirely independent of the steel confrontation. A good example of what could occur had taken place well before the late-

May "crash," when IBM announced earnings that failed to meet expectations. In response to the news, IBM stock plunged more than 50 points.

Were stocks overvalued in late 1961, making the market susceptible to a serious drop? Comparisons were often made to 1929. As was discussed in chapter 6, however, recent research suggests that stocks were not badly overpriced in 1929, despite the conventional "overspeculation" explanation of the crash. What about the 1962 crash? Did stock prices fall sharply because they had been "too high," or was the ex post facto conventional wisdom wrong again?

On the face of it, there does seem to be substantial evidence that stock prices may well have been "too high" before the 1962 market break. In December 1961 the P/E ratio of the Dow Jones Industrials peaked at 23.7 to 1, which was high not only by historic standards but by standards that would prevail for most of the remainder of the century. *Barron's* calculated that the average P/E ratios of 300 leading stocks based on their 1961 highs was 23.3 to 1, significantly higher than the 14.9 to 1 peak P/E multiple of the 1953–1957 bull market. A subsequent, much more comprehensive calculation of *median* P/E ratios for all New York Stock Exchange–listed stocks showed that in 1961 half had P/E's greater than 19.98 to 1; not only was this number higher than any value attained in the previous bull market, it was higher than any median P/E ratio registered until the spectacular bull market of the 1990s.[20] And of course, in 1961 the leading "glamour" stocks routinely traded at P/E multiples more than twice those of the overall market.

It was the glamour stocks (as well as the smaller, "emerging" growth stocks) that suffered the most in the 1962 market setback. While the Dow Jones Industrial Average of established companies fell approximately 25% from the December 1961 top to the May 1962 bottom, leading glamour stocks dropped faster and farther. A sampling of 25 top growth stocks showed an average decline of 34% over this period.* Vickers Associates re-

---

*The growth stocks surveyed were AMP, American Home Products, Baxter Labs, Bristol-Myers, Coca-Cola, Disney, Eastman Kodak, Fairchild Camera, General Electric, Honeywell, IBM, ITT, Johnson & Johnson, Merck, MMM, Pepsi, Pfizer, Polaroid, Procter & Gamble, Revlon, Schering Plough, Sears, Texas Instruments, Upjohn, and Xerox.

ported that the "favorite fifty" Over-the-Counter Industrials plunged an average of almost 40%, with declines exceeding 50% in ten cases.[21]

An oft-quoted remark from the mid-1950s about growth stock valuations seemed appropriate. An anonymous observer remarked, "These glamour stocks remind me of a person riding a bicycle. All goes well while you are moving ahead, but if you try to stop the bicycle falls over."[22] With the benefit of hindsight, this became the accepted explanation of what happened in 1962. Hints that earnings growth was not living up to lofty expectations hit the growth and emerging growth stocks hard. The lackluster growth rates of the late 1950s simply could not justify swollen stock valuations. When the collapse came, it pulled down the high P/E multiples of the glamour stocks and those of the broader market as well. (By June 1962 the P/E ratio of the Dow Industrials had fallen from more than 23 to under 16 to 1.)

This interpretation, much like the overspeculation explanation of the 1929 boom and bust, seems clear-cut. Unfortunately, an examination of events immediately subsequent to the 1962 market break muddies the conclusion somewhat. Unlike the post–1929 crash market, which rallied briefly but then slid into a prolonged decline precipitated by the Depression, stock prices recovered robustly in late 1962 (after the Cuban missile crisis). The Dow Jones Industrials broke through the December 1961 high in 1963, and eventually established a new high slightly over 1,000 in early 1966. Thus an investor who bought the Dow Industrial stocks at the "overpriced" high of 734.51 in December 1961 would, over the next four years, achieve a compounded rate of return (including dividends) of approximately 11%, roughly the historic average rate of return for stocks over the century. Had he simply ignored the unpleasant volatility of 1962, the long-term investor would have made out just fine.

Perhaps even more surprisingly, the investor who owned the high-multiple "glamour" stocks before the 1962 break also did quite well over the long term, if he had the stomach to ride out the severe downdrafts of 1962. An investor holding stocks of the same 25 companies listed earlier, from the market peak in December 1961 until early 1966, would have achieved a 17% compounded annual rate of return (including dividends). Hardly convincing evidence that these stocks were badly overpriced before the 1962 crash.

What the events of 1962 illustrated unquestionably was that the growth stocks were significantly more *volatile* (risky) than the rest of the market. With higher expected returns came higher risk; the growth stocks fell much faster, then recovered much quicker, than the broad market. While this concept may seem unremarkable, it was to be at the root of a raging debate at the end of the decade between a new generation of impertinent academic researchers on one side and high-profile portfolio managers on the other. For the first time, formerly ignored voices of scholars like Louis Bachelier and Harry Markowitz would finally make themselves heard on Wall Street.

An SEC investigation of the 1962 market "crash" concluded that "neither this study nor that of the New York Stock Exchange was able to isolate and identify the cause of the market events [of late May 1962]." The SEC noted that "there was some speculation at the time that these events might be the result of some conspiracy or deliberate misconduct. Upon the basis of the study's inquiry, there is no evidence whatsoever that the break was deliberately precipitated by any person or group or that there was any manipulation or illegal conduct in the functioning of the market."[23] These conclusions marked a significant watershed; never again would "manipulation" be seriously considered as an explanation of a major market move. The days of Jay Gould and Jesse Livermore were gone forever.

But what of the stunning recovery that reversed the crash in prices on May 29? And why was the crash of 1962 of significantly lesser magnitude than the crash of 1929? (The Dow Industrials dropped 45% in the 1929 crash, but only 25% in the 1962 break.) The SEC was silent on this score, but subsequent research has provided indications that high margin requirements, combined with heavy buying by institutions, ultimately worked to cushion the 1962 drop.

By the spring of 1962, the Federal Reserve had increased margin requirements to 80%, meaning that investors were required to put up a minimum of 80% of the cost of any stock they purchased. (They could therefore legally borrow only 20% of the purchase price from their broker, using the stock itself as collateral.) In 1929, on the other hand, there were no legal margin requirements; each brokerage firm could determine on what basis it would lend money collateralized by its customers' stocks. The president of the New York Stock Exchange estimated that before the 1929 crash, the average margin required by member firms was 40%, meaning that customers could borrow 60% of the value of their purchases.[24] (Of course, an "average" margin requirement of 40% implied that some brokers were even more generous, allowing their customers to put up less than 40%.) Clearly, these margins provided a much smaller cushion than the 80% margin required in 1962; when prices dropped substantially in 1929, many "margined" investors were forced to sell as the value of their collateral fell to the point at which it was no longer sufficient to secure their loans. This forced selling in turn exacerbated the overall decline, which in turn forced more margined investors to sell, and so on. In 1962, however, because of the much stiffer margin requirements, very little forced selling occurred.

In addition, the rapidly increasing participation of large institutions in the stock market of the early sixties provided a reservoir of buying that apparently offset the panic selling of the crash. The steady flow of pension fund money into stocks reached a point in 1962 at which, for the first time ever, more than 50% of trustee-managed pension fund money was invested in equities (excluding the large AT&T fund that was still 90% in bonds).[25] More surprisingly, and contrary to what had been feared, the public also poured money into mutual funds at the time of the crash. On May 29, the day the market bottomed, $26.9 million in new mutual fund shares were purchased, as opposed to only $6.9 million worth of share redemptions. This was the largest one-day differential between mutual fund purchases and sales on record.[26]

A *Barron's* study found that in the second quarter of 1962 (the period that included the crash) mutual funds bought more stocks ($865 million versus $772 million) and sold less ($523 million versus $531 million) than in the previous quarter. Of the funds surveyed by *Barron's*, 22 were net sellers during the period of the crash, while 57 were net buyers. For the entire year, new mutual fund sales came to $2.7 billion, down $350 million from 1961 but still the second highest level on record. Redemptions actually declined for the year, to $1.1 billion from $1.2 billion in 1961. A subsequent study of institutional activity for the period from 1960 to 1968 confirmed that mutual funds generally tended to stabilize the market, acting counter to short-term market trends (such as the 1962 market break).[27]

While it is always risky to state with any degree of certainty *why* something happened in the stock market, it does appear that institutions were the heroes of 1962. The large cash reserves of pension and mutual funds provided an important safety net that cushioned, then reversed, the 1962 crash. Instead of becoming a destabilizing force, institutional involvement in the market seemed to have the opposite effect.

On November 15, 1962, the Kennedy administration announced it would seek an income tax cut. The Wall Street reaction was generally positive, even though such a move would likely widen the federal budget deficit. For years conservative opinion had considered inflation to be the primary threat to economic well-being, and deficit spending was seen to be inflationary. But now most of the business community accepted the idea of a tax cut as a means of stimulating needed growth. Even *Business Week*, traditionally fearful of inflation, admitted that "reducing the tax burden today . . . is the only way to correct the nation's slow rate of economic growth."

By the fall of 1963, much of the Wall Street animosity toward the Kennedy administration had dissipated. With stocks moving into record territory, the balm of rising prices soothed away old grievances. The market's resiliency after the 1962 "panic" was seen as a positive sign; once again, stocks had shrugged off adversity and resumed their climb. The same glamour stocks that had been punished so severely in mid-1962 came roaring back, leading the market higher. The old-line Dow Industrial stocks also did quite well; only the smaller, emerging OTC issues generally failed to share in the recovery. But just as Wall Street and Washington seemed finally to have reconciled, entirely unexpected events originating outside the Street abruptly brought the "Kennedy market" to a tragic end.

An implausible figure by the name of Anthony "Tino" DeAngelis was to be a leading player in the turbulent events that would buffet the market in late November 1963. DeAngelis did not appear to be the sort of man who could precipitate a major stock market crisis. His five-foot-four-inch frame was burdened by 240 fleshy pounds, making him seem wider than he was tall. Thin wire-rimmed black spectacles perched precariously on his round face, poking out from thick, graying black hair combed straight back from his temples. His rumpled suits usually looked as if he had slept in them. DeAngelis was rarely seen in the canyons of the financial district around Wall Street; instead his base of operations was a giant "tank farm" across the river in Bayonne, New Jersey. And the items in which he dealt were not stocks or bonds but vegetable oils.

DeAngelis was the principal behind Allied Crude Vegetable Oil Refining Corporation, which had grown in a few years to become the largest supplier of vegetable and fish oils used to make margarine, salad dressing, vitamin extracts, and paint, among other products. Self-described as the King of Salad Oil, DeAngelis drove around in a large Cadillac and always ostentatiously carried a thick wad of bills. He had an unsavory business history, including a corporate bankruptcy and accusations that he had cheated on government contracts. Two New York banks had closed accounts he controlled because of suspicions that he was kiting checks. But this had not prevented him from borrowing huge amounts of money based on the security of vegetable oil warehouse receipts.

Allied effectively used much of the borrowed money to speculate in commodities futures, buying immense quantities of vegetable oil contracts. But by mid-November 1963 it was evident that the "bets" DeAngelis had made in the futures markets had gone horribly wrong. Allied was unable to meet the ever-increasing demands for more margin to cover its losses. On November 20 the Produce Exchange was forced to close, as officials desperately tried to liquidate Allied's massive holdings without creating a catastrophic drop in prices. Up to this point, the crisis had not affected the stock market. But that would soon change.

Two New York Stock Exchange member firms were caught in the Allied web. The venerable Ira Haupt & Company, and Williston & Beane, found that Allied's failure left them on the hook for millions of dollars they could not pay. Due to internal errors within the firms, monies that should have been used for stock market transactions had been paid to meet the commodities contracts. Suddenly the crisis was no longer confined to the commodities market. The New York Stock Exchange members faced a collapse that was also likely to wipe out the accounts of their stock market customers, which were unsecured obligations of the two firms.

On Thursday, November 21, as a realization of the magnitude of the crisis spread, the stock market dropped sharply, recording the largest single-day loss of the year. Unsettling rumors, always the by-product of uncertainty, abounded. Reports began to circulate that some of the warehouse receipts upon which Allied had borrowed money were forged.

Worse, quick inspections of Allied's storage tanks in Bayonne began to reveal that much of the supposedly certified oil did not exist. It was even feared that American Express, which had certified many of the Allied warehouse receipts through a subsidiary, might be forced into bankruptcy.

On the morning of Friday, November 22, the New York Stock Exchange faced a major crisis. Ira Haupt & Company alone had 20,700 customers; many had left their stocks and cash balances at the firm for safekeeping.[28] If stock market customers lost securities and monies they held with New York Stock Exchange member firms, investor confidence in the stock market would be jeopardized, even if the failure of those firms was due to difficulties in the commodities market. Worse still, inevitable demands for government intervention would result.

New York Stock Exchange president G. Keith Funston was determined to head off this unpleasant eventuality. But he faced a problem: he didn't have any control over the banks that were Haupt's principal creditors. If any one of the banks chose to initiate action against Haupt, customer assets would be tangled up in legal proceedings that might last years.

Funston hastily arranged a meeting with the Haupt bankers early Friday afternoon. Everything hinged on the outcome; if he was unable to persuade the bankers to hold off, Haupt would fail, with potentially disastrous ramifications for the entire market. But then, by horrible coincidence, at virtually the precise moment the bankers were scheduled to arrive, the shocking news that President Kennedy had been shot in Dallas swept through the Exchange. The market, already jittery because of the salad oil scandal, plunged, in the steepest drop ever recorded. The Dow Jones Industrial Average plummeted 24 points (3.3%) in 27 minutes, on trading of 2.6 million shares. Funston, stunned by the totally unexpected tragedy, immediately decided that the Exchange should be closed. Unfortunately, he lacked the authority to order a closing on his own. In a scene that resembled a black comedy, he scrambled to locate a quorum of the Exchange governors, many of whom were out to lunch. In the meantime, hundreds of millions of dollars of stock values were shredded in the panic.

Trading was finally suspended at 2:07 p.m. Many people, already struggling to deal with the unfolding salad oil debacle, were overwhelmed by the juxtaposition of crises that Friday afternoon. One man, Fred Hediger, who was president of Garnac Grain Company, one of Allied's big export customers, said, "A guy got a phone call from Bayonne and was told that oil was missing. I jumped into my car to go to Bayonne and heard on the radio that Kennedy had been assassinated. I thought, this must be a plot by the Russians or the underworld—too many crazy things are happening at once."[29]

The horrendous news of the assassination blotted out press coverage of the salad oil scandal, but behind the scenes Exchange authorities worked frantically to resolve the matter before trading resumed the following week. Williston & Beane was to be saved by a cash investment by Exchange members Walston & Company and Merrill Lynch. Funston then patched together a plan whereby the Exchange, through assessments of members, would put up $12 million to pay off the Haupt customer accounts, and Haupt's bankers would hold off on attempts to collect the $24 million they were owed by Haupt. But the Haupt partners balked; they would ultimately be liable for any monies the Exchange was unable to recover once the firm was liquidated, and they didn't like it.

The Haupt partners were in a terrible position. Most of them had been completely unaware of the problems with Allied until a few days earlier. They were rich, successful men who suddenly realized that they were about to be wiped out. As the Haupt managing partner described his colleagues, "They were all in a state of shock."[30] To many of the partners, it almost seemed better to let events play out and hope that they might salvage something rather than accept the Exchange plan that promised almost certain personal ruin.

The Stock Exchange was closed on Monday, November 25, out of respect for the slain President. Negotiations dragged on all day and into the night. A great deal of pressure was exerted on the recalcitrant Haupt men; there were even veiled threats that if the partners prevented a settlement and thus allowed a financial panic to occur, they would be effectively blackballed from securing other employment on Wall Street. Finally, after agonizing for hours, the partners capitulated and signed the agreement a few minutes after midnight on the morning of November 26.

By the opening of trading on Tuesday, President Lyndon Johnson's firm handling of the very tense situation, combined with the resolution of the salad oil scandal, removed much of the crisis atmosphere that had dragged the market down the previous Friday. In the most explosive single-day rally in history, the Dow Industrial Average jumped 32 points to 744, a gain of 4.5%. Johnson personally called Funston to congratulate him on the market's performance. In later months, as the broad rally continued, Johnson delighted in citing stock market gains, as if they were expressions of his own popularity.

The chaotic events of November 20 through November 27 were finally over, as was the Kennedy market. Tino DeAngelis pleaded guilty to several counts of fraud and conspiracy and was trundled off to prison. The vast majority of the nearly $200 million lost by the corporate victims of his salad oil scheme was never recovered. However, the Exchange's quick action in the Ira Haupt case established the principle that Exchange authorities would act to protect the integrity of customer accounts at member firms even if they were not legally required to do so. This helped solidify public confidence in the market and established a precedent that would eventually lead to the creation in 1970 of the federally chartered but privately owned Securities Investor Protection Corporation. The SIPC insured the holdings of investors who left securities and money on deposit with their brokers. Much as the Federal Deposit Insurance Corporation had done for the banking industry, the SIPC would eliminate the specter of debilitating runs on reputedly troubled brokers by panicky customers. Such "brokers' panics" (like that of 1907) would never happen again.

During the Kennedy market the growth psychology embraced by aggressive investors was for the first time wedded to pro-growth government economic policy. In an indirect but very important way, the basic ideas behind growth investing were ratified by Washington. Conservative elements of the Wall Street community were now much more receptive to growth strategies, even if they risked higher inflation. But there were other risks associated with a growth stock investment strategy, as the roller-coaster performance of glamour stocks in 1962 had amply shown. It would be this tension between the risk and reward associated with growth investing that would spark a heated debate on Wall Street, and in academia, and ultimately come to redefine the way money was invested in the stock market.

Dow Jones Industrial Average, 1960–1969

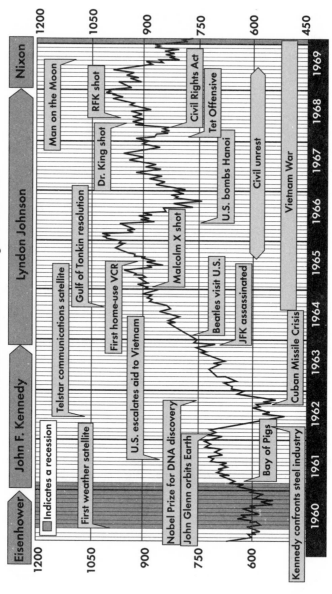

Eisenhower | John F. Kennedy | Lyndon Johnson | Nixon

Indicates a recession

First weather satellite

Telstar communications satellite

U.S. escalates aid to Vietnam

Gulf of Tonkin resolution

First home-use VCR

Nobel Prize for DNA discovery

John Glenn orbits Earth

Bay of Pigs

Malcolm X shot

Beatles visit U.S.

JFK assassinated

Cuban Missile Crisis

Kennedy confronts steel industry

Man on the Moon

RFK shot

Dr. King shot

Civil Rights Act

Tet Offensive

U.S. bombs Hanoi

Civil unrest

Vietnam War

1960 1961 1962 1963 1964 1965 1966 1967 1968 1969

1200 1050 900 750 600 450

© *Dow Jones & Company Inc.*

ORANGUTANS

WILLIAM SHARPE WAS a self-described computer nerd.[1] As such, he was well suited to take advantage of the impressive advances in computing power that had been made by the late 1950s, when he was pursuing his doctorate in economics at UCLA. In the course of his studies, Sharpe bumped into Harry Markowitz, who, only a few years older than Sharpe, was then completing the work on risk-reward relationships in portfolio theory (discussed in chapter 9) that would ultimately win him a Nobel Prize. Sharpe, under Markowitz's guidance, homed in on a vexing problem inherent in the Markowitz approach to selecting the most risk-efficient portfolio: how to ensure proper diversification by calculating the extent to which the securities included in the portfolio moved together (covariance).

Under the Markowitz regime, the covariance of returns of each selected stock with every other possible stock had to be calculated individually. Even given the greatly enhanced computational powers of new computers, this was a daunting task. But Sharpe had an insight, which would eventually help win him a Nobel Prize. Instead of laboriously attempting to calculate how different stocks moved relative to each other, he would try to identify a "basic underlying factor" that influenced the movement of all stocks, and compare each stock with that single factor.

Sharpe quickly determined that the "basic underlying factor" influencing the returns of individual stocks was the overall market itself.

Markowitz himself had observed, "The returns on most securities are correlated. If the Standard & Poor's Index rose substantially, we would expect United States Steel to rise. If the S&P rose substantially, we would also expect Sweets Company of America to rise. For this reason, it is more likely that U.S. Steel will do well when Sweets Company does well."[2] In other words, the movements of U.S. Steel stock and Sweets Company stock were related to each other by virtue of the fact that they were both influenced by the entire market.

Like many great insights, this observation seems intuitively obvious. But it had very significant implications. According to Sharpe, an analyst seeking the most risk-efficient portfolio need now only calculate the relationship of each stock with the overall market. If a stock is more volatile (risky) than the market, its addition to a portfolio will make the portfolio more volatile (risky). Likewise, the addition of a less volatile stock will lower the risk of the portfolio. Sharpe found that about one-third of the movement of an average stock was a reflection of the movement of the overall market, while the rest was explained by the stock's relationship to other stocks in similar industries, or by the unique characteristics of the stock itself. Significantly, however, he found that in a properly diversified portfolio the non-market-related factors cancelled each other out, leaving the influence of the market as the primary factor affecting the value of the entire portfolio.

Sharpe's ideas were published in *Management Science* magazine in January 1963. In the article, Sharpe estimated that by using his approach, the mainframe computer time required to select a "Markowitz" diversified portfolio from a hypothetical universe of 100 stocks would be cut from 33 minutes to 30 seconds. It was now possible for virtually any investment manager to put together a "risk efficient" portfolio that would maximize expected return for a given level of risk.

But this was only the first step. By 1964, Sharpe's idea had evolved to the point where it could be used to create a comprehensive method for valuing financial assets such as stocks. In this Capital Asset Pricing Model, the expected return earned by a stock consisted of the sum of the "risk free" rate of return (defined as the interest rate paid on a riskless asset like a U.S. government bond) and a *risk premium* (representing the additional return, over the risk-free rate, that an investor must expect to receive as compensation for taking the extra risk involved in purchasing the risky asset). The risk premium, in turn, was determined by two factors: an "alpha" factor, which represented the specific return due to the unique characteristics of the stock itself, and a "beta" factor, which represented the influence of the overall market's return on the individual stock. (The so-called beta coefficient simply represented the degree to which an individual stock moved with the market; for example, a beta of .75 meant that the stock was expected to move up or down about 75% as fast as the overall market moved, while a beta of 1.5 meant that the stock was expected to move 1½ times as fast as the market.) Since in a diversified portfolio the alphas of the different stocks tended to cancel out, the beta became predominant and was termed the "systematic" (or market-related) risk. The risk premium of a given stock was thus a function of this beta risk.

Sharpe's work on the Capital Asset Pricing Model eventually led to a revolutionary conclusion. Given the assumptions of the model, the most risk-efficient portfolio that an investor could select was the market itself; in other words, an investor should buy proportional amounts of all stocks in the market rather than attempting to select only certain stocks that would hopefully outperform the market. This startling assertion ultimately provided the intellectual basis for "index" funds—that is, mutual funds that arbitrarily invested in all stocks included in a given index, such as the Standard & Poor's 500 Industrials. But that would come much later. In 1964, Sharpe's research, like that of Markowitz before him, was largely ignored by the Wall Street community.

One man who could not be ignored was Eugene Fama. A third-generation Italian American from Boston born in 1939, Fama had first been introduced to the stock market while working his way through college. One of his professors published a stock market advisory letter recommending stocks based on a form of what would come to be called "momentum" investing, which sought to identify uptrends in stock prices that would presumably continue. Fama's job was to find workable buy and sell signals based on his professor's system.

He soon confronted a paradox. While he could develop systems for trading that seemed to work on historical data, they invariably broke down when used to predict future market moves. Curious about this and other market-related questions, Fama enrolled in business school at the

University of Chicago, which had become the unchallenged center of academic inquiry into the stock market.[3]

His timing was perfect. In January 1964, two Chicago professors, James Lorie and Lawrence Fischer, produced the first comprehensive study of stock market returns made possible by advances in the computational power of computers. The study covered the period from 1926 to 1960 and found that an investor who bought into the stock market in 1926 and reinvested all dividends would, by 1960, have multiplied his money by nearly 30 times, representing a 9% annualized rate of return.[4] Because the period analyzed included the 1929 crash and subsequent Depression, these results surprised many people. The 9% return greatly exceeded that received by bond investors over the same period, confirming Lawrence Smith's work of 1924, which had first made the case for stocks over bonds but had seemingly been discredited in the 1930s. The Fischer-Lorie study implied that impressive long-term results could be achieved simply by buying and holding a portfolio representative of the entire market. This dovetailed neatly with William Sharpe's conclusion that the most risk-efficient portfolio an investor could buy was a portfolio representing the entire market.

Fama waded into the discussion with his Ph.D. dissertation in 1965, published in the *Journal of Business*, in which he defined the term "efficient capital market." In such an *efficient market*, securities are instantaneously priced to reflect all information available to market participants. It is therefore theoretically impossible to predict future price moves based on current publicly available information. In effect, Fama confirmed the prescient insight the young French mathematician Louis Bachelier first developed in 1900. In an efficient market, no one could really hope to "beat" the market, because the market already perfectly reflected the sum total of all relevant data.

But there was more. Nine months after publishing the article in the *Journal of Business*, Fama wrote a simplified version for the *Financial Analysts Journal* entitled "Random Walks in Stock Market Prices." Comparing the movement of stock prices to the "random walk" of a drunk stumbling from point to point, Fama argued that price movements in an "efficient market" were random, representing adjustments to unpredictable news items that, when made public, would immediately be reflected in the price of stocks. Fama did not invent the term "random walk," but his work certainly popularized the expression.

Fama became something of a celebrity, appearing on television talk shows, and was profiled in *Forbes*, *Fortune*, and *The Wall Street Journal*. As he put it modestly, "Insofar as you can become famous for writing an article for an academic journal, I became famous."[5] Unlike Harry Markowitz, whose landmark research had been largely ignored by Wall Street in the previous decade, Fama could not so easily be dismissed. If what he and William Sharpe argued was true, then most of what highly paid Wall Street portfolio managers did was useless. Since no one could reasonably hope to outperform a truly "efficient" market, there was no reason for portfolio managers to exist.

Needless to say, the efficient market research coming out of the University of Chicago met with a hostile reaction on Wall Street. John Hartwell, a leading money manager, argued that since trading by individual investors still made up a large portion of overall market activity, and since "most individuals make hash of their portfolios," there was no doubt professional managers would be able to outperform the market. "It is a basic fact," he declared, "that we should look upon performance as something that is attainable, has been attainable and can be attained with a great deal of consistency if one organizes to do it."[6] Pierre Rinfret, a well-known economist with experience in investment management, claimed, "The value of investment advice is substantial . . . I will say to the random theorists, as was said to the aeronautical engineer whose airplane crashed, 'Go back to the drawing boards.' It's interesting, but highly inconclusive."[7]

Once again, just as most market practitioners had refused to accept the mounting empirical evidence refuting the basic tenets of technical analysis, Wall Street rejected the work of Eugene Fama and William Sharpe. They were, after all, simply obscure academics far removed from the practical realities of the market. There were other players much closer to the action who were far more intriguing.

One of those players who fired across the heavens in the 1960s like a shooting star was Gerald Tsai. Born in Shanghai to westernized parents (his father had been educated at the University of Michigan and was the Shanghai district manager for Ford Motor Company), Tsai credits his mother with fostering his interest in the stock market. His mother, according to Tsai, was "a very smart woman. She was always buying and selling real estate, gold bars, stocks and even cotton."[8] When Tsai learned about Wall Street early in his life, he yearned to make it big in the American market. Sent to the United States for college, he graduated with a master's degree from Boston University in 1949 and, three years later, was introduced to the man who would help him realize his dream: Fidelity Fund owner Edward Johnson.

"Mr. Johnson" hired Tsai as a junior stock analyst in 1952. Johnson was so impressed by the young man that in 1957, at the tender age of 29, Tsai was given his own fund to manage. Named Fidelity Capital, the new fund was to be aggressively growth oriented. Though it started with less than $10 million under management, good performance and favorable publicity helped Fidelity Capital raise new money rapidly. By 1964, the fund's assets totaled $223 million.

Tsai was certainly in his element. "I liked the market," he said. "I felt that being a foreigner, I didn't have a competitive disadvantage there . . . If you buy GM at 40 and it goes to 50, whether you are an Oriental, a Korean, or a Buddhist doesn't make any difference."[9] Johnson gave Tsai a great deal of leeway to run the fund as he saw fit. One of Johnson's favorite expressions was, "Do it by yourself. Two men can't play the violin."[10]

Tsai concentrated his fund's holdings in a relatively few "glamour" stocks and relied heavily on technical analysis to time his moves. The fund's turnover rate* was extremely high, frequently exceeding 100%. Johnson spoke glowingly of his protégé: "It was a beautiful thing to watch his reactions. What grace, what timing—glorious."[11] The Capital fund was hit hard during the May 1962 market debacle, but made a stunning recovery when prices came back at year-end, and racked up impressive gains as the glamour stocks boomed over the next few years.

---

*The turnover rate in a fund portfolio is a measure of how frequently the fund manager buys and sells stocks. The rate expressed is the percentage of the total number of shares in the portfolio that is transacted each year; for example, if a portfolio manager transacted 1 million shares of stocks in a 1-million share portfolio, the turnover rate would be 100%.

The "inscrutable" Tsai soon became the center of attention; a frequently heard question was "What is the Chinaman doing?" Other portfolio managers tried to imitate his stock selection actions, which often had the effect of creating a self-fulfilling prophecy; their "mimic" buying would push the prices of stocks Tsai held higher, creating large gains for Tsai's portfolio.

Ironically, over the years Tsai managed Fidelity Capital, the other principal Fidelity fund, Fidelity Trend, often outperformed Fidelity Capital. But Tsai possessed the intangible qualities that made him a media star, while the shy, reclusive Johnson did not. Tsai was the first of a series of "go-go" fund managers whose ability to attract attention was almost as important as the investment results they produced. In 1965 Johnson informed Tsai that he planned to eventually turn over the management of the Fidelity organization to his son Ned. But Tsai wanted to be "number one, not number two," as he himself put it. Realizing he would never be number one at Fidelity, he resigned to set up his own mutual fund.[12]

The cult of "performance" was just starting to take hold on Wall Street, fired by a strong bull market and the availability of data comparing the records of different mutual funds. In the 1950s no such information existed, meaning that investors who bought fund shares were forced to rely solely on the representations of the salesmen who sold them the shares. By the 1960s, however, data compiled by firms such as Arthur Lipper & Company provided an independent means of comparing mutual fund results. The existence of the comparative data created an environment in which great emphasis was placed on short-term performance. New money flooded into funds that had done well but quickly dried up for funds that lagged behind. The great "performance" race was on.

Tsai was a beneficiary of the new environment because he had a good track record to exploit. In 1965 the 29 leading "performance" funds averaged a gain of just over 40%, while the Dow Industrials rose only 15%. Fidelity Capital, in the last year of Tsai's reign, gained approximately 50%, on a turnover rate of 120%.[13] Using this record as a powerful marketing tool, Tsai announced plans in 1966 to launch his new Manhattan Fund. Originally intending to raise $25 million from investors, Tsai was overwhelmed with the demand for shares, eventually taking in an incredible $270 million.

Tsai set up shop in a suite of rooms at 680 Fifth Avenue, ensconcing himself in a corner office with beige carpeting and a large leather-covered bull. He told reporters he set the thermostat at 55 degrees to keep a clear head at all times. *Institutional Investor* reported that Tsai ran Manhattan Fund

> *just like Fidelity Capital. He loaded it up with all his big glamour favorites. To facilitate his chartist maneuverings, he built an elaborate trading room with a TransJet tape, a Quotron electronic board with the prices of relevant securities, and three-foot-square, giant loose-leaf notebooks filled with point-and-figure charts and other technical indicators of his holdings. Adjoining the trading room was erected "Information Central," so aswarm with visual displays and panels that slid and rotated about that it resembled some Pentagon war room. Three men were hired to work full-time maintaining literally hundreds of averages, ratios, oscillators and indices, ranging from a "ten-day oscillator of differences in advances and declines" to charts of several Treasury issues, to 25-, 65-, and 150-day moving averages of the Dow.*

Of course, few observers recognized it at the time but only a few weeks before the Manhattan Fund commenced operations, the market (as measured by the Dow Industrials) reached a long-term top of 1,001.11, on February 9, 1966. While the Dow would flirt with the 1,000 level again in 1968 and 1972, it would not decisively break through that important psychological barrier until many years later, in 1982. Ironically, just as Tsai began to pour the Manhattan Fund's newfound resources into stocks, the end of the great bull market that had made his reputation was in sight.

For the time being, though, nimble, fast-trading "go-go" funds were very much in vogue. New York Stock Exchange president Funston declared that the emphasis on performance "is the most significant change in the marketplace today."[14] Most of the performance fund managers were relatively young—usually in their thirties. It was almost as if anyone older was presumed to be too tainted by past experience, somehow unable to adjust to the new market realities.

Competition for results was fierce. One anonymous fund manager, quoted by *Institutional Investor*, said, "You can really feel the pressure. It's as bitterly competitive as a pro football league with a tight race. Every day, we have our salesmen calling up, saying give us a record to sell, give us performance. Every day, we check the gains or losses of our portfolio against our competitors. When one of my competitors outperforms me, I check: how did he do it? . . . It's a business that's going to burn up people pretty rapidly, because the guys who are good in one kind of market aren't good in the next, and the pressure is there all the time."

Many so-called gunslinger portfolio managers would, along with Tsai, ride the crest of the wave until it broke. Three men in particular came to symbolize the times. Known as the "three Freds" (Fred Alger, Fred Carr, and Fred Mates), they would each parley number-one performance rankings for one year into reputations for investment "genius" that would attract numerous clients and many millions of dollars.

Frederick Moulton Alger III was a scion of a wealthy Michigan family. His parents sent him to the prestigious Milton Academy, where the 1952 yearbook described him as "Fearless Fred."[15] Then it was on to Yale; upon graduation Alger took a job at a regional brokerage house where his father was a director. It was there that young Fred developed his interest in investing, describing it as "a mystery story which, if you could figure it out, would make you a lot of money." Studying for his MBA at the University of Michigan in 1958, Alger concluded that he had unique insights in the field of finance. "I could see things that others just couldn't see," he said.[16]

Alger got his chance in 1965, when he was given the reins at the very small Security Equity Fund. Starting with only $375,000 in assets, the fund rocketed to a 77.5% gain for the year by purchasing concentrated positions in growth stocks. These results brought Alger much-needed publicity. They also attracted the amorous glances of Bernard Cornfeld, a natural showman whose Investors Overseas Services had pioneered the concept of a "fund of funds," which took in money from investors outside the United States and in turn invested the money in different American mutual funds. Under U.S. law, no American registered investment company could own more than 3% of any other investment company. But because IOS was based overseas, it was beyond the reach of American regulations and faced no such restriction.

Cornfeld wanted to capitalize on Alger's one-year success to form the Fred Alger Fund, which would be part of the IOS group. Cornfeld joked that he chose the name Alger Fund so that he would "know the schmuck to blame if it goes wrong."[17] Cornfeld's past success had been based on successful marketing that downplayed the onerous charges his investors were subjected to. Fees and front-end charges sometimes took as much as 50% of an investor's first-year contributions to the funds, and, on top of that, every quarter IOS took 10% of all gains as a performance bonus, even if the gains had not actually been realized by selling the appreciated securities.

Cornfeld agreed to split this "performance bonus" with Alger, who then immediately went to work investing the money Cornfeld provided to him. Alger quickly hit upon a strategy that promised to generate good short-term results. Aware that Gerald Tsai was about to pour his Manhattan Fund's freshly raised $270 million into the market, Alger bought the stocks that he thought Tsai would buy, reasoning that Tsai's massive purchases would undoubtedly force prices higher. As Alger put it, "We assumed Gerry would buy pretty much what he had at Fidelity Capital, and that he'd concentrate in about fifty stocks . . . So that's what we bought."[18] The strategy worked. "A couple of months later," Alger explained, "we read in the newspaper that Manhattan Fund was 80% invested, and that day we went 40% into cash. But the edge we got in those months while Tsai was buying the portfolio of his new fund gave us the second best performance record in the country for the whole year."

On the whole, Alger attributed his good performance in the 1960s to an ability to anticipate changes in the direction of the entire stock market. "We have," he stated flatly, "the best sense of timing in the market. Our stock selection is no good—I can't think why—but our timing is superb."[19]

Another of the "three Freds" who dominated the go-go performance fund era was Fred Carr, of the Enterprise Fund. A native of Los Angeles who attended Los Angeles City College, Carr got his start in the brokerage business after a stint in the army in Korea. In 1962 he secured a position he described as "director of research slash West Coast" at Ira Haupt & Company. When that firm drowned in salad oil, Carr moved on to work in research and sales at another small firm before getting his chance to manage a stock portfolio in 1965.[20] In his thirties, like Alger, Carr was openly contemptuous of the traditional management style of other mutual funds. "The Enterprise Fund will no longer trade an imposing building or pinstriped suits for capital gains," he declared.[21] "When your objective is to double the value of your holdings in a year, anything short of that is a mistake, and a decline is something of a catastrophe."[22]

In person Carr was unfailingly polite, speaking softly in a high-pitched voice. But he relentlessly tried to purge his organization of all traces of emotion, insisting on cold, dispassionate analysis. Unlike Tsai and Alger, Carr did not concentrate his investments in high-flying glamour stocks. (He frequently said that performance managers who chased after high P/E growth stocks were operating on the basis of the "greater fool theory," meaning that they paid too much for stocks on the dubious assumption that others would pay even more for them in the future.[23]) Carr preferred instead to seek out well-managed small firms that would be the growth stocks of the future. By 1968 he held positions in about 300 companies, most of them small. "I'm delighted to concentrate if there's a reason," he explained, "but not to turn away profit. If you can find a half-a-million-dollar investment, that's still a lot of money."[24]

The approach seemed to work. The Enterprise Fund gained 117% in 1967 (which ranked it number one for large funds) and followed up with a gain of 44% in 1968, which was among the best records for that period as well. As of September 30, 1968, Enterprise had assets of $784 million, including new sales in the first seven months of 1968 that totaled a phenomenal $325 million.

The best-performing small fund for 1968 was operated by a 36-year-old named Fred Mates, and was, not surprisingly, called the Mates Fund. Created in mid-1967 with assets of about $700,000, the fund showed a spectacular gain of 172.3% by December 1968. *Institutional Investor* described Mates as a "cross between a used car salesman and an aging Hell's Angel." He was short, wiry, and wore a shaggy hairpiece appropriately styled for the late 1960s. Mates, unlike Tsai and Alger, disdained technical analysis, making his investment selections purely on the basis of fundamentals.

Mates evidenced a quirky sense of social responsibility; at one point he considered buying shares in D. H. Baldwin, a well-known piano maker, but refrained from doing so when he discovered that a division of the company made bomb fuses. "Why should we buy somebody who makes money killing people?" he asked rhetorically.[25] He announced plans to "make poor people rich" by cutting the minimum investment in his fund to $50 and called his office the "kibbutz of Wall Street," comparing his young staff to "flower children."[26]

Associates professed to see in Mates some of the same characteristics of "genius" attributed to other investment "stars," like Alger, Carr, and Tsai. A vice president of the Mates Fund said of Mates, "Fred will watch a company for a long time . . . Then all of a sudden one more piece of info will come in and Fred will announce that at last the company 'smells right' . . . When he tries to tell you why, you can follow it about 90% of the way but then he leaves you. That last 10% is too subjective. That is the area where artists work."[27]

While "artists" like Mates were at work revolutionizing portfolio management, conservative voices echoed the old refrain that the bull market was a product of "overspeculation." One such voice that could not be ignored was that of Federal Reserve chairman William McChesney Martin. Martin repeatedly warned of impending financial difficulties as the stock market soared to new heights. Then, on June 1, 1965, he took direct aim at the market itself, citing "disquieting similarities" with the situation that had existed in 1929.[28] Once again, the old bugaboo of the 1929 crash was raised, this time by the man who had more direct power over the American economy than any other individual.

Stock prices, which had already slipped in the days before Martin made his pronouncement, fell further. Later that month Martin again voiced concerns; eventually the Dow Jones Industrials dropped 10% from their earlier highs. Analysts spoke of the "Martin market," and many economists openly derided what they perceived to be Martin's inordinately gloomy assessment. Others argued that it was inappropriate for the Fed chairman, whatever his views, to make public judgments on the level of stock prices. In July the market recovered, appearing to shrug off Martin's warnings. Perhaps stung by the criticism, Martin thereafter refrained from commenting directly on stock prices, although he was not hesitant about expressing other concerns about the economy. His silence on the subject of stock prices set something of a precedent; not for another 30 years would a Fed chairman actively attempt to "jawbone" the market.

By 1966, however, the great bull market seemed to have run out of steam. For the rest of the decade, the major market averages failed to gain much ground. This directionless period marked the beginning of the end of the "performance cult" on Wall Street; Gerald Tsai of the Manhattan Fund was to be the first "fallen star." After its formation in 1966, the Manhattan Fund achieved impressive results for about two years, as the market continued to favor the traditional glamour stocks that Tsai preferred. As late as May 1968, the press treated Tsai as an almost mystical figure. *Newsweek* described him as "something of a mystery man" who "radiates total cool . . . from the manicured tips of his fingers to the burnished black tops of his slip-on shoes," and made reference to Tsai's "blank, impassive—friends actually call it inscrutable—gaze."

But as the year wore on, Tsai's "inscrutable gaze" clouded. The Manhattan Fund ended with a 7% loss for the year, even though the overall market (as measured by the Dow Industrials) gained 5%. The fund ranked dead last, 310 out of the 310 funds rated by Arthur Lipper & Company. (Tsai's former employer, Edward Johnson at Fidelity, didn't do much better. Fidelity Trend and Fidelity Capital ranked 301 and 303 respectively.)

The traditional glamour stocks that had made Tsai's success now threatened to break him. The glamours were no longer the market leaders, and Tsai failed to adjust to the new environment. Repeating the lament so often heard from adherents of technical analysis, Tsai blamed his own failings, not his methodology, for his misfortune. "The charts kept telling us [the glamours] were not the most desirable areas, but we were too dumb to realize," he said.[29] The cult of performance that had earlier so benefited Tsai proved to be quite fickle; in 1968 the Manhattan Fund was hit with $181 million of redemptions versus only $57 million in new purchases.[30]

In August 1968, Tsai sold his mutual fund management company to CNA Corporation for the equivalent of roughly $30 million in cash. He joined CNA in an executive capacity, but he continued to play an active role in the Manhattan Fund, stating that he'd spent the last several months of 1968 revising the portfolio "to meet the economic challenges of 1969."[31] That effort was unsuccessful; 1969 was not a good year for the Manhattan Fund, and 1970 would be even worse. (Of the 45 stocks the Manhattan Fund held at the end of 1969, half would either go bankrupt or lose at least 90% of their value the following year.[32]) Tsai's supporters blamed the poor performance on his failure to concentrate on running the Manhattan Fund, noting that after the CNA transaction he devoted an increasing amount of time to other activities. Tsai's detractors, however, argued that the source of his difficulties was far more basic. As they saw it, Tsai was "always a trader, never an investor," and in a different market environment he was "like a fish out of water."[33] Whatever the case, his sale of his mutual fund company to CNA was certainly made at the top of the market. In that sense, he proved himself a very adept trader indeed.

Quick denouements were also suffered by the "Freds." Fred Mates, after racking up incredible gains in his Mates Fund in the first eleven months of 1968, stumbled badly at the end of the year when the SEC suspended trading in one of his fund's principal holdings, Omega Equities, stating that the stock was being traded on the basis of "incomplete and inaccurate information."[34] Mates had purchased 300,000 shares of Omega at $3.50 in September, but the shares Mates purchased were in so-called letter stock, shares that were sold directly by Omega to Mates without having been registered with the SEC. To purchase such unregistered stock, the buyer had to sign a letter to the effect that he did not intend to resell it, and in fact was prohibited from reselling to anyone else who would not sign a similar letter. The advantage to the issuing company was that it could raise money quickly without having to wade through the cumbersome SEC registration process. The advantage to the buyer was that the price of the letter shares was usually set at a significant discount below the market price for unrestricted stock. This was the case in the Mates Fund purchase of Omega Equities. When Mates purchased the letter stock directly from the company at $3.50 per share, unrestricted stock was trading in the OTC market at $24.

Mates then performed a feat of accounting legerdemain that was, while technically legal, extremely misleading. He quickly marked the price of Omega Equities on his books up to about $16, which represented roughly a 30% discount from the market price. (The discount theoretically reflected the fact that the stock could not be readily resold.) Obviously this transaction instantaneously created a large "paper" profit for the Mates Fund, showing a gain in excess of 350%. By December 1968 more than one-third of the Mates Fund portfolio was in similar letter stock.

But when the SEC suspended trading in the registered stock of Omega Equities, many Mates Fund investors, aware that Omega represented a significant chunk of the fund portfolio, rushed to redeem their Mates Fund shares. Buried under an avalanche of redemption requests, and unable to raise money fast enough to meet the redemptions (because so much of the portfolio was locked up in illiquid letter stock), Mates was forced to suspend redemption from his fund. When investors were finally allowed to redeem shares seven months later, Omega Equities was marked down to 50 cents per share and the Mates Fund had been forced to liquidate most of its holdings. By 1974, Fred Mates had left the mutual fund business entirely, moving on to open up a New York City singles bar appropriately called Mates.

Shortly after the Mates Fund withered away to a fraction of its former size in 1969, Fred Carr abruptly found himself at the end of his meteoric career at the Enterprise Fund. Carr's strategy of investing in small companies with good potential worked well in 1967 and 1968, when small stocks were in vogue. The thinly traded stocks rose rapidly in the face of buying by large funds such as Enterprise. But when the stock market turned down in 1969, the situation quickly became ugly. The same lack of liquidity that allowed these stocks to rise rapidly in a strong market meant that they could fall just as fast if large holders tried to sell. Enterprise Fund, which had ranked number one among large funds in 1967 and number ten in 1968, fell to 329 in 1969. Carr was forced out in November. A competitor said of Carr's departure from Enterprise, "I think Carr saw even worse coming. They've got a lot of thin stocks they can't get out of if the market stays bad and the redemptions pour in—and he ran before the whole place collapses."[35]

While Gerald Tsai, Fred Mates, and Fred Carr disappeared from the mutual fund management scene in the 1970s, the last of the three "Freds," Fred Alger, was to remain a Wall Street fixture for years. Unfortunately, the original Fred Alger Fund did not. The fund had achieved impressive early results in 1966 when Alger bought the stocks he assumed Gerald Tsai would buy, and had also benefited from the practice of buying letter stock at discount prices, then arbitrarily valuing it higher.[36] But the performance slackened with the market in 1969, and in early 1970, Alger left the fund that bore his name. (Alger claims that he left because of disagreements with Investors Overseas Services head Bernard Cornfeld, but other sources indicate he was fired.[37]) Cornfeld himself was forced out of IOS less than a year later, and his organization was taken over by the soon to be notorious Robert Vesco, who proceeded to systematically loot the funds. While Fred

Alger certainly cannot be blamed for the criminal activities of Vesco, the fact remains that investors who held shares in the Fred Alger Fund were largely wiped out.

Once separated from Cornfeld and IOS, Alger went on to compile an impressive record as a portfolio manager. Even his apparent success raised troublesome questions, however. When Alger later proposed to establish his own mutual funds, he was accused of inflating his performance statistics in order to attract investors, and the SEC launched an investigation of the performance claims. The ensuing controversy highlighted the difficulty of measuring a manager's "performance." Since Alger had managed money for a wide variety of different clients under different circumstances, the question of precisely what to include in the performance calculations arose. Alger's critics accused him of selectively including only those accounts in which his record was good. Ultimately Alger agreed to a consent decree with the SEC involving relatively trivial matters in which he did not admit wrongdoing.

The Alger case illustrated the problems associated with measuring long-term performance. As one pension consultant put it, "There are a lot of ways you can make your record seem better than it is, and no generally accepted standards on what you can put into a performance record . . . Everyone in the world claims they've outperformed the averages."[38] Another fund manager noted that even the definition of the term "performance fund" was very imprecise and tended to bias reported results for all such funds. He observed that "all capital gains funds try to be performance funds. The ones that achieve a [good] record are performance funds. The ones that don't, aren't, and say that wasn't their intention."[39]

How, then, is it possible to evaluate the true performance of the go-go funds of the 1960s, aside from anecdotal accounts of fallen "stars"? One comprehensive attempt was made by three scholars from the Wharton School; they found that while on average mutual funds in the period 1960–1968 roughly matched the performance of the overall stock market, there was some evidence that performance funds (defined in the study as "high risk" funds) did better than the market averages, particularly in the period 1964–1968. But the study (which concluded in 1969) also found that these same funds underperformed the market when stock prices turned down in 1969.[40] In effect, the performance funds exaggerated moves in the overall market, rising faster in bull market periods but falling faster in bear market environments.

The Wharton study also found that, unsurprisingly, the emphasis on short-term performance induced mutual fund managers to speed up the pace at which they bought and sold stocks. The old "buy and hold" strategy had seemingly fallen by the wayside. In 1960 the turnover rate for mutual fund portfolios had been only 17.6%, up only slightly from the 13.1% figure for 1953. But then the pace of trading exploded, reaching 46.6% (for the average fund) in 1968. As has been seen, the turnover rate for the most aggressive performance funds was significantly higher still.

The new stars of the go-go era liked to see themselves as mavericks who sought to shake up the stodgy, conservative Wall Street establishment. (Fred Alger and Fred Carr in particular frequently referred to themselves in this way.) Undeniably, the notion that a professional manager would buy and sell stocks in rapid-fire progression, frequently turning over his entire portfolio in a single year, was revolutionary. But behind the frenetic pace of trading often lay investment philosophies that, far from being radical, were in fact throwbacks to earlier eras, and that completely ignored recent scholarly research on the stock market.

Gerald Tsai and Fred Alger, among others, made frequent use of technical analysis to time their market moves. Technical analysis was certainly nothing new or revolutionary, having originated with the Dow theory in 1900. The fund managers who employed these techniques seemed blissfully unaware of the accumulating body of academic data refuting the validity of this approach. Likewise, many of the performance managers disdained diversification, preferring instead to concentrate in a few issues, and made no allowance for the greater risk such an approach entailed. They were either unaware of (or chose to ignore) the implications of Harry Markowitz's and William Sharpe's work on risk-efficient portfolios, which mandated a well-diversified portfolio as the means of achieving the best possible results consistent with risk. In effect, their attitude was not much different from old-style investors such as Gerald Loeb, who had written in his 1935 classic *Battle for Investment Survival* that "once you obtain confidence, diversification is undesirable. Diversification [is] an admission of not knowing what to do and striking an average."

Far from being pathfinders exploring new frontiers in investing, most of the performance managers of the 1960s combined a mishmash of traditional investment techniques with a penchant for frenetic activity and a flair for publicity. They briefly rocketed to success, claiming investment "genius," in the hot market of the mid-1960s, but soon fell back to earth in the bear market that followed. John Kenneth Galbraith perhaps put it best when he sought to define "genius" in the context of stock market speculation. "Genius," he said succinctly, "is a rising market."[41]

By late 1968, over 250 articles and papers, as well as 89 books and pamphlets, had been written examining the issues of portfolio risk management and market efficiency raised by Markowitz, Sharpe, and Fama.[42] For the most part, perhaps because the material was often published in obscure scholarly journals, the research was ignored outside the academic community. In the few instances when Wall Street participants deigned to comment (as in the case of Fama's "efficient market" research), the response was usually derisive.

But Wall Street could not ignore a landmark study completed for the Bank Administration Institute in December 1968 entitled "Measuring the Investment Performance of Pension Funds," which was compiled by University of Chicago professors Lorie, Fischer, and Fama. The impetus for the report came from traditionally conservative pension fund managers in bank trust departments, who found they were losing clients to the more aggressive performance managers. The bank trust officials, and the Chicago professors, were concerned that performance managers were not being held accountable for the risk they were taking to produce exceptional returns. "The bankers felt that the best way they could counter performance was to get some kind of risk adjustments to the statistics," said one participant in the discussions that led up to the study. "They wanted to be able to point out to their clients that, okay, the performance types were raking up big gains but, for God's sake, will you look at the risks."[43] In effect, the study probed the same question Harry Markowitz had first examined in 1952: What is the appropriate trade-off between risk and reward in portfolio management?

Not surprisingly, the BAI report concluded that a "complete evaluation of the manager's performance must include examining a measure of the degree of 'risk' taken in achieving [a] rate of return." It further concluded that "much evidence shows a direct correlation between variability in rate of return and degree of risk," and that the variability of returns was "the most satisfactory way to estimate the degree of risk . . ."[44]

The following year Eugene Fama threw down the gauntlet to Wall Street fund managers, questioning whether it was possible to consistently outperform the market when risk was fully taken into account. Writing in the *Journal of Finance*, Fama conceded that it was very difficult to empirically test the thesis that the market was efficient. He then suggested the issue be framed differently. Fama proposed to seek out approaches to stock market investment that promised to "beat the market"; if none of these systems could actually be shown to succeed over the long run, then, he argued, prima facie evidence of market efficiency could be said to exist.

Fama first considered technical analysis. Citing the voluminous work done on the subject, he concluded that since past prices could not be shown to be correlated in any way with future prices, there was no statistically significant advantage to be gained by studying past data. Hence technical analysis in any form was useless. Fama defined this as the *weak* form of market efficiency.

He then moved on to fundamental analysis—that is, the examination of business and economic fundamentals as a means of predicting stock prices. He cited a long list of studies that showed that stock prices changed well in advance of definable "new information" (earnings, dividends, mergers, etc.). Hence it was not possible for the security analyst to achieve excess returns by analyzing such information. He defined this condition as *semi-strong* market efficiency.

Finally Fama moved on to what he called *strong* market efficiency, a state of affairs in which even what he called monopolistic information would not enable anyone to beat the market. ("Monopolistic" information was defined as both "inside" information and the alleged ability of some sophisticated investors to successfully anticipate future developments that would influence the market.) Here Fama's conclusions were not as definitive, but even so, he stated that there was only "limited evidence" that the use of such "monopolistic" information enabled some people to outperform the market.

Fama was careful never to say that all fundamental analysis was useless. But the thrust of his argument was that with so many professional managers striving to beat the market, it became progressively more difficult for any one of them to consistently do so. In a way, he was making an observation not very different from the one made ten years earlier by Ben Graham, who had decried the fact that it was no longer possible to get the future "for nothing." Graham's "value" approach to investing depended on inefficiencies in the market that allowed some stocks to be underpriced. But as more sophisticated players began to search out such opportunities, their actions made the market more efficient and eliminated the opportunities. In effect, Fama was arguing that the very success of Graham and his fellow "value" investors had made their approach obsolete.

Gradually, what Fama, Sharpe, and the other academics were saying began to sink in. Cracks began to develop in the heretofore impervious facade of disdain Wall Street portfolio managers had presented to the Chicago researchers. One leading money manager, Peter Bernstein of Bernstein, McCauley dated his conversion to the day he had lunch with William Sharpe in 1969. Sharpe asked Bernstein bluntly, "Do you beat the market?"

Bernstein was forced to admit that no one had ever asked him that question before; it had always been assumed that all competent investment managers would outperform the market. As time passed, Bernstein found himself more and more troubled by Sharpe's seemingly innocuous question.[45] Eventually he came to conclude that he and most other professional money managers were kidding themselves when they assumed that they could easily achieve returns superior to the overall market. In effect, they had *become* the market; by 1969 nearly 70% of trading on the New York Stock Exchange was executed on behalf of institutions, up from about 25% at the beginning of the decade. To ask professional money managers to beat the market was to ask them to beat themselves.

But what of the many managers who still claimed that they could achieve superior returns? Some years later, Warren Buffet proposed the following coin-tossing contest. Suppose 225 million Americans all join a game in which each player bets one dollar a day on whether the toss of a coin will turn up heads or tails. Each day, the losers turn over their dollars to winners, who then stake the money on the next day's bet. The laws of chance predict that after ten tosses, only 220,000 people will still be in the contest, and each will have won a bit over $1,000. Ten days later, only 215 people will still be playing, but at that point each will have won

$1,050,000. Some lucky players would, according to Buffet, undoubtedly write books entitled *How I Turned a Dollar into a Million in Twenty Days Working Thirty Seconds a Day*. But then, Buffet said, some rude professor would point out that if 225 million orangutans engaged in a similar contest, the results would be the same—"215 egotistical orangutans with 20 straight winning flips."[46]

Dow Jones Industrial Average, 1970–1974

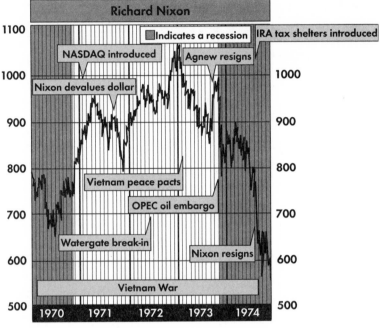

© *Dow Jones & Company Inc.*

12

BURSTING APART

O N APRIL 22, 1970, H. Ross Perot earned a dubious distinction no one had matched before: he lost nearly half a billion dollars in the stock market in one day. The stock of the company he had founded, Electronic Data Systems, plummeted from $160 to around $90 per share, and the value of Perot's 9 million shares dropped from nearly $1.5 billion to less than $1 billion. The dollar amount of Perot's loss represented more than the entire wealth possessed by J. P. Morgan at the time of his death in 1913, adjusted for subsequent inflation.[1]

Perot liked to portray himself as a neophyte on Wall Street, an East Texas country boy with a pronounced hillbilly twang who was decidedly out of place in the sophisticated precincts of eastern finance. A former IBM computer salesman, Perot had gone out on his own in 1962, forming Electronic Data Systems with a $1,000 investment. The company designed, installed, and operated computer systems; by a fortuitous twist of fate, EDS was in the right place at the right time to capitalize on the federal government's new Medicare program, which in 1965 created an instant demand for computerized billing systems.

Enticed to go public at the height of the small-stock boom in 1968, Perot sold shares of EDS at $16.50 each. At that price, the paper value of his remaining shares was more than $200 million. EDS was earning only $1.5 million per year, but was growing rapidly. Its stock price rose quickly in spite of a generally weak stock market in 1969, and held up even as the overall market slipped in the spring of 1970. But on April 22, the reality of an ugly bear market finally caught up with EDS.

EDS was traded in the Over-the-Counter market, still a loose collection of independent dealers connected only by telephone wires. Starting early on April 22, the various dealers who made markets* in EDS began to drop their quoted prices in the face of selling pressure. It didn't take much to initiate the decline; with no central mechanism through which prices could be reported and displayed, dealers were reluctant to commit their own capital to provide liquidity in an uncertain environment. In effect, the primitive state of the OTC market meant that no one (including the dealers) really knew the full picture at any given time. With the dealers in the dark and unwilling to buy stock, the market simply disintegrated.

There were unsubstantiated rumors after the EDS collapse that an old-fashioned bear raid, reminiscent of the 1920s, sank EDS stock on April 22. A representative of the investment banking firm that had originally underwritten EDS said, "No one can prove it, but it certainly appears that there was an organized raid of some kind on the stock."[2] Bear raid or not, the real problem was the nature of the OTC market itself. A patchwork of poorly capitalized dealers with no central reporting mechanism could not hope to deal with difficult environments such as existed in the spring of 1970. Ross Perot survived the April 22 debacle, poorer on paper but otherwise unscathed. But the flaws in the OTC market exposed by the EDS experience (and similar incidents) provided a powerful impetus for reform. The following year, the NASDAQ market system (creating electronic links between dealers that provided much-needed transparency) was established to make some semblance of order out of the OTC chaos.

What so suddenly happened to EDS stock on April 22 was typical of what had already happened to many other stocks over the preceding weeks and months. A vicious bear market pulled the Dow Jones Industrial Average back to levels not seen since 1963, representing a decline of 40% from the 1968 highs. But the Dow fared much better than the glamour stocks of

---

*A "market maker" is a dealer who stands ready to buy and sell a stock at all times, presenting a "bid" at which he is willing to buy, and a higher, "asked" price at which he is willing to sell. The dealer makes his profit on the "spread" between the two prices.

the 1960s and smaller OTC companies like EDS. The New York Stock Exchange Composite Index declined 50% from its peak to the 1970 low, while many glamour and small-cap stocks fell as much as 80%.

Declines of this magnitude shocked professional portfolio managers and individual investors alike. One stunned manager lamented to *Institutional Investor*, "You expect to see declines of 20% to 30% in a bear market, and you prepare for it. But 80%? No one can be ready for that." The painful 1970 experience led to much soul searching. Why did the drop occur, and how should portfolio managers and investors react to it?

Some observers declared that the market had become "irrational," subject to increasingly erratic fluctuations. A European banker noted, "The value of American industry now fluctuates as much as 5% in one day." He asked, "Have you Americans become so hysterical you no longer have any sense of value?"[3] Performance fund managers, so recently basking in accolades, now became goats. Their frenetic trading style was presumed to contribute to market volatility, forcing prices of their favorite stocks too high in bull markets, then crushing the same stocks as they all tried to get out at the same time in bear markets.

But was the increased volatility of the market truly a sign of irrationality? Economist Henry Wallich suggested it was not.[4] Instead, Wallich argued, higher volatility was the inevitable result of the market's focus on future growth rather than current dividends. Changes in expectations of future earnings rapidly impacted on current stock prices, creating volatility. In addition, changes in interest rates disproportionately affected growth stocks because so much of those stocks' value depends on a discounted stream of future earnings. The further into the future investors attempt to project earnings, the more the value of that earnings stream will be affected by a change in the interest rate at which the future earnings are discounted back to the present.

In Wallich's view, the damage done to growth stocks in 1970 was a logical response to higher interest rates. He observed that rates had risen "more drastically in recent years than in any comparable prior period" and noted that long-term corporate bond rates of 9% to 10% were "outside the realm of civilized financial experience." (By comparison, corporate bond interest rates had averaged 2.5% in 1950.) These high rates sharply depressed the present value of the growth stocks' future earnings stream.

Unless expectations of future growth increased to offset the effect of higher rates, the prices of growth stocks must decline.

Future earnings growth was crucial. In theory, the present value of future earnings should not be adversely affected by inflation, because the nominal amount of future earnings will be increased by inflation, and these higher nominal earnings should offset the effect of higher interest rates in making the present-value calculations. Over the long run, stocks should be a good hedge against inflation. But, as John Maynard Keynes once said, "In the long run, we're all dead." In the short term in the early 1970s, stocks did not prove to be a good inflation hedge at all.

There are several possible reasons stocks might perform poorly over the short run in periods of inflation. One is that in "cost-push" inflation, where prices are forced higher by rising costs of raw materials or labor, businesses may be unable to pass all those costs on to the consumer, resulting in a profit squeeze. (The large increases in OPEC oil prices in the early 1970s created this type of "cost-push" inflation.) Another reason is that corporate taxes do not properly adjust for inflation. In effect, corporations pay tax on illusory profits, reducing real after-tax earnings. (Depreciation, inventories, and capital gains are all calculated for tax purposes in terms of "nominal," not "real," dollars, resulting in an "inflation tax.") And finally (probably most important), fears that the Federal Reserve will act to restrain inflation by attempting to slow the economy can hurt the stock market.

This unpleasant reality created a paradox for growth stock owners. Fear of inflation had originally been the driving force behind growth investing. But, at least in the short run, the early 1970s showed that inflation could prove quite bad for stocks because of inflation-induced interest rate increases, dislocations in earnings, and fears of Federal Reserve action.

An article in *Barron's* in June 1970 starkly defined the harsh new environment. Entitled "Equity Backlash," the article quoted bond market authority Sidney Homer, who argued that inflation and the resulting rise in interest rates had fundamentally distorted the capital markets. Irreversible changes had occurred in the relationship between the debt (bond) and equity (stock) markets. As discussed in chapter 9, bond interest yields had risen decisively above stock dividend rates in the late 1950s, and permanently remained above dividend rates thereafter. The relationship between interest rates and dividends that had held since the dawn of organized markets had been abruptly overturned. Now, Homer said, another assumption of market traditionalists—that the stock and bond markets usually moved in opposite directions—was most likely no longer valid. Historically, a booming economy had caused stocks to rise but bonds to fall, as increased corporate profits spurred stocks higher while increased corporate demand for funds forced interest rates up (and thus bond prices down). In the new environment, the same inflation that drove down bond prices would also hurt stocks. Homer anticipated that in the future the bond and stock markets would move down together under the stress of inflation.

Homer could not have been more prescient. He described in a nutshell precisely what would happen in the 1970s, when the stock market's love affair with inflation was shattered. Several empirical studies performed in the 1970s would corroborate what a casual observer could readily see— that, contrary to all accepted wisdom, stock prices fell in the face of anticipated (and unanticipated) inflation.[5] As the Federal Reserve periodically tightened money to restrain inflation, both stock and bond prices plunged. It was a scenario that would be repeated again and again.

The painful experience of 1970 had another important effect. Professional investment advisers, shaken by poor performance, were finally forced to reconsider their reflexive rejection of the troublesome new theories of stock market behavior coming out of academia. The principle that Harry Markowitz and William Sharpe had struggled to impart—that risk was integrally related to reward, and that portfolio returns were only meaningful when evaluated in terms of the risk involved—finally began to sink in. The BAI study completed in late 1968 had laid the groundwork; in 1971 the message was reinforced by an SEC institutional investor study that concluded, "Although work needs to be done on risk measurement, there is evidence that the volatility of rates of return on institutional portfolios provides a useful measure of the risk borne by portfolio shareholders." William Sharpe's beta coefficient (the volatility of an individual stock relative to the market) quickly became a popular means of measuring risk.

Under the new "beta" regime, all performance figures would be adjusted for volatility (risk). Thus if a portfolio manager bought very volatile stocks, with an average beta of 2.0 (stocks, on average, that moved twice as fast as the market), he would be expected to outperform a rising market by a factor of two to one. Anything less would mean that he had actually underperformed on a risk-adjusted basis. After adjusting for this "market risk," a manager's stock selection prowess would be evaluated on the basis of achieved "alphas"—that is, how well his individual stock picks did after separating out the influence of the overall market. (Recall that "alpha," in the Capital Asset Pricing Model, represents the portion of an individual stock's return that is specific to that stock and not affected by the performance of the overall market.) Merrill Lynch was a leader in adopting the new performance criteria. The firm hired William Sharpe as a consultant and launched a risk-adjusted performance analysis service. The service produced a "reward-to-variability ratio" that could be used to evaluate portfolio performance.

The implications of the new approach were revolutionary. It quickly became clear that much of the market-beating performance claimed by investment advisers vanished when subjected to risk analysis. A San Francisco–based investment adviser summed it up this way: "Do you realize what's at stake? What the implications are? A lot of people are simply going to be put out of business. I mean, what are they really doing? What value are they adding to the process? What passes for security analysis today, in my opinion, is 150,000 percent bullshit. I don't believe that wide acceptance of this concept will be easy, or shall we say, made with good grace. But whether it is accepted or not, the truth is the truth."[6]

Professor James Lorie warned investment advisers to "give up conventional security analysis," claiming "its occasional triumphs are offset by its occasional disasters and on the average nothing valuable is produced."[7] According to Lorie, the manager should establish a beta for the level of risk his client was willing to take, and stick to it, diversifying sufficiently to get rid of alphas. Lorie's ideas represented the essence of the "efficient market" viewpoint. If stocks were efficiently priced, no amount of fundamental (and certainly not technical) analysis of those stocks would improve returns. Alphas were effectively random and therefore unpredictable; the impact of the alphas of individual stocks should be diluted (and hopefully eliminated) by diversification, leaving only the overall market (beta) risk to be managed.

Suddenly beta theory was respectable. *Institutional Investor* noted how an "obscure statistical term" had become "the big new thing on the street, the new way to play the game." An investment adviser interviewed by the magazine commented that "it's getting to be that if you don't know all about beta these days, you've had it." By 1971 several mutual funds had been formed that were explicitly managed using beta analysis. Beta advocates firmly believed that the problems money managers experienced in the 1969–1970 market downturn would have been less severe if there had been a general awareness of how much risk was being taken. To them, beta was an essential measure of that risk.

The beta approach was, of course, not without critics. Many Wall Street professionals refused to accept the implication that they could effectively be replaced by computers. Edward Zinbarg of Prudential observed that if "everyone could forecast betas, and everyone knew the answers, you wouldn't have a stock market."[8] Zinbarg rejected the notion that a good market analyst provided no added value. Speaking to the New York Society of Security Analysts, he complained: "You've all heard the comment, 'Well, big deal. You did very well just because you took on more risk.' It's the kind of disparaging comment that comes in all the [volatility] literature. But the fact is, dammit, I did take more risk. I was smart enough to take more risk and you weren't."

Others were quick to point out flaws in the beta approach. Since most research indicated that less than one-half, and perhaps only about one-third, of the typical stock's return could be accounted for by the market (the remainder being the alpha factor, which was not defined with any theoretical or empirical precision), managers focusing exclusively on beta were by definition ignoring most of what made individual stocks move. Perverse results could follow. For example, in a slowly declining industry (such as steel or railroads), stock prices might be less volatile. But did that truly mean that those stocks were less risky? Very low beta stocks also generally tended to have high individual alphas. Thus a fund manager who selected low beta stocks to minimize risk might well be taking on more stock-specific alpha risk than he bargained for.

Merton Miller, a professor of finance at the University of Chicago, summed up the limitations of the beta approach. He stated, "Betas may help you do your job a bit more systematically, and they may be useful in evaluating past performance," but he conceded the approach was not helpful "in spotting undervalued securities or putting together better portfolios."[9] Another observer remarked, "If you have a volatility measure but you can't predict the market, then it isn't worth a damn. It's like having the fastest car in the world with no steering mechanism."[10]

Of all institutional managers in the early 1970s, pension fund advisers embraced the beta approach most enthusiastically. But, according to critics, the concept was probably least well suited to these funds. The proper question for long-term investors, the critics argued, was, "will they get where they are going," not "what kind of bumps [volatility] they will have along the way." Ironically, the beta critics claimed that pension managers attempting to fund very long term obligations might actually benefit from a sharp market decline in a volatile portfolio of stocks, in that the decline would enable the managers to buy more stocks at low prices.[11]

While beta management gained favor as a result of the 1970 bear market, it was by no means embraced by all portfolio managers. In fact, one of the most pronounced developments in institutional stock investment in 1971–1972 ran directly counter to the beta approach of careful risk-adjusted diversification. The new trend was to concentrate institutional portfolios in roughly fifty large capitalization growth stocks, nicknamed by the press the Nifty Fifty. These stocks (representing industries such as computers, electronics, retailing, drugs, and brand-name consumer products) had a sufficient number of shares outstanding to make possible large institutional holdings, guaranteeing a liquid market when portfolio managers sought to buy or sell substantial blocks. The Nifty Fifty companies were often called one-decision stocks, meaning that they should be bought and never sold.

The P/E ratios for these stocks were high, reflecting anticipated future growth. Multiples of 40 and 50 to 1 were not uncommon; some of the Nifty Fifty sported ratios of 70 or 80 to 1. And they tended to pay low dividends, quite often less than half the dividends paid by other large capitalization companies. The Nifty Fifty had been hit hard in the 1970 bear market, just as in the 1962 market break. But after both 1962 and 1970, they came roaring back once the market environment improved. Over the long term, they had consistently provided returns superior to those of the market as a whole. Since these companies had performed so well for so long, the reasoning went, no portfolio manager could really be faulted for owning them.

The prices of most Nifty Fifty stocks peaked in December 1972, along with the overall market. They then dropped sharply in the severe 1973–1974 bear market. The failure of the Nixon administration's wage and price controls, combined with the sudden inflationary impact of OPEC oil price increases, once again forced the Federal Reserve to aggressively tighten monetary policy. Since the unprecedented inflation had caused businesses seeking to beat raw-material price increases to quickly build up inventories, firms were caught with huge excess stocks of goods when the tight money policy choked off demand. A classic "inventory liquidation" recession set in, resulting in a precipitous 15% drop in industrial production from 1973 to 1975, the most severe recession since World War II. Inflation and recession combined to create the worst of all possible scenarios.

Much as in the post–1929 crash period, conventional wisdom set in that the Nifty Fifty stocks had been grossly overvalued at their 1972 peak, leading to the substantial declines most of them suffered in the ensuing market drop. An article in *Forbes* summed up this (after the fact) conventional wisdom:

> *What held the Nifty Fifty up? The same thing that held up tulip-bulb prices in long-ago Holland—popular delusions and the madness of crowds. The delusion was that these companies were so good it didn't matter what you paid for them; their inexorable growth would bail you out.*
>
> *Obviously the problem was not with the companies but with the temporary insanity of institutional money managers—proving again that stupidity well-packaged can sound like wisdom. It was so easy to forget that probably no sizable company could possibly be worth more than fifty times normal earnings.*

The semiretired but much respected 80-year-old Benjamin Graham joined the chorus. Employing the familiar "speculative bubble" argument, Graham said, "Take a stock that has earnings growth of 15% per year. That's rather remarkable, but let's take it as an example. So long as the P/E just stays at its present level, the buyer will get a 15% return—plus dividends, if any—which will be so attractive to other investors that they will want to own that stock too. So they will buy it and in doing so they will bid up the price and hence the P/E. This makes the price rise faster than 15% so the security seems even more attractive. As more and more 'investors' become enamored with the promised rate of return, the price lifts free from underlying value and is enabled to float freely upward, creating a bubble that will expand quite beautifully until finally and inevitably it *must* burst. In other words, if you start low, you'll have a rise, and if you have a rise, you'll have satisfaction and that will bring a further rise, and so on. It won't go on forever. It may go too far, but never forever."[12]

Were the Nifty Fifty really overpriced in late 1972, or was the "conventional wisdom" wrong again, as it had been after the 1929 crash? An interesting insight is provided by Wharton professor Jeremy Siegel in his 1999 book, *Stocks for the Long Run*. Siegel studies the performance of a representative list of Nifty Fifty stocks over the 25-year period following the December 1972 market peak, and concludes that on a risk-adjusted basis the returns of the group roughly matched the market return over that period as measured by the Standard & Poor's Industrials. Siegel concluded that the Nifty Fifty as a group were not grossly overpriced in 1972, the conventional wisdom of later years notwithstanding.

This result is significant in that it is similar to the conclusions presented in chapters 6 and 10, where growth-influenced stock valuations preceding the 1929 and 1962 crashes were shown not to be excessive either, given that investors who bought stocks at those "high" prices still earned good returns going forward. There were no "speculative bubbles" waiting to burst, as has so often been portrayed. In each case (1929, 1962, and 1972), P/E multiples were substantially higher than they had been in earlier years, leading to fears that stocks were "too high" (particularly when the market dropped sharply thereafter). But in each case, when viewed from a long-term perspective, the valuations do not appear to have been unreasonable. The successively higher valuations should instead be seen as part of a long-term trend, away from conservative standards that had prevailed earlier, and toward the more aggressive standards that would be typical of the future.

The question of whether or not "bubbles" exist is integrally related to the credibility of the "efficient market" theory. By definition, an efficiently priced market should not be susceptible to irrational bubbles. That the popular interpretation of bubble pricing can be disproven in important instances provides crucial support for the efficient market theory. (Even Benjamin Graham finally threw in the towel. Shortly before his death in 1976, he conceded, "I'm on the side of the efficient market school of thought."[13])

The intellectual revolution on Wall Street did not end with the concept of market efficiency. Fischer Black, a tall, courtly MIT professor given to few words, soon dropped another bombshell. Working with his colleague Myron Scholes, Black resolved a problem that had been perplexing theorists for some time: how to value options. As they pertain to the stock market, options are contracts that enable the holder to purchase (or sell), at his discretion, a given stock at a given price (called the strike price) within a given amount of time. The advantages to the option buyer are that by owning the option he can benefit from the movement of a stock without actually having to put up the full amount of money necessary to purchase or sell short the stock, and that his potential loss is limited to the amount he pays for the option.

Options on major stocks were traded in the Over-the-Counter market in the 1960s. Market professionals thought that speculators paid too much for them, and therefore the professionals usually preferred to sell options to individual buyers. Because no options valuation model existed, the price of the options was determined on an ad hoc basis, based on the length of time the option would exist and the level of interest rates. (The higher the interest rate, the greater the value of the option, because the option holder effectively acquires a claim on a stock's prospective returns by making an investment smaller than would be required if he actually bought or sold the stock itself, thereby freeing up money that he can put out at interest elsewhere.)

But Black and Scholes (as had others before them) recognized that the ad hoc approach to valuing options was missing a crucial element. Some account had to be taken of the likely price movement of the particular stock on which the option was written. Theorists had previously struggled to incorporate some notion of the stock's expected returns into an option pricing formula, but without success. The Black-Scholes insight was that the value of the option did not depend on the expected return of the underlying stock but instead on the *volatility* of that stock, defined as the expected range (up or down) through which the stock price tended to move over a given period of time. The more volatile the stock, all other considerations being equal, the more valuable the option.

For example, assume an investor wishes to purchase options on two stocks, both trading at $50 per share. The first stock is a relatively stable (nonvolatile) utility that tends to move slowly over time. The second stock is a highly speculative technology company subject to sharp price moves based on rapidly changing investor expectations. Each option gives the option buyer the opportunity to buy each underlying stock at $50 for three months.

Clearly the option on the technology stock would be worth more, because the likelihood of a substantial rise in the price of the technology stock sometime during the three-month life of the option is much greater than the chance of a big gain in the utility stock. (The chance of a large loss in the technology stock is also much greater but is of little concern to the option buyer because the most he can lose is the amount he pays for the option, regardless of how far the technology stock falls.)

A colleague of Black and Scholes, Robert Merton, then took the idea one step further, developing the concept of a "replicating portfolio" to explain in simple terms why a stock's volatility, not its expected return, was the essential input necessary to value an option. Again take the example above of options to buy 100 shares each of two stocks at $50 per share, with each stock trading at $50. Assume, for simplicity, that the nonvolatile utility stock would either rise to $55 or fall to $45 over the life of the option, while the volatile technology stock would either rise to $70 or fall to $30 over the same period.

Merton deduced that the seller (writer) of the options could "hedge" his risk by purchasing 50 shares of each stock and charging a price (premium) for the option that would completely insure him against loss. In the case of the utility stock, the option premium would be $250 for a 100-share option. If the utility stock rose $5, to $55, the option buyer would exercise his option to buy 100 shares at $50. Since the hedged option seller would own only 50 shares of stock, he must go into the market to buy the other 50 shares at $55 and then deliver them to the buyer at $50, taking a $250 loss; this loss would be exactly offset by the $250 premium he received for selling the option. On the other hand, if the utility stock fell $5, to $45, the option seller would lose $250 on the 50 shares he owned but have no other obligation since the option buyer would not exercise his option to buy the stock at $50 if it were selling in the market at $45. Again, the option premium of $250 would exactly offset the option seller's loss.

The reasoning is exactly the same in the case of the technology stock. However, the fair price of the option is quite different. Since the technology stock is much more volatile (moving up or down $20 per share within the given time, rather than just $5, as in the case of the utility), the option premium necessary to indemnify the option seller against risk would be $1,000 per 100-share option rather than $250 (using the same assumption that he buys 50 shares of stock at $50 to "hedge" his risk).

Obviously these examples greatly oversimplify reality. There are many more than two discrete prices at which any given stock can trade at in the future. To deal with the different scenarios, Merton made a crucial assumption—that *continuous* efficient markets would allow the option seller to constantly modify his "hedge" as the stock price moved around, so that he could protect himself in all eventualities. This assumption seemed quite reasonable on the academic "drawing board," and in fact would become the basis for huge new markets in so-called derivatives (securities whose value is determined by their relationships to other securities). But, unknown to Merton and others at the time, the assumption would prove to be fatally flawed in important respects. It was a ticking time bomb destined to explode disastrously in the future.

In the short run, however, all was well. By coincidence, the Chicago Board of Trade inaugurated trading in stock options the same year that Black and Scholes published their new "model" for pricing options. Option traders routinely made use of the Black-Scholes model to price their transactions. An entire new market had been created in response to the work of a few academics.

As university scholars pressed the investment community from one side, the federal government weighed in on the other. In 1974, Congress passed landmark legislation establishing regulations under which pension and retirement plans would operate. Called the Employee Retirement Income Security Act (ERISA), the legislation mandated standards for employer-operated pension plans and made possible the liberalized plans for individuals that would subsequently spur greatly increased participation in the market. ERISA also codified acceptance of the principles of risk assessment developed by scholars; the legislation formally ratified the replacement of the old Prudent Man rule by the new concept of diversified risk management, stating that a fiduciary could demonstrate prudence "by diversifying the investments of the plan so as to minimize the risk of large losses." Some lawyers believed that the best antidote to lawsuits under the act would be for managers to demonstrate that they ran their portfolios according to "modern portfolio theory."[14]

After explosive growth in the 1950s and 1960s, stock investments made by corporate pension plans fell from 71% of assets in 1972 to 54% in 1974, in response to the disastrous market performance of the early 1970s.[15] ERISA would reverse this trend, resulting in increasing investment in equities by corporate pension funds for the remainder of the century. In addition, although it did not apply to government pension plans, ERISA would provide the rationale by which various ultraconservative state plans at last overcame their resistance to equities. Finally, ERISA inspired the Keogh and IRA plans that would eventually be developed, providing the means by which massive amounts of capital have been injected into the stock market by individuals saving for retirement. In short, ERISA was the engine that would drive the greatest accumulation of capital in history, through modern pension and retirement plans. Few pieces of regulatory legislation have had a greater impact.

In this turbulent era, the New York Stock Exchange was under siege by both the SEC and large institutional customers displeased with its minimum commission schedule. This rule prevented Exchange member firms from reducing commission rates charged to customers and was widely viewed as anticompetitive price-fixing. Institutions were particularly aggrieved because the commission schedule provided for no quantity discounts; the rate charged on a 10,000-share trade was 100 times the rate charged for a 100-share trade, even though the actual costs associated with executing the larger transaction were nowhere near 100 times the execution costs of the smaller transaction. Under relentless pressure from the government and its biggest customers, the Exchange was finally forced to agree to the elimination of fixed commission rates effective May 1, 1975 (to become known as May Day).

Dire predictions emanated from affected brokers, who feared that the traditional means by which business was done would be destroyed. They were right. The brokerage industry would undergo severe dislocations in the years ahead. But at the same time, the reduction in transaction costs (first for institutions but eventually also for individuals) caused an explosion in trading volume. The active trading that can be seen today, both by institutions and by individuals (often transacting on the Internet for less than $10 per trade), would not have been possible without the May Day reforms.

By December 1974 the market (as measured by the S&P 500) was down nearly 60% from its 1968 high, adjusted for inflation. The magnitude of the decline was second only to the disastrous 85% plunge (in real terms) of 1929–1932. While the market recovered substantially in 1975, a great deal of damage had been done. The old rules seemed no longer to apply. Inflation, once a friend to the market, had suddenly become a dangerous enemy. Controversial academic research, which could no longer be ignored, had undermined some of the basic principles upon which Wall Street had operated for generations. Regulators pressed Wall Street on several fronts. The public, after eagerly embracing the market in the 1960s, turned tail and ran; the percentage of American household wealth invested in stocks, which had hit 24.3% in 1968, fell to only 8.5% by 1978. (The 1968 figure would not again be exceeded until 1998.) The P/E ratio for the Dow Jones Industrials bottomed at 6.2 to 1 in 1974, the lowest since before the 1920s boom. The growth-induced expansion of P/E multiples that had dominated the twentieth century had seemingly been reversed. Taking note of these unprecedented shocks, investment adviser Peter Bernstein exclaimed that "all the known parameters [of stock market investing] were bursting apart."[16] He was right. The world of stock investing had been turned upside down. And much more was to come.

Dow Jones Industrial Average, 1975–1982

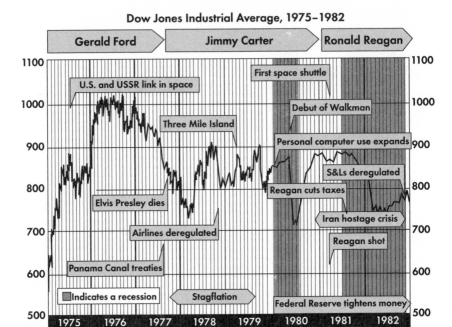

Gerald Ford · Jimmy Carter · Ronald Reagan

First space shuttle

U.S. and USSR link in space

Debut of Walkman

Three Mile Island

Personal computer use expands

S&Ls deregulated

Reagan cuts taxes

Elvis Presley dies

Iran hostage crisis

Airlines deregulated

Reagan shot

Panama Canal treaties

■ Indicates a recession · Stagflation

Federal Reserve tightens money

1975 1976 1977 1978 1979 1980 1981 1982

© *Dow Jones & Company Inc.*

13
CRUNCH

PAUL VOLKER DID not look the part. As the newly installed chairman of the Federal Reserve Board, Volker was without doubt the most powerful man in the American economy in 1979. But he made no effort to project the austere, dignified image typical of a central banker. Instead, his tendency to slouch his six-foot-seven-inch frame, wear ill-fitting suits, and smoke cheap cigars gave him a common, homey appearance. One colleague recalled, "In formal meetings with the governors of various central banks, [Volker's] legs would be spread out over the coffee table, and cigar ash would be falling over his belt and his trousers."[1]

President Jimmy Carter's nomination of Volker to the Fed post received nearly universal acclaim. Even so, the new chairman took office under very difficult circumstances. The economy was laboring through a four-year expansion beset with foreign trade imbalances, weakness in the dollar, large federal budget deficits, high interest rates and persistent inflation. *Barron's*, although generally supportive of Volker, noted tartly that he had "been present at the creation" of many of the problems plaguing the economy, having held positions in the Treasury Department in both the Johnson and Nixon administrations, when the nation's inflation and foreign exchange problems had originated. It would now be his task to clean up the mess.

In a surprise Saturday-evening news conference on October 6, Volker proclaimed his intention to do just that. He announced a full 1% hike in the discount rate, to an unprecedented 12%, and put in place curbs on the ability of banks to issue additional credit. His message was clear: the Fed was slamming on the brakes. Volker believed that in the past the Federal Reserve had eased up prematurely in attempts to combat inflation. (In 1970 the Fed loosened monetary policy in response to the Penn Central Railroad bankruptcy and resultant turmoil in the money market, while in 1975 it had backed off in the face of a severe recession and strains on the banking sector.) The inflationary forces plaguing the economy had never truly been extinguished. Volker was determined to do things differently. He would persist in the unpleasant task until the job was finally done.

The drastic Fed action precipitated what was called the "October Massacre" in the financial markets. Stocks and bonds dropped sharply; during the ensuing two weeks, the Dow Jones Industrials fell nearly 10% before recovering. *Barron's* termed the market action a controlled panic. By untimely coincidence, the drop occurred almost exactly 50 years after the 1929 crash. The press was, of course, full of predictable comparisons; once again, the noted sage John Kenneth Galbraith was trotted out by *The New York Times* to opine that something like the 1929 crash could happen again.

Pessimistic comments abounded. The economist Otto Eckstein said that the "board's action guarantees a recession," while Albert Cox at Merrill Lynch somberly concluded that there was a "very real possibility of a long, and ultimately deep, slide in business activity."[2] John Heimann, the U.S. Comptroller of the Currency, rocked Wall Street by suggesting that tight money could cause some major banks to fail. Interest rates hit unprecedented levels; Treasury bills were auctioned by the government at 11.5%, the highest rate ever paid, and interest charged on margin accounts held by stock investors reached 17%.

But beneath the headlines lay another story. The stock market reaction to the new Fed policy was not as bad as had first appeared; in fact, the market regained all its losses in the months immediately following the "October massacre." When compared with the severe slides the market had taken earlier in the decade, the 1979 drop was relatively mild. Prescient observers noted that at last the market seemed to be acting as the inflation hedge it was supposed to be.[3] This appeared to confirm the opinion prevalent in academic circles that while the market in the short run might provide poor protection against inflation, share prices had to rise in the long run in an inflationary environment because the value of the real businesses the shares represented must by definition be worth more when expressed in depreciated dollars.

But it would not be easy. The financial tug-of-war between tight money and high interest rates on one hand and inflation on the other would continue for some time, with the stock market trapped in the middle. External shocks generated by the clash between tight money and inflationary forces could have devastating repercussions. Such a shock occurred early in 1980, when one of the most improbable financial machinations in American history collapsed, wreaking havoc on the markets.

The story of what would become known as Silver Thursday began in the early 1970s. The principal players would be Bunker, Herbert, and Lamar Hunt, sons of the legendary oil wildcatter H. L. Hunt. The senior Hunt was a fervent apostle of extreme right-wing views, believing that Calvin Coolidge had been the last good President and that succeeding administrations had left the country "susceptible to Communism."[4] For a time, H. L. Hunt was possibly the richest man in America. Like many wildcatters, H. L. was an inveterate gambler, a trait his sons seemed to inherit. They also inherited his political opinions, viewing modern democratic governments as "welfare states" that would ineluctably debase the currency (that is, create inflation).

Believing that only "hard" assets provided protection against government-induced inflation, the Hunt brothers took an interest in silver, which they were convinced was cheap relative to the other traditional metallic standard of value, gold. By the mid-1970s they were confirmed "silver bugs." Believing in an almost messianic vision of an inflationary Armageddon, they were not interested in playing the silver market merely to capture moderate profits from small swings in the price, like most silver traders. They had far bigger objectives in mind. Backed by an inherited fortune variously estimated to have been between $6 billion and $14 billion, the Hunts entered the silver market like rampaging bull elephants in the proverbial china shop.

While the Hunts to this day deny it, most observers believe that the brothers' objective was to "corner" the market in silver. The effect of such a corner would be to squeeze the many commercial interests and other speculators who would in the normal course of business have sold silver short. Once the Hunts controlled the available supply of the metal, they could then force the "shorts" to come to them to buy back the metal they were short, at prices set by the Hunts. A silver corner would in theory have consequences similar to those of the Northern Pacific corner described in chapter 2, devastating the shorts who were caught on the wrong side of the market.

The commodities futures markets provided an excellent vehicle for the Hunts' machinations. A "futures contract" is simply a transaction entered into by a buyer and a seller that will be consummated ("settled") at a specified date in the future. On that date, the seller is obligated to deliver to the buyer a stipulated amount of the commodity in question, unless the seller has reversed his position in the futures market by buying back a like contract for delivery on the same date. The advantage to the Hunts (and other market participants) is that until the actual settlement date, the buyers and sellers are only required to put up a minimal margin (typically totaling 5%) of the value of the contract, and to post additional "maintenance margin" if the price of the contract moves against them in the market.

The Hunts poured their billions into silver. By January 1980, the Commodity Futures Trading Corporation (the regulatory body supervising the commodities markets) became alarmed, estimating that the Hunts and their allies controlled contracts for 77% of all the privately held silver in the world. The regulators increased margin requirements, but this only made matters worse; the shorts were forced to come up with tens of millions of dollars to meet their obligations under the new rules. Silver prices spurted higher, incredibly breaking through $50 per ounce on January 21, 1980, up from about $9 per ounce only six months earlier.

Finally the regulators and the commodities exchanges took draconian action to forestall disaster. Rules were imposed arbitrarily to prevent further buying of silver by the Hunts or anyone other than legitimate industrial users and shorts who were buying back silver they had previously sold. The Hunts were trapped; they could not buy, and there was no one to sell to.

By March 1980, silver had declined to the point where the Hunts, despite having inherited a multibillion-dollar fortune, actually began to run short of money. In addition to their huge hoard of silver, they had accumulated large stockholdings in such companies as Columbia Pictures, Global Marine, First National Bank of Chicago, and the brokerage firm through which they directed much of their business, Bache, Halsey, Stuart, Shields. As the price of silver fell (along with the prices of many of their stockholdings), they were continually required to put up more margin. They had exhausted much of their available credit, and the very high interest rates prevailing in early 1980 made their existing credit lines extremely expensive.

On March 14 they were hit with a body blow from an unexpected source. The Federal Reserve took another step in its efforts to squeeze out the inflationary forces the Hunts feared. A policy of "special credit restraint" was announced, under which member banks were advised in no uncertain terms to cease providing loans to finance speculative activity. Technically this program was voluntary, but few banks were prepared to openly resist it. Unlike 1929, when a similar directive by the Fed to cease funding speculation was openly spurned by Charles Mitchell of First National City Bank, in 1980 the banking community quickly fell in line with Fed policy. It was generally assumed that the Fed was specifically targeting the Hunts; whatever the case, the effect of the new policy on the brothers was devastating. They could expect to borrow no more money from U.S. banks to meet future margin requirements.

The price of silver continued to slide, and the Hunts, for the first time, found themselves unable to meet their margin calls. Bache, Halsey, Stuart, Shields put up some of the money for them, but even this additional margin was quickly consumed by falling prices. Worse still, Bache itself was now placed in a precarious financial position. Even though the Hunt brothers still possessed substantial assets that were not encumbered by loans, those assets were illiquid and could not be sold easily to raise cash. Because of Federal Reserve policy, banks would not lend to them. The day of reckoning had finally arrived. Herbert Hunt offered a sobering assessment of what would occur if silver continued to plummet. He said simply, "All the Hunt family will be washed out. We will go broke."[5]

The panic spread to the stock market, where rumors flew that Bache and several other firms connected with the Hunts' commodity speculation, including Merrill Lynch, might fail. Unable to raise enough money by selling silver, Bache dumped blocks of stock the Hunts had also posted as collateral for their loans, exacerbating the stock market drop. On March 27, dubbed Silver Thursday (reminiscent of Black Tuesday in 1929), the stock market decline degenerated into a rout.

Then suddenly the market reversed itself. Much as had occurred in 1962 at the bottom of the May "crash," a stunning rally in stock prices erased most of the day's losses. There was no news or action by any government or private entity that could explain the abrupt reversal. In coming years, critics of the "efficient market" hypothesis would cite examples of unexplained volatility such as this as proof that the stock market was not truly efficient. (An efficient market should in theory not be subject to violent swings that are not in direct response to new information.) But this academic debate lay in the future. For the present (late March 1980), market participants were stunned by the wild ride but grateful that they had somehow weathered the storm.

The silver market also stabilized, enabling Bache to unload some of the metal it had taken from the Hunts as collateral for loans. In the short term, disaster was averted, but it had been a very near thing. Bache and several smaller dealers had barely survived. Gerald Corrigan, assistant chairman at the Federal Reserve, later commented, "I did feel that if there had been a sizable default [such as Bache], it could have gotten very nasty indeed."[6] Most major market participants, and all the regulators, realized all too clearly just how close the financial system had come to a breakdown.

While the immediate crisis had abated, serious problems remained to be dealt with. There were still large loans outstanding to the Hunts from various commercial banks. The U.S. Comptroller of the Currency, John Heimann, set out to determine the extent of the obligations that remained, and whether any banks were endangered by their exposure to the Hunts. He was shocked to discover that the brothers had been able to borrow well over $1 billion from a number of different banks and brokers without any of the individual lenders being aware of the total extent of the Hunts' borrowings. The Hunts had simply refused to provide the bankers with consolidated statements detailing the magnitude of their debts, and the bankers, not wanting to miss out on what was viewed as profitable business, did not press them on the issue.

Like detectives quietly seeking to ferret out information, Heimann and his auditors probed for weak links among the banks that had lent money to the Hunts and soon found one. The First National Bank of Chicago already had serious problems, created by bad investments and the extremely high interest rates that then prevailed. It also had large loans outstanding to the Hunts. Rumors began to circulate that the bank might be in trouble. Heimann knew that he faced a potential crisis.

In 1907, J. P. Morgan had worked frantically to stem a banking crisis precipitated by panicky withdrawals from banks and trust companies by small depositors. By 1980 small depositors were protected by Federal Deposit Insurance up to $50,000 and were thus unlikely to panic. But all major banks held deposits that were significantly greater than $50,000, and many of these deposits were controlled by relatively sophisticated managers who made it their business to be aware of the financial condition of the institutions in which they had placed their funds. Heimann could easily foresee a run on big banks caused solely by fearful large depositors. He was already struggling to save the First Pennsylvania Bank, the thirty-fifth largest in the country, which was slowly being strangled by the high interest rate environment. If First Pennsy failed, followed by the collapse of First Chicago, the nation's ninth largest bank, it could be 1907 all over again, on an unimaginably larger scale.

Attention focused on the Federal Reserve, the nation's "lender of last resort," and chairman Paul Volker. Volker believed that it would be necessary to bail out both First Pennsy and First Chicago to save the rest of the banking system, but he fully recognized that a Hunt default could swamp those efforts. Volker was left facing what must have been a very unsavory prospect. He grudgingly recognized that it might become necessary for the government to bail out the Hunts as well.

The Hunts understood the bind Volker and the bank regulators were in. The brothers adamantly refused to engage in any fire sale of their assets (including their large remaining silver holdings), preferring instead to force a resolution of the crisis that was more palatable to them. In a sense they were playing a form of financial Russian roulette, implicitly threatening to commit financial suicide if an arrangement acceptable to them was not worked out. They knew that a complete collapse of their finances could have potentially catastrophic consequences for the banking system and the economy.

The only solution seemed to be to refinance the Hunt loans. If new lenders could be found who would loan long-term money to the Hunts, the existing creditors could be paid off. The Hunts did have other, illiquid assets (primarily oil properties) of substantial value. But to allow the Hunts to borrow large sums against them would seemingly violate the Fed's proscription against bank loans made to finance "speculative" endeavors.

In the end the Fed blinked, and the loans went through. Volker would always deny that he had in any way initiated or organized the refinancing, although clearly the final resolution of the Hunt difficulties removed a very dark storm cloud that had hung over the markets and the banking system. Critics accused the Fed chairman of "bailing out the Hunts." In a sharply worded editorial entitled "Too Rich to Fail," *Business Week* lambasted the central bank for sanctioning "an arrangement that gives the Hunts what amounts to a second chance to benefit from rising silver prices . . . They [the Hunts] played a dangerous game for high stakes. They guessed wrong, and they lost. They should be forced to liquidate other assets and cover their losses—just as any speculator would have to."

Bunker Hunt took the decline in his fortunes in stride. When asked how it felt to lose billions, he shrugged and said, "A billion dollars isn't what it used to be." But the incident had broader implications that reached far beyond the Hunts' personal misfortunes. The Federal Reserve had demonstrated its intent to use its powers to stabilize the markets in times of great distress, even when by so doing it would give comfort to players in the markets who did not deserve assistance (the Hunts), and even though the stabilization effort required the central bank to temporarily put aside its own policies of credit restraint.

At the time of the 1963 "salad oil" debacle, the New York Stock Exchange had intervened to protect customers of Ira Haupt & Company, establishing an important precedent that led to the formation of the Securities Investor Protection Corporation, which removed a significant element of risk (brokerage firm failures) that had in the past led to stock market panics. The 1930s reform legislation that provided federal deposit insurance for banks had already greatly reduced the risk of bank runs, another former cause of panics. Now, in 1980, the Fed's decision to effectively bail out the Hunts indicated a proactive willingness to intervene in the markets to forestall crises that, if left unchecked, could wreak havoc on the financial system and the stock market.

This is an extremely important point. The risk of external shocks to the stock market had been sharply curtailed. While there was (and is) no guarantee that other, unanticipated shocks will not occur in the future, it is clear that government stabilization programs have made the stock market inherently less risky than it was in the past.

There was no way to incorporate the notion of catastrophic financial risk into accepted modes of "beta" risk analysis. This and other difficulties with the beta approach begin to disillusion some of those who had first supported the concept. In 1980, *Institutional Investor* went so far as to run an article entitled "Is Beta Dead?" A prominent beta critic, 40-year-old UCLA finance professor Richard Roll, claimed to have uncovered a significant defect in beta analysis. Arguing that the notion of the "market" should include the market for all investment assets, not just stocks, Roll said that all proxies for the market used by beta analysts (such as market averages like the Standard & Poor's 500) were imperfect. To Roll, the whole idea of a beta coefficient was meaningless, since it was ultimately only as good as the index to which it was applied. Roll suggested instead that an appropriate model of stock market risk should include a number of factors, such as interest rates, currencies, and inflation, and not be based on a single factor like beta risk.

A "single factor" model (like the Capital Asset Pricing Model) was appealing because of its simplicity. But Roll was not alone in pointing to its deficiencies. Other scholars began to produce evidence that beta analysis provided poor forecasts of actual performance; betas tended to change over time, and often the alphas of individual stocks proved to be quite significant and did not entirely disappear with diversification. Tentatively, other potential models were proposed, all using more than one factor to measure risk. Some of the suggested variables were a company's asset replacement cost, stock price to book value ratio, financial (credit) risk, cash flow, unfounded pension liabilities, and the impact of changing rates of macroeconomic growth. Ironically, just as ERISA was pushing professional money managers to embrace beta analysis, new academic research caused them to question it.

Opinions varied all over the map. One portfolio manager ventured cautiously, "I think beta has some information in it. But it may be such an imprecise measure of risk that we have to be very, very careful how we use it."[7] Others were less equivocal. One beta critic declared, "If Roll is right, advanced mathematics will become to investors what the *Titanic* was to sailing."[8] A defender of the Capital Asset Pricing Model rebutted this view, warning, "People who have always been antagonistic to using the highest scientific standards in finance could use Roll's work to throw us back into the stone age."[9]

While the debate over beta raged on, another basic assumption underlying the Capital Asset Pricing Model took a hit from an entirely different quarter. In the Capital Asset Pricing Model, individual stocks are assumed to be efficiently priced, meaning that all relevant available information is instantaneously incorporated in the stock price and that individual investors or portfolio managers therefore cannot hope to outperform the market by betting that some stock prices are "wrong" (undervalued or overvalued). But just as the "efficient market hypothesis," conceived by academics, began to receive grudging acceptance among Wall Street professionals, scholars began to chip away at it. Fischer Black, fresh from helping devise the Black-Scholes options pricing formula, published an article in the *Financial Analysts Journal* with the quirky title "Yes Virginia There Is Hope." Black examined the investment recommendations made by the widely distributed *Value Line Investment Survey* and concluded that an investor who diligently followed Value Line's advice would have outperformed the market by a statistically significant amount. In a truly efficient market, this should not be possible. Black effectively took up the challenge laid down in 1968 by Eugene Fama, who had said that the efficient market hypothesis could be assumed to be true if no trading methodology could be shown to systematically beat the market. Black seemed to have found such a market-beating approach, which consisted simply of following Value Line recommendations. He wryly noted, "It appears that most investment management organizations would improve their performance if they fired all but one of their securities analysts and then provided the remaining analyst with the Value Line service."

This result was particularly galling to advocates of the efficient market theory. The *Value Investment Line Survey* was readily available to all investors. If such a straightforward strategy beat the market, could the market really be all that efficient after all?

A trickle of other studies followed that found "anomalies" that seemed to undermine the efficient market hypothesis. Wharton professors Marshall Blume and Irwin Friend analyzed stock market returns from 1928 to 1968 and found that the returns of small firms exceeded the returns from large firms, even when adjusted for risk.[10] The implication seemed to be that the market for small-capitalization stocks was not as efficient as that for large-cap companies. (This result encouraged the formation of mutual funds that specifically invested in small-cap stocks. The Wall Street community had now learned that academic research could be a useful marketing tool.)

Studies were published that isolated a "day of the week" effect, showing that stock prices tended to act differently on different days of the week. A 1977 analysis of low P/E stocks found that those stocks tended to perform better than did other stocks, implying that they were not efficiently priced.[11] But the most crucial blow to the notion that markets were perfectly efficient was struck by Yale professor Robert Shiller.

Shiller studied the aggregate dividends and earnings of the S&P 500 between 1871 and 1979 and concluded that the value of the market as measured by the index fluctuated far more than could be explained by changes in subsequent cash flows (dividends) to investors.[12] According to the efficient market theory, the market should adjust instantaneously to new pieces of information pertinent to particular companies or to the overall market. While the market might initially overreact or underreact, it should quickly reach a new equilibrium state incorporating the newly available data. (The overreactions and underreactions were assumed to be randomly distributed, therefore unpredictable.) But Shiller found that stock prices moved far too often and too much for those moves to be solely attributable to new information. How could the market be truly efficient if prices bounced around so much more than was justified by changes in substantive information? The Silver Thursday roller-coaster ride was just one example of this inexplicable market behavior. Shiller concluded that the "excess volatility" was caused by the irrational behavior of investors. Hence the market was not by any means perfectly efficient.

Doubters of the efficient market hypothesis seized upon this new evidence. They derided the university "eggheads" who continued to push the idea, calling them zealots. One humorous anecdote, often repeated by the critics to illustrate their belief that the efficient market theorists were divorced from reality, concerned an imaginary University of Chicago professor who spotted a $100 bill on the sidewalk. According to the story, the professor adamantly insisted that the bill was not really there. If it were, he reasoned, someone would have picked it up already.[13] Even the sidewalk "market" for lost currency was presumed to be efficient.

As the debate over the merits of the Capital Asset Pricing theory continued, Volker's Fed persisted in its tough policy of monetary restraint. Ultimately tight money precipitated two recessions, but when the Fed finally eased in late summer 1982, in the midst of the most severe economic downturn since World War II, inflation had at last been tamed.

The stock market had been battered by the experience. Even though it had held up fairly well through the early months of Fed tightening, the 1982 recession and the resultant drop in corporate profits had finally pulled prices down. In early August 1982, the Dow Industrials stood at 777, down 25% from the 1972 high. Broader market indexes showed similar nominal declines; more important, adjusted for the severe inflation of the 1970s, stock prices in August 1982 were down fully 75% from their peaks of a decade earlier. It was the efforts to restrain inflation (notably through a tight money policy) that depressed stock prices, not the inflation itself. In theory, the proposition that stocks were a good long-term hedge against inflation was still valid. But it was also quite evident that short-term anti-inflation policies could do a great deal of damage.

What about valuations? Nominal P/E ratios for major market averages in the early 1980s were in single digits, levels unseen since the 1940s. At first glance, these extremely low P/E's seemed to indicate that the trend toward higher valuations that had been in existence since the 1920s (interrupted only by the Great Depression) had been reversed. But was this interpretation correct?

In a word, the answer is no. The reason is conceptually quite simple, but is extremely important nonetheless. Price-earnings valuations are very sensitive to interest rates; higher rates mean that the discounted future value of earnings or dividends (upon which stock prices depend) is greatly reduced. High rates also create competing investment opportunities; for example, if essentially riskless money market funds pay double-digit returns, as they often did in the late 1970s, stocks become less attractive investment alternatives. Therefore, P/E ratios tend to fluctuate inversely with interest rates.

The effect of interest rates on stock valuations is presented graphically in the figures below. Two charts for the earnings-price ratio (the reciprocal of the more familiar price-earnings ratio) are shown for the postwar period; the first chart is not adjusted for interest rates, while the second one is. Conceptually, the earnings-price ratio represents the amount of earnings a stock investor buys when he purchases stock, expressed as a percentage of the price. If a company earns $10 per share, and its stock is selling for $100, for example, its earnings-price ratio is .10, meaning that the shareholder is buying 10 cents of earnings for every dollar he invests in the

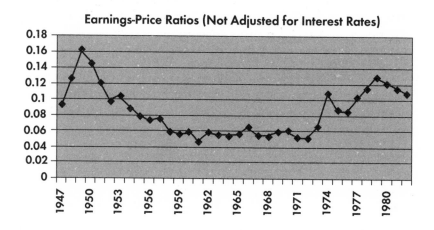

Earnings-Price Ratios (Not Adjusted for Interest Rates)

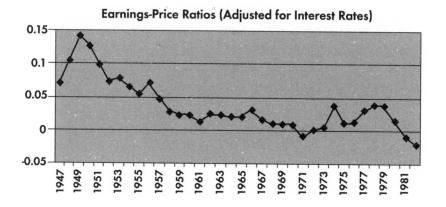

Earnings-Price Ratios (Adjusted for Interest Rates)

stock. The *lower* the earnings-price ratio, the *higher* (more expensive) the price of the stock is relative to its earnings.

The earnings-price ratio is used here because it best facilitates comparison with interest rates. How does the amount of *earnings* an investor can buy through stock purchases compare with the amount of *interest* he can buy through bond purchases? From the first graph, it appears that stocks became steadily more expensive (lower earnings-price ratios) through the 1950s, only to have that trend reversed in the 1970s. But when interest rates are taken into account (by subtracting the interest rate paid on government bonds from the earnings-price ratio), a very different picture emerges. It becomes clear that much of the apparent tendency for stocks to become cheaper in the 1970s was the result of rising interest rates, not a reversal of the long-term trend toward higher valuations.

Unfortunately, the notion that stock valuations had not dramatically declined when adjusted for interest rates was of little use to stock investors who had no way of adjusting their investment results for high rates. By 1982 only 16% of American households owned stock either directly or indirectly, a lower percentage than in the late 1960s. Whatever the merit of stocks as a long-run inflation hedge, the disastrous short-term performance of equities in the 1970s certainly tarnished the reputation of stocks as a good investment vehicle in times of inflation.

With the benefit of twenty-twenty hindsight, however, it can be said that in spite of the seemingly dismal investment climate in late summer 1982, the stock market was poised to rise. Volker's credit "crunch" had done its job. Inflation was finally under control and interest rates were coming down as the Fed at last eased its tight money policy. The Reagan tax cuts promised to stimulate the economy. Few market participants recognized it at the time, but Wall Street stood on the threshold of the greatest bull market ever.

14

RETURN OF THE BULL

O N A SEPTEMBER night in 1976, a 35-year-old University of California at Berkeley finance professor was plagued by sleeplessness. As he
tossed about in bed, Hayne Leland found his thoughts occupied by something his brother John had said. John Leland worked for a major investment management firm in San Francisco and had expressed disgust at the
incredibly shortsighted behavior of many portfolio managers who had pan-
icked and sold out of stocks after the 1973–1974 bear market.[1] Those
managers then missed the strong rebound in stock prices that occurred in
1975 and found themselves significantly underweighted in equities in a rising market.

As he pondered his brother's remarks, Hayne wondered if it might be
possible to devise a means by which worried investment managers could
protect themselves against bear markets, without having to liquidate their
entire portfolios. He was well aware of the landmark work done by Fischer
Black and Myron Scholes, creator of the Black-Scholes model for valuing
options. What was needed, Leland reasoned as he lay in bed, was a "put
option" on the market as a whole that a portfolio manager could purchase
to "insure" his holdings against a bear market. (A "put" option is the opposite of a "call" option; the holder of the "put" is entitled to sell a specified security at a specified price during a specified period of time.)

Unfortunately, the type of long-term market puts necessary to provide
such "insurance" didn't exist. But Leland remembered a crucial element in-

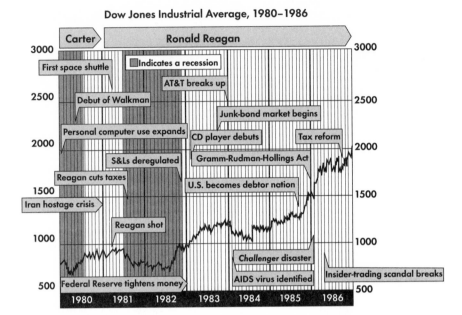

Dow Jones Industrial Average, 1980–1986

Carter

Ronald Reagan

- First space shuttle
- ▨ Indicates a recession
- AT&T breaks up
- Debut of Walkman
- Junk-bond market begins
- Personal computer use expands
- CD player debuts
- Tax reform
- S&Ls deregulated
- Gramm-Rudman-Hollings Act
- Reagan cuts taxes
- U.S. becomes debtor nation
- Iran hostage crisis
- Reagan shot
- Challenger disaster
- AIDS virus identified
- Insider-trading scandal breaks
- Federal Reserve tightens money

3000 — 2500 — 2000 — 1500 — 1000 — 500

1980 1981 1982 1983 1984 1985 1986

© *Dow Jones & Company Inc.*

herent in options pricing theory—the notion of a "replicating portfolio," discussed in chapter 12. Since it should be possible to construct a package of securities that would exactly replicate (hedge) the price movements of an option, could not that "replicating portfolio" be used in lieu of an actual options contract to accomplish the same purpose?

Leland's insight provided the basis for what would be called portfolio insurance. His idea was made much more practical by the creation of stock index futures in 1982. These contracts allowed investors and portfolio managers to buy or sell an entire market index—such as the Standard & Poor's 500 Industrials—without having to actually buy or sell every stock included in that index. The equity futures were similar to the silver futures traded by the Hunt brothers (and to other commodity futures), with one important exception. In the case of commodity futures, the seller of the contract was obligated to deliver the physical commodity to the buyer at the end of the contract period. In stock index futures, however, the seller and buyer settle up in cash. If the value of the stock index moved higher after the futures transaction was made, the seller would have to make up the difference to the buyer, and vice versa if the stock index went down. The messy necessity of delivering exact numbers of shares in the many different stocks that made up the index was avoided.

To "insure" a stock portfolio, the portfolio manager would sell an amount of futures dictated by the Black-Scholes model. The nature of the replicating (hedging) process was such that it was necessary to sell more futures contracts as stock prices declined, and to buy back those futures contracts as prices rose. Obviously there was a potential cost involved in this process; if the market was very volatile (meaning that prices moved back and forth frequently), the portfolio insurer might be required to repeatedly sell futures at lower prices, then buy them back at higher prices, thus incurring a loss. This loss could be viewed as the "premium" paid for the synthetic put option that was being "replicated." In effect, it was the premium paid for the portfolio insurance.

In theory, the futures market would closely track the "cash" market (the market for the stocks that actually made up the index in question), enabling portfolio insurers to use the futures contracts as a good proxy for the overall market. The mechanism by which futures prices were kept in line with actual "cash" prices was "index arbitrage," an activity that soon became commonplace after the equity futures markets were created. The dictionary definition of "arbitrage" is "the purchase of securities in one market for resale on another market in order to profit from a price discrepancy." Index arbitrageurs buy all the stocks that make up an index and simultaneously sell the index futures when the price of the futures is too high, or do the reverse when the price of the futures is too low. To accomplish this quickly for a large number of stocks, computerized trading was necessary—hence the oft-used phrase "computer trading" (or "program trading"). It was assumed that index arbitrage would always keep the futures prices in line with cash prices.

According to Leland, portfolio insurance was ideal for pension funds that needed to meet certain defined obligations but could afford to take more risk once the ability to meet those obligations was guaranteed. Likewise, it was an appropriate tool for investment managers who thought they could select individual stocks that would outperform the overall market (stocks that had positive alphas, in terms of the Capital Asset Pricing Model) but feared a severe bear market that would drag all stocks down. As Leland put it, portfolio insurance was comparable to a "run with your winners, cut your losses" strategy.[2]

Leland and other apostles of "portfolio insurance" were quite successful in selling the idea; by 1987 close to $100 billion in institutional portfolio values was reportedly "insured." Some observers expressed concern about the potential impact of these insurance strategies in a down market, in that the strategies called for selling more futures contracts as prices fell. This might exacerbate market weakness by creating even more selling pressure at the worst possible time, in much the same sense that margin-call selling accelerated the 1929 collapse. But little attention was paid to this possibility. Most portfolio insurance clients were quite happy with the protection they believed they had purchased.

From the August 1982 lows, the stock market roared ahead over the next several years, propelled by a rapid economic recovery, declining interest rates, and rising corporate profits. The market was driven primarily by institutions, which accounted for approximately 70% of all trading volume. Feeding the institutional appetite for stocks was a continuing flow of pension money (due to ERISA) into equity investments, and of personal savings into equity mutual funds. During the bull market of the 1980s, the concept that long-term investment in stocks was a reliable means of building wealth finally became broadly accepted by middle-class Americans. The conventional wisdom, repeated over and over again, was that a steady policy of investing personal savings in a diversified portfolio of stocks would enable the average investor to achieve solid returns with an acceptable degree of risk.

Perhaps the most effective advocate for this "gospel" was a soft-spoken, affable portfolio manager for the Fidelity organization named Peter Lynch. Lynch had developed an interest in the stock market at an early age and got his first exposure to the world of professional investing while working for Fidelity during the summer between his first and second years at the Wharton Graduate School of Business. Lynch immediately noticed discrepancies between what he had been learning in the classroom at Wharton and what he observed at Fidelity. Wharton at the time was a bastion of efficient market theorists, while the portfolio managers and analysts at Fidelity operated as if the concept of market efficiency didn't exist. Their objective was to consistently locate and purchase stocks that would outperform other stocks, something that in a truly efficient market should not be possible. Yet the Fidelity managers clearly believed it was possible, and that it had been done before. Lynch noted that they spoke almost reverentially of legendary Fidelity "stars" like Edward Johnson and Gerald Tsai.

As Lynch put it, the heavily quantitative, theoretical analysis he was exposed to at Wharton "taught me that the things I saw happening at Fidelity couldn't really be happening."[3] He went on to say, "It's hard to support the popular academic theory that the market is [efficient] when you know somebody who just made a twentyfold profit in Kentucky Fried Chicken, and furthermore, who explained in advance why the stock was going to rise."[4] Lynch was also troubled by the seeming inconsistency between the idea of market efficiency and the fact that stock prices appeared to move around more than they should. (In this sense, he intuitively grasped the more rigorous argument made by economist Robert Shiller, cited in chapter 13, that stock prices are far more volatile than they should be if the market were truly efficient.)

As his graduation from Wharton neared, Lynch made one additional, and very important, observation. He noticed that Wharton professors were not paid nearly as much as Fidelity managers and analysts. Lynch therefore decided to "cast [his] lot" with Fidelity, forswearing academia for the real world.[5] After a short apprenticeship as an analyst, he was given control of the Fidelity Magellan Fund, then totalling approximately $20 million in assets. His career as perhaps the most successful fund manager ever was about to begin.

Lynch promptly went on a buying spree, adding stocks to his new fund portfolio. He believed that investing was quite simple, and would tell anyone who asked that success in the market was more a matter of the application of common sense than the result of esoteric analysis. He later said that he would not buy any company if his 14-year-old daughter could not comprehend its balance sheet, and he scrupulously avoided businesses, such as high-technology companies, that he "did not understand." Lynch was openly disdainful of most Wall Street professionals. He later remarked, "Twenty years in this business convinces me that any normal person using the customary three percent of his brain can pick stocks just as well, if not better, than the average Wall Street expert."[6]

Lynch freely admitted that he "stumbled" upon many of his best stock picks in "extracurricular situations."[7] He bought Taco Bell after enjoying a burrito at a Taco Bell store in California. He found out about La Quinta Motor Inns stock because someone at a Holiday Inn told him about it. He investigated Volvo because both his family and friends owned Volvos and liked them. He was introduced to Apple Computer because his kids had one and because the systems manager at Fidelity bought several for the firm. He bought Pier One after it was recommended by his wife, who shopped at one of the company's stores.

Why was such a simple, commonsense approach to investing successful? Because, according to Lynch, the stock market was dominated by institutions that acted in ways not conducive to achieving good results. Investment decisions were often made by committee, a practice that ensured mediocrity and a tendency to run with the herd rather than to pursue innovative ideas. (Fidelity managers were given a great deal of independence so as to avoid this problem.) Also, in Lynch's view, most professional managers were excessively risk averse, which caused them to invest in proven, well-known companies rather than to seek out interesting new opportunities. The old maxim "You'll never lose your job losing your client's money in IBM" was appropriate, Lynch believed.[8] Rarely would a portfolio manager be chastised for buying a tried-and-true company like IBM, even if it did not perform well. But if he lost money in a speculative stock like La Quinta Motor Inns, his judgment would inevitably be questioned.

Throughout the late 1970s and 1980s, Lynch consistently beat the market, outperforming the Standard & Poor's 500 in all but two of the years he managed the Fidelity Magellan Fund. He became a high-profile spokesman for the mutual fund industry, granting interviews and making frequent public appearances. His pithy maxims and down-to-earth approach to investing attracted many people, both to his fund and to the idea of investing in common stocks. In Lynch's straightforward view, history had proven stocks to be superior long-term investments, although he frequently cautioned against attempts to predict short-term swings. Market declines should not be feared; instead they presented opportunities to buy more stock at cheap prices. And, most important, the efficient market theory notwithstanding, Lynch clearly believed it was possible to consistently achieve above-average returns by the persistent application of commonsense investment techniques.

There is no question that Peter Lynch and a few other "star" investment managers inspired many amateur investors to hope they could beat the market, either through investing on their own or by selecting good mutual fund managers to invest for them. The astounding success of the weekly PBS television program *Wall Street Week with Louis Rukeyser,* which included interviews with leading portfolio managers, provided evidence of the seemingly insatiable public appetite for information about the stock market, and the growing faith in the wisdom of professional managers. *Wall Street Week* would be the precursor of the all-financial-news-all-the-time networks of the 1990s, like CNBC, CNNfn, and Bloomberg. The mass marketing of investing to the general public, first begun by Charles Merrill in the 1940s, had at last truly arrived.

Did Peter Lynch's success really prove that the market was not efficient, and thus could be consistently beaten? Was it reasonable for the average investor to assume that he could somehow duplicate Lynch's results? Analysts attempting to answer these questions must confront the same tricky problems that arose a generation earlier when the go-go fund managers of the 1960s claimed similar abilities to "beat" the market. A simple statistical analysis of Lynch's record at Fidelity Magellan certainly seemed to indicate that his results were not the product of luck alone. Wharton professor Jeremy Siegel calculates the odds of Lynch's achieving the results he did by chance alone at only 1 in 500,000.[9]

But this analysis overlooks Lynch's tendency to concentrate his many holdings in certain industries. For example, at one time he owned 150 different savings-and-loan stocks in Magellan's portfolio. Likewise, when he decided he liked the convenience-store industry, he not only bought Southland Corporation, the parent of 7-11, but also invested in Circle K, National Convenience, Shop & Go, Hopping Foods, Fairmont Foods, and several others.[10] Lynch's practice of making concentrated bets on entire industries meant that the Magellan Fund was more risky than a broadly diversified market basket of stocks, because there were strong positive covariances between many of the securities in his portfolio. It also means that it is more difficult to judge whether Lynch's ultimate success was the result of luck or superior skill (or perhaps some of both).

Intuitively, it is hard to believe that the straightforward, commonsense approach to investing that Lynch employed can consistently beat the market. If investing in stocks is so "simple," as Lynch repeatedly says it is, then why can't everybody do it successfully? On the other hand, the same thing could be said about other fields of endeavor. Take professional baseball, for example. Conceptually, the act of hitting a pitched ball with a bat is "simple." But only a tiny fraction of the population can perform this simple task well enough to play in the major leagues, and only a small fraction of those can manage to do it successfully even 30% of the time (a .300 hitter).

Nobel Prize–winning economist Paul Samuelson has been a passionate defender of the idea that the market is efficient. But even he concedes that it is at least theoretically possible that a few individuals can consistently earn above-market returns, properly adjusted for risk. As he puts it, "People differ in their heights, pulchritude and acidity, why not in their P.Q., or performance quotient?"[11] However, Samuelson argues persuasively, those select individuals must be few and far between, if they exist at all. He concludes that it is pointless for investors to endlessly search for such tiny needles in huge haystacks.[12]

Did Peter Lynch stand head and shoulders above other portfolio managers? Or was he simply one of Warren Buffet's fabulously lucky "orangutans"? Unfortunately, there is no way to know for sure.

Much of the money that flowed into Lynch's Fidelity Magellan Fund, and other mutual funds, came via a new instrument—the 401(k) plan. The first such plan, a delayed response to the 1974 ERISA legislation, was introduced in 1981. The idea quickly caught on, along with the more general notion of defined-contribution, as opposed to defined-benefit, retirement plans.

In traditional, defined-benefit pension programs, an employer would be required to guarantee a certain "defined" level of payments to retirees; how the employer chose to invest money to fund those future payments had nothing to do with the amount to be paid out. Thus if an employer chose to invest its pension assets in the stock market, and earned good returns, the benefits of the good returns, over and above what was necessary to provide the "defined" benefits, would accrue to the employer.

In defined-contribution plans, like the 401(k), an employer (or a self-employed individual) would make certain "defined" contributions to the plan. The benefits actually received by the retiree would then depend on the returns earned by the plan. If the funds were invested in stocks, and those investments did well, the beneficiary could receive amounts much larger than any defined-benefit plan contemplated.

In the early 1980s, most pension and retirement plans were defined-benefit in nature. A substantial portion of those funds was actually invested in stocks, but the benefits to be received by retirees were not linked to stock market returns. This state of affairs changed rapidly in the 1980s and 1990s; by the mid-1990s, the majority of pension and retirement funds were defined-contribution plans, giving millions of plan participants a very important stake in the stock market, a stake they had not had before.

The profound transformation of public attitude that made these changes possible is stunning, when viewed from the perspective of the time frame covered in this book. If anyone had seriously suggested in the 1930s that retirement savings (or Social Security funds) be invested in stocks, he would have been deemed absolutely crazy. As discussed in chapter 6, respected financial writers in the 1930s labeled stocks as speculations, not investments. Even by the late 1950s, traditionalists still considered stocks to be so risky that they expected stock dividends to exceed bond interest rates to compensate investors for those risks.

Over time, the tireless efforts of advocates from Charles Merrill to Peter Lynch, as well as the research of academics such as Harry Markowitz and William Sharpe, had decisively changed the way investors looked at risk, and the stock market. All sorts of historical analyses could be (and were) presented by Peter Lynch and others to show that stock returns, over the long run, were stable and consistent. A diversified portfolio of stocks, held over the long term, in a regulated market free from the abuses of earlier years, was no longer seen by most people as being unduly risky. Instead, it became a standard, and sizable, component of the savings of millions of Americans.

But had abusive behavior really been banished from the market by government regulators? One of the greatest obstacles Charles Merrill had confronted in his efforts to restore public confidence in the stock market was the lingering perception that the market was basically crooked, with the deck stacked against small investors. The federal reform legislation of the 1930s had been designed to "clean up" the game, establishing a set of rules under which the market would operate. Blatant manipulative activity was now confined to peripheral operators like Serge Rubenstein, who did not, and could not, affect the large-capitalization stocks that made up most of the market. By the 1980s, supervision of the market by the SEC and other authorities was accepted as a given. But was the regulation really as effective as advertised? More fundamentally, was the market now truly fair?

This question is important because ultimately public acceptance of stock market investing requires that most investors believe they are not at an unfair disadvantage when competing against market professionals. If Peter Lynch could succeed by applying simple, commonsense formulas, then so could anyone else, unhindered by unscrupulous operators lurking behind the scenes. But in the 1980s a series of high-profile scandals raised the possibility that at least one important type of abusive behavior—insider trading—was still quite prevalent.

A ban on trading on the basis of "material nonpublic information" (more commonly known as inside information) had been a cornerstone of the 1930s reform legislation. Originally directed at officers and directors of companies, who, in the course of their normal activities, would be privy to nonpublic information about the company's affairs, in the 1960s the prohibition against insider trading was broadened to include brokers, bankers, lawyers, accountants, and even clerical employees who might become aware of such information. In short, almost anyone who knowingly possessed inside information and acted on it by trading in the stock market would be breaking the law.

But the reality of enforcement was such that very few cases were ever pursued by regulatory authorities. The SEC, charged with policing the markets to prevent insider trading, had in its more than four decades of existence brought only fifty cases against persons alleged to have profited from inside information. In each instance, the cases had been civil, not criminal, with the proscribed punishment being "disgorgement," or the repayment of profits made by trading illegally. The risks to prospective inside traders seemed to be limited and well-defined; they would probably not be caught, and if they were, the worst outcome was that they would simply have to give back the money they had made illicitly.

The issue came to the fore in the 1980s, with a dramatic upsurge in corporate merger activity. The virulent inflation of the late 1970s, and the Fed's efforts to squelch it, had a perverse effect on certain companies that possessed significant hard assets, such as real estate or oil. Current earnings of these companies were depressed by the recession, and the discounted value of future earnings was reduced by high interest rates. Thus the stock prices fell. But at the same time, the value of the companies' hard assets was increased by inflation, creating anomalies whereby the per share net asset value of a company could be higher than its stock price. In other words, the corporation would be worth more if it was broken up and its assets sold than it was as an ongoing entity.

Aggressive firms began to seek out "asset plays," attempting to locate and acquire firms that were valued by the stock market at a price below the value of their assets. Hence the merger boom of the 1980s. When one corporation sought to take over another, it would usually offer to pay a premium for the shares of the firm to be acquired, to ensure that the stockholders of the potential acquisition voted in favor of the deal. The result was that the stock of the target company often spiked up sharply when news of the merger proposal was announced. This clearly created significant profit opportunities for anyone who had advance knowledge of a deal.

A peculiar breed of professional traders known as risk arbitrageurs specialized in merger and acquisition transactions. The term "risk," as it related to risk arbitrageurs, distinguished their activities from those of other arbitrageurs, such as the index arbitrageurs discussed earlier. Index "arbs" engaged in relatively low-risk transactions in which they bought or sold stock index futures versus buying or selling comparable amounts of the stocks that made up the index. In the final analysis, they were perfectly "hedged." But "risk arbs" played a far more dangerous game, engaging in simultaneous transactions in different securities where there was no "perfect" hedge available. In a narrow sense, as applied to corporate takeover transactions, this usually meant buying the shares of a company to be acquired, and selling the shares of the acquirer. The risk element arose because the possibility always existed that the merger the risk arbs were betting on would not be consummated, in which case their losses could be substantial.

For years, risk-arbitrage trading had been frowned on by conservative Wall Street firms. It was considered to be an inappropriate activity for reputable investment banks to engage in, and risk arbitrageurs were seen as being very "different" from conventional investment bankers. Daniel Tisch, who headed the Risk Arbitrage Department at Salomon Brothers, admitted, "Most of us have some personality defect. You have to, to want to gamble with this much money."[13] Another partner at Salomon put it more bluntly. "The best arbs," he said, "are twenty-four-hour-a-day manipulators, round-the-clock schemers and compulsive liars who'd tell their widowed mother to bail out of a hot stock if they wanted to buy her position."[14]

Ivan Boesky was ideally suited for a career in risk arbitrage. The son of a well-to-do Russian immigrant, he attended a fashionable prep school but liked to pretend that he had worked his way up from more humble origins. He frequently told a story of how as a youth he had sold ice cream from an old truck for dimes and nickels. According to the story, the hard work necessary to make small change instilled in him a truer appreciation for "the green stuff."

After a desultory academic record at three colleges, Boesky eventually received a degree from Detroit Law School. He did marry well, however, wedding the daughter of a wealthy real estate developer. After drifting from job to job on Wall Street, he finally set up shop on his own, financed by his wife's money. He had discovered the great game of risk arbitrage, and it was to make him rich.

Immediately, Boesky began to rock the boat. Seeking still more capital to support an aggressive trading style, he broke with the secretive tradition of risk arbitrageurs and sought publicity for himself and his firm. He hired a public relations company and managed to get himself quoted frequently in the press as an "expert" on corporate takeovers and the trading of securities involved in corporate transactions. Much like Jesse Livermore a half century earlier, Boesky skillfully used the media to market himself and attract backers. He also attracted the ire of his competitors, most of whom were far more experienced than he and were understandably resentful of his grandstanding.

There was another, unspoken reason the established "arbs" were disturbed by Boesky's publicity seeking. The arbitrage community operated on or near the fine line separating legal from illegal use of information. The arbs were subject to the same insider-trading laws that applied to corporate officials and their outside advisers. Many in the arb community were concerned that if more attention was focused on risk arbitrage and the large profits frequently reaped by its practitioners, government regulators might begin to take notice and ask bothersome questions. Ivan Boesky was a highly visible lightning rod who threatened to unwittingly attract a bright flash of unwanted scrutiny to a heretofore secretive business.

This concern was well-founded. Stocks of companies involved in mergers often moved dramatically before the deals were actually announced, action that could only be the result of traders acting on the basis of inside information. This pattern was a source of irritation to the principals involved in conceiving and implementing corporate mergers and acquisitions. If the stock of a company that was to be acquired suddenly traded up before a deal was completed, the transaction itself could be jeopardized. Sir James Goldsmith, who was an active participant in several major corporate acquisitions, once decided to test the ability of his investment bankers to keep a secret. He asked them to conduct research on three companies that were not takeover targets, then waited to see what happened. He was not surprised when shortly thereafter one of his presumed targets was openly bandied about the Street as the subject of a takeover rumor.

H. Ross Perot had a similar experience when he was negotiating to sell

Electronic Data Systems to General Motors. As Perot described it: "We had a good meeting and the stock [EDS] went up; we had a bad meeting and the stock went down. I finally called the guys in and I said, 'Now, if this happens anymore, I'm going to find out who did it . . . this is rotten, absolutely rotten.' And interestingly enough, it stopped."[15]

In April 1985, *Business Week* published an article analyzing the performance of stocks of companies that were targets of acquisitions. The study showed that in 72% of all cases, the stocks rose before the actual merger announcement was made. The results infuriated SEC chairman John Shad, who had already publicly threatened to come down on insider trading "with hobnail boots." Commission staffers searched for an opportunity to aggressively enforce the insider trading rules. They soon found it.

On May 22, 1985, an odd letter arrived at the main offices of Merrill Lynch in New York. The letter was unsigned, with no return address, and had been postmarked in Venezuela. The typed text was full of grammatical and spelling errors, but its meaning was clear. The anonymous author wanted to alert Merrill Lynch to a pattern of apparent insider trading that was occurring through one of its offices.

When it was turned over to the SEC, the letter set in motion an investigation that eventually led to a Swiss bank office in the Bahamas. Someone dealing through the bank, hidden behind the cloak of secrecy provided by Swiss and Bahamian banking laws, had demonstrated an uncanny ability to buy stocks involved in mergers before the actual announcements, realizing large profits. The SEC kept pressuring the bank, and the Bahamian authorities, until it was finally given the name of the man behind the trades. He was a pudgy, flamboyant New York investment banker named Dennis Levine.

Levine had been trading on information obtained from his own work on pending merger transactions, as well as tips he received from other investment bankers and lawyers involved in similar deals. But there was more. Reluctantly, Levine revealed that he had also funneled information to Ivan Boesky, who used it in his risk-arbitrage business. In return, Boesky agreed to pay Levine a percentage of the money his firm made using Levine's information. The SEC had repeatedly investigated Boesky between 1983 and 1986, suspecting correctly that his well-publicized success as a risk arb might have been attained through the use of illicit information. But agency staffers had never been able to come up with hard evidence to back their suspicions. Levine would now provide it.

Once Levine's arrest was announced, Boesky knew the game was up. In an effort to save himself, he agreed to cooperate with prosecutors by providing incriminating evidence on others involved in illicit trading. One such individual was star investment banker Martin Siegal, at first appearance a very unlikely culprit. Siegal had been the youngest graduate of the Harvard Business School in 1971; tall, with an athletic build and movie-star looks, he seemed destined for success on Wall Street. But even though he quickly became one of the top investment bankers involved in merger transactions, Siegal's rapidly rising personal income was not sufficient to keep pace with the even more rapidly rising cost of supporting his way of life. He was entranced by the trappings of wealth Boesky displayed, watching in awe as Boesky arrived at tennis games in a pink Rolls Royce, or when Boesky ordered every item on the menu at expensive restaurants so that he could sample each one and then decide which to eat. Most of all, Siegal was impressed with Boesky's palatial estate in Mount Kisco, New York. Siegal wanted to have what Boesky had, and he made a pact with the devil to get it.

Boesky told prosecutors about the arrangement he had made with Siegal, which called for Boesky to pay Siegal a secret cash "bonus" each year based on the value of the information Siegal provided. As a result, Siegal was arrested. But the investigators wanted more than just Siegal. They had reason to believe that Boesky had had improper dealings with one of the most powerful figures on Wall Street, a man who had revolutionized the way the Street did business. That man was Michael Milken.

Michael Milken, of Drexel Burnham Lambert, was the apostle of what had become known as the junk bond revolution. By outward appearances he was hardly a natural salesman. Obviously shy, of lean stature, and wearing a toupee with curly brown hair that hid his premature baldness, Milken looked more like a meticulous accountant than a flamboyant promoter. Citing the academic studies he had come across while studying for his MBA at Wharton, Milken argued that bonds of lesser credit quality were unnecessarily shunned in the marketplace and therefore presented intriguing opportunities for investors. He tirelessly preached the gospel to insurance companies, pension funds, and newly deregulated savings and loans. According to Milken, and a growing legion of believers who accepted his argument, a diversified portfolio of high-yield bonds would, over time, yield a significantly higher return (even allowing for the greater possibility of default) than would a portfolio of investment-grade bonds. An early *Wall Street Journal* article about Milken noted the daring mixed with his shyness and self-effacement and went on to declare that "Mike Milken . . . is undisputed king of the junk bond market."

Milken's junk bonds provided a means of raising the money necessary to finance many of the corporate takeovers that were the lifeblood of arbs like Boesky. The two men developed a close relationship, which included a Milken-arranged junk bond deal that raised more capital for Boesky's firm. But the relationship ultimately proved to be too close. Milken was intimately involved in the investment banking activities of Drexel Burnham and therefore privy to advance knowledge of Drexel client merger transactions. Milken, and Drexel, could not legally trade on this information. But Boesky could, if the connection to Drexel was kept secret. The two men worked out an arrangement to do just that.

The government waited as long as possible to publicly disclose Boesky's plea bargain, seeking to obtain more evidence on Milken and others Boesky attempted to implicate. Finally, the official announcement was made on Friday afternoon, November 14, 1986, after the stock exchanges closed. Boesky would plead guilty to an unspecified felony charge, pay a whopping $100 million fine, and accept a lifetime ban from the securities industry. As the details of the deal were announced, an army of process servers fanned out around the Street, slapping subpoenas on figures implicated by Boesky.

The reaction in the Street, and in the press, was intense. It was clear from the terms of the plea bargain that Boesky was cooperating with investigators, meaning that he was probably implicating others. Fear swept the risk-arbitrage community. Almost everybody who was anybody would have had dealings with Boesky at one time or another. Who could be the targets of the ongoing probe? The uncertainty spilled over into the stock market, sending prices sharply lower, with stocks involved in takeovers especially hard hit.

Paranoia paralyzed the arb community, but fear quickly turned to anger as additional details of the Boesky settlement became public. The SEC, concerned about the potential market impact if Boesky was forced to dump his large stock positions after making his guilty plea, had permitted him to begin liquidating his firm's holdings well before the plea was announced. Many arbs, as well as other observers, were outraged. In effect, they claimed, the SEC had unfairly permitted Boesky to unload in advance of the inevitable market decline, selling off his holdings to other arbs and investors who were unaware of the impending announcement. One arb, speaking to *The Washington Post*, claimed, "The SEC has unwittingly aided one of the largest insider trader scams in history."[16]

Further criticism of the government came as exaggerated press reports implied that Boesky had made significantly more money from his insider trading with Dennis Levine than the government had calculated when it determined the fine he would pay. Far from being portrayed as having achieved an astounding success, the investigators began to be seen as incompetents who had mishandled one of the most important criminal cases of the century. Prosecutors were shocked by the vehemence of the reaction, which reached Congress, where formal hearings were demanded. One SEC official, speaking to colleagues, likened the experience to discovering the vaccine for polio, then being criticized for having killed monkeys in experimental trials.[17]

Eventually, as the sordid details of Boesky's activities became known, the public was astonished by stories that read like cheap cloak-and-dagger novels. Siegal, in clandestine meetings, had received suitcases stuffed with cash from unsavory Boesky operatives, and at one point actually feared that Boesky intended to have him killed. Boesky himself wore a hidden microphone, attempting to obtain incriminating evidence on others. And one fellow risk arbitraguer, John Mulheren, became so enraged with Boesky's revelations that he loaded an assault rifle, two semiautomatic pistols, and a shotgun into his car and set off to kill Boesky, only to be stopped by policemen who had been warned by Mulheren's wife.

Boesky was eventually sentenced to three years in prison, while Milken received ten years. The junk bond market collapsed under the weight of the investigation and an economic slowdown at the end of the 1980s, taking Drexel Burnham into bankruptcy. As one government attorney put it,

Boesky "played fast and loose with the rules that govern our markets, with the effect of manipulating the outcome of financial transactions measured in the hundreds of millions of dollars." Prosecutors would ultimately describe Boesky's cooperation as unprecedented, giving "the government a window on the rampant criminal conduct that has permeated the securities industry in the 1980's."[18] But what was the reaction of the general public to these events? Was the public's confidence in the stock market, so painstakingly built up beginning with the regulatory reforms of the 1930s, jeopardized?

The answer appears to be no. In spite of incontrovertible evidence of widespread insider trading in advance of significant corporate events (noted by the 1985 *Business Week* survey and similar studies), the investing public seemed to shrug off the Boesky-Milken revelations. There is no evidence to indicate that investors came to see the market as less fair, or more risky, because of the insider-trading scandals. Much as in the 1920s, investors seemed more concerned with the direction than with the integrity of the market. As described in chapter 5, lurid accounts of pools and other manipulative activity prevalent in the 1920s did not deter public interest in stocks. If anything, investors seemed to believe that they could somehow play the same game, hitching a ride with the big operators. It was only during the prolonged bear market of the early 1930s that manipulative activity came to be seen as a serious problem. After the fact, manipulation was blamed (erroneously) for causing the crash, and even the Depression. But in the 1980s, as well as in the 1920s before the crash, no one seemed to care as long as the market was going up.

After a sharp sell-off on November 17, 1986, in the wake of the Boesky plea bargain announcement, the stock market resumed its rise. By mid-1987 the market (as measured by the S&P 500) stood nearly three times higher than its August 1982 level. The average daily trading volume on the New York Stock Exchange had risen from 70 million shares to 180 million. The P/E ratio of the S&P expanded to more than 20 to 1, up from under 9 to 1 at the 1982 market trough. The rambunctious bull market was powered by whopping increases in corporate earnings, with 20% and higher year-to-year gains quite typical, and by falling interest rates, which (as explained in chapter 13) justified higher P/E ratios. (Roughly one-third of the rise in stock valuations in this period can be attributed to falling rates.) But increasing corporate profits and declining interest rates did not fully account for the upward move in valuation multiples. The long-term secular trend toward higher market valuations that had characterized the years since 1920 (interrupted by the Depression) continued, and accelerated, in the 1980s. By mid-1987, stock price valuations (adjusted for interest rates) were the highest they had ever been.

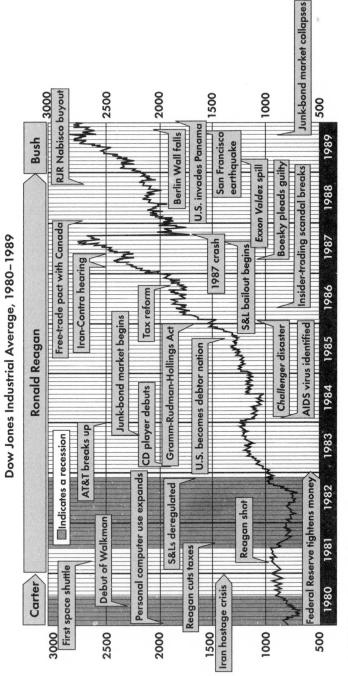

Dow Jones Industrial Average, 1980–1989

Carter | Ronald Reagan | Bush

First space shuttle
Debut of Walkman
Personal computer use expands
S&Ls deregulated
Reagan cuts taxes
Iran hostage crisis
Reagan shot
Federal Reserve tightens money

■ Indicates a recession
AT&T breaks up
Junk-bond market begins
CD player debuts
Gramm-Rudman-Hollings Act
U.S. becomes debtor nation

Free-trade pact with Canada
Iran-Contra hearing
Tax reform
1987 crash
S&L bailout begins
Challenger disaster
AIDS virus identified

RJR Nabisco buyout
Berlin Wall falls
U.S. invades Panama
San Francisco earthquake
Exxon Valdez spill
Boesky pleads guilty
Insider-trading scandal breaks
Junk-bond market collapses

3000
2500
2000
1500
1000
500

1980 1981 1982 1983 1984 1985 1986 1987 1988 1989

© 2000 Dow Jones & Company Inc.

15
AN ACCIDENT WAITING
TO HAPPEN

WHEN RONALD REAGAN appointed Alan Greenspan chairman of the Federal Reserve Board in 1987, critics openly questioned whether Greenspan was up to the job. The retiring chairman, Paul Volker, had attained near-legendary status by successfully vanquishing inflation. Greenspan lacked stature in comparison to Volker; some critics also questioned whether he was too close to Reagan to be truly independent. Greenspan was criticized for what appeared to be his blithe acceptance of the administration's optimistic view of the economy, ignoring large budget and trade deficits, and was derided for stating publicly that he saw no signs of incipient inflation. Alan Abelson of *Barron's* facetiously blamed Greenspan's optometrist, who, according to Abelson, "obviously fitted the new chairman of the Federal Reserve with faulty eyeglasses."

But Greenspan's measured, professorial demeanor was deceiving. He was well aware of the potential dangers lurking on the economic landscape. Shortly after assuming office at the Fed, he initiated a secret study designed to anticipate future crises and to develop contingency plans for meeting them. Greenspan was most concerned with identifying specific "flash points"—such as a major bank failure, the collapse of the dollar in foreign exchange markets, or a stock market crash—that could imperil the financial system. His aides immediately went to work on the project. Neither they, nor Greenspan himself, had any inkling of how soon it would be needed.

By 1987, about 30% of American households owned stocks, either directly or indirectly through mutual funds and defined-contribution pension plans. Institutions thoroughly dominated stock trading; less than 20% of stock market volume was transacted by individuals acting for their own accounts.

The institutional dominance of the market was reflected in a rapidly increasing turnover rate. Turnover on the New York Stock Exchange (defined as the annual Exchange trading volume divided by the total number of Exchange-listed shares outstanding), which had fallen to an all-time low of 12% in 1940, rebounded to exceed 80% by the mid-1980s. Professional portfolio managers tended to trade more frequently than individuals, particularly since the elimination of fixed commission rates on New York Stock Exchange stocks in 1975 greatly reduced transaction costs. In addition, new products (like stock index futures) enabled institutions to buy and sell large baskets of stock quickly and cheaply, further increasing the pace of trading activity.

The total value of the U.S. stock market grew from roughly $1.4 trillion in 1980 to nearly $3 trillion by early 1987. This increase occurred in spite of the unprecedented number of corporate acquisitions that had so enriched risk arbitrageurs like Ivan Boesky, and that effectively took billions of dollars' worth of shares out of circulation. The rise in share prices accelerated in 1986 and the first half of 1987; by August of 1987 the market (as measured by the S&P 500) was up 30% since the beginning of the year.

However, the downward trend in interest rates that had spurred part of the increase in valuations during the post-1982 bull market reversed in 1987. Rates began to rise, due to a more restrictive Federal Reserve monetary policy and fears of resurgent inflation. At the same time, dividends paid on stocks hit an all-time low; even the large-capitalization, established companies represented in the Dow Jones Industrial Average paid average dividends of merely 3%.

The stock market began to trend lower in September, with the pace of the decline accelerating in early October. Concerns were expressed about the potential impact on the market of new program trading systems (such as the index arbitrage discussed in chapter 14). Writing about the early October market slide, *The Wall Street Journal* took note of these sentiments, referring to "fears that some computerized trading techniques, such as portfolio insurance, could deal a nasty blow to an already fragile market."

Things quickly got worse. The week ending Friday, October 16, witnessed a steep decline in prices, with the biggest drop occurring at the end of the week. On Friday the Dow Industrials fell more than 100 points, or 4.6%, the sixth largest percentage loss since World War II. New York Stock Exchange trading volume soared to a record 344 million shares, bursting the old mark of 302 million. The Friday loss wiped out $145 billion in equity values.

Then on Monday, October 19, a tidal wave hit. The selling actually began overseas, in markets located in time zones ahead of New York. East Asian markets sold off sharply from the opening of business; European markets followed as the sun moved west. By the 9:30 a.m. opening in New York, market participants were braced for disaster.

The panic actually began in Chicago, on the floor of the Chicago Mercantile Exchange, where stock index futures contracts had been traded since 1983. The "Merc" opened before the New York markets, and immediately futures prices plummeted. Within seconds, prices of the S&P 500 index futures had plunged 20.75 points, more than the entire drop on the previous Friday.

Normally the index arbitrageurs described in chapter 14 would be expected to step in, buying futures with the intention of selling the stocks included in the index, locking in a profit if the price they paid for the futures contract was less than the aggregate price at which they sold the index stocks. But no one knew with any degree of certainty where stock prices would open in New York. The index arbs sat on their hands, and the futures fell lower and lower.

As the 9:30 opening arrived in New York, the market-making specialists on the floor of the New York Stock Exchange struggled to find prices at which they could balance supply and demand and commence trading in the stocks for which they were responsible. But the imbalance of sell orders was so great that many stocks could not be "opened"; there was no reasonable price at which demand equaled supply. Even one hour later, by 10:30, 95 blue-chip stocks had failed to open, representing in market capitalization 30% of the S&P Index, and including 11 of the 30 Dow Jones Industrials. The Dow average itself, calculated on the basis of its component stocks that had started trading, was down 94 points, or 4.5%. More realistically, if the remaining stocks that had not yet opened had been somehow included in the computations, the Dow Industrials would likely have been down at least 200 points, or nearly 10%.

The gaping discrepancy between the reported values of the major averages, which were based only on the stocks that had begun trading, and the reality of where prices would have to be in order to equalize supply and demand had not been anticipated by academics such as Hayne Leland, who had invented portfolio insurance. They had always assumed that index arbitrage would keep futures prices in line with cash prices at all times, allowing portfolio insurers to transact in futures at prices very representative of the actual cash values. But the arbitrage mechanism broke down under great stress on October 19. Since it was virtually impossible for the index arbs to predict where (or even if) they could sell the stock included in the market indexes, they were unwilling to buy futures, at almost any price. When the portfolio insurance computer models flashed signals requiring that more futures contracts be sold, there was no one to sell to, and futures prices collapsed.

The big gaps between the actual futures prices reported from the Merc and the theoretical prices derived from available stock quotations made it appear that the futures market was "predicting" further sharp declines in stock prices. This encouraged more selling of stocks, both by index arbs, who wanted to sell stocks first so they could then buy the "cheap" futures, and by other traders, who feared that the depressed futures prices presaged lower stock prices. As the market decline accelerated, the futures-cash relationship quickly spiraled out of control.

By 11 a.m., New York Stock Exchange volume hit 154 million shares, a record for 90 minutes of trading. The market briefly stabilized, only to plunge again in early-afternoon trading. As one New York Stock Exchange specialist described it, "From 2 pm on, there was total despair. The entire investment community fled the market."[1] The trading floor specialists, and many "upstairs" stock dealers,* were forced to take on ever-increasing in-

---

*The term "upstairs dealers" refers to traders at investment banking and brokerage firms who are not physically located on the floor of the Stock Exchange.

ventories of securities as they were besieged by sellers. In a normal environment, specialists and dealers attempt to turn over their inventories of stock quickly, but on October 19, particularly as the decline accelerated in the late afternoon, this simply wasn't possible. No precise statistics are available on what percentage of stocks sold ultimately ended up in specialist and dealer inventories instead of being placed with natural buyers. But it is clear that the amount was significant, and unprecedented.

The bloodletting was mercifully suspended at 4 p.m., when the market closed. The Dow Jones Industrials had fallen an incredible 508 points, on a record-smashing volume of 608 million shares. The decline of 22.6% was nearly *twice* that of the worst single day of the October 1929 crash. Reporters pressed government officials, including President Reagan, for a comment. Reagan admitted he was perplexed, saying, "Everyone is a little puzzled. There is nothing wrong with the economy."[2]

In response, 79-year-old John Kenneth Galbraith chimed in with his usual reference to 1929. "After the 1929 crash," Galbraith pointed out, "the universal phrase was, 'The economy is fundamentally sound.' Expect to hear that out of Washington over the next few days."[3] Perhaps concerned about inevitable comparisons to Herbert Hoover, Reagan did not comment further on the market.

The crisis by no means ended with the market's close on October 19. In fact, the real drama, played out largely behind the scenes, was only beginning. As the exhausted stock-exchange specialists and upstairs dealers tallied up their bloated inventories, they recognized that they would require substantial additional financing to pay for the stock they had been forced to buy. But they were in for a very rude awakening when they contacted their banks to borrow the necessary money. Almost without exception, the banks, scared by the day's events, refused to lend more money, even though they had long-standing relationships with the firms in question. Suddenly the specialists, and many dealers, were confronted with the shocking possibility that they might be forced to default, bringing the entire New York Stock Exchange market-making mechanism down with them.

During the market's late-afternoon collapse, Alan Greenspan was on an airplane en route to a speaking engagement in Dallas. At the time he departed from Washington, the Dow Industrials had been down 200 points but appeared to be stabilizing. Immediately after disembarking in Dallas, Greenspan inquired as to how the market had finally closed. When told the Dow had ended down "five-oh-eight," he at first breathed a sigh of relief, assuming the response meant 5.08 points. He was quickly disabused of that notion.

Hurrying to consult by telephone with other Fed officials, Greenspan moved to implement the contingency plan previously developed to deal with such a catastrophic event. He issued a terse one-sentence statement, declaring, "The Federal Reserve, consistent with its responsibilities as the nation's central bank, affirmed today its readiness to serve as a source of liquidity to support the economic and financial system."[4] This announcement served notice that the Fed would reverse its policy of monetary restraint and flood the banking system with liquidity. At the same time, in private conversations with major banks, Federal Reserve officials pressured the banks to reverse their decision not to provide loans to distressed stock market dealers. The Fed invited the banks to borrow as much as they needed from its "discount window" in order to make such loans, and "encouraged" the banks to look at the broad picture—the need to protect the entire financial system—rather than their own narrow interests.

The arm-twisting worked, and the specialists and dealers got their emergency loans. The Federal Reserve also entered the money market aggressively, pumping in liquidity that forced the federal funds rate down from 7.5% to 6.75%. But no one knew if this would be enough. Everything depended on what happened in Tuesday's stock trading session.

First indications were positive, with stocks opening higher than Monday's close; shortly after trading commenced, the Dow Jones Industrials were up approximately 200 points. Many of the overburdened specialists and dealers were able to dispose of their excess inventories. But the rally quickly evaporated, and prices began to fall as if the market had hit an air pocket. One by one, Exchange specialists were forced to suspend trading in major stocks, citing "order imbalances." This meant that there were many more sellers than buyers; after the previous day's terrifying experience, the specialists were in no mood to try to make up the difference with their own depleted capital.

The New York Stock Exchange suspended operation of the automated order entry system that allowed index arbs using computer programs to send large batches of sell orders directly to the Exchange floor. This effectively shut down the index-arbitrage process because it was physically impossible for the arbs to execute orders for hundreds of individual stocks manually. Now no matter how low the futures traded, there was no efficient means of arbitraging the discount against the stocks that made up the indexes.

By midday, the stock market had effectively ceased to function. Many major stocks could not be traded because of the order imbalances, and "derivative" securities like futures and options therefore could not be priced. Some major investment banking firms carrying large inventories of stocks faced catastrophic losses and secretly urged the New York Stock Exchange to close. Felix Rohatyn of Lazard Frères later said, "Tuesday was the most dangerous day we had in 50 years. I think we came within an hour [of the disintegration of the market]."[5]

It was as if everything had stopped. The fate of the market, and perhaps the broader economy, seemed to be suspended in a precarious balance. Then, slowly at first, the balance shifted. Buyers began to come in, and the market mechanism sputtered to life. Stocks in which trading had stopped reopened, usually at better prices than had been feared. Slowly the shaky rally built up momentum. At the close of trading, prices were firm and rising. The immediate crisis seemed to have passed, but it had been a very near thing.

Many explanations have been offered for Tuesday's turnaround. One of the most persuasive focuses on the spate of corporate stock repurchase announcements made that day, when one large company after another announced (and often immediately implemented) plans to buy back stock in meaningful quantities, providing crucial support for the market. Another possible reason for the turnaround was the decision of the New York Stock Exchange to cut off the automated order system, eliminating index-arbitrage selling pressure at a critical juncture. While both of these explanations have validity and were likely factors contributing to the final outcome Tuesday, their relative importance can never be known with certainty. As is usually the case with dramatic market reversals, the complete explanation will always remain a mystery.

One fact does stand out, however. As was also the case during the 1962 "crash," the rapidly growing body of mutual fund shareholders did not panic during the 1987 collapse. Mutual fund redemptions were not excessively high, and did not lead to the much-feared scenario in which fund portfolio managers would be forced to dump large blocks of stock to make good on redemption requests from their investors. (For example, during the week of October 19 only 3% of Peter Lynch's Fidelity Magellan shareholders redeemed their shares.[6]) The idea that Peter Lynch and others had worked so hard to sell—that short-term market fluctuations could be ignored because stocks would perform well over the long run—had obviously been accepted by most individual investors. Even a disaster like October 19 could not shake this belief.

On Wednesday, October 21, the market rallied substantially. For the next several months, it would seesaw back and forth in a fairly narrow range, but with substantial day-to-day volatility. Numerous predictions were made that the abrupt market break presaged a recession, but an economic slowdown did not develop in 1988. Undoubtedly the aggressive effort by the Federal Reserve to provide liquidity and to encourage banks to lend to distressed broker-dealers was crucial. The Fed had performed the same role that J. P. Morgan had assumed in 1907, when he struggled to provide funding for imperiled financial institutions. Had it not been for the Fed's timely intervention, it seems quite likely that the stock market panic of 1987 could have provoked a broader financial panic, which would have done great damage to the overall economy.

In the days following the crash, many people rushed forward to offer explanations for what had happened. The market break was said to be the result of the failure of the Senate to confirm Robert Bork to the Supreme Court (showing Reagan to be a lame duck), mistaken Fed monetary policy (either too tight or too loose), or concerns about the ever-present budget and trade deficits. Donald Trump said that there were "too many things wrong with the country" and claimed that he had sold out all his stocks before the crash.[7]

One explanation that received a great deal of attention involved proposed legislation to disallow tax deductions for interest paid on money borrowed to finance corporate takeovers. The legislation was designed to put an end to the merger binge of the 1980s, which had been financed with borrowed money (often junk bonds), and had been endorsed by an important congressional committee shortly before the crash. Critics pointed to the fact that stocks involved in mergers were particularly hard hit on October 19 and cited the proposed legislation as a likely cause.

But the attention of market participants, and of regulators, quickly focused on a high-profile culprit—index arbitrage—and, more specifically, portfolio insurance. The chairman of the New York Stock Exchange, John J. Phelan, had previously expressed concern that options and futures trading based on indexes could exacerbate a market downturn. On the evening of October 19, he said that such a "waterfall" effect seemed to have occurred.[8]

A subsequent SEC report examining the causes of the crash focused on this issue. The report concluded that up to 20% of the volume in S&P stocks on October 19 was created by portfolio insurance selling through the futures markets. (Recall that portfolio insurance strategies, as explained in chapter 14, often required the sale of more equity futures as stock prices declined.) More ominously, during the fateful 1 p.m. to 2 p.m. period when the market began to disintegrate, portfolio insurance selling may have accounted for as much as 40% of the total volume. In this view, the final resounding crash in the last hours of trading on October 19 might not have occurred if portfolio insurance selling had not pushed the market over the cliff.

Unfortunately, there is a flaw in this explanation. Virtually every major stock market in the world "crashed" on October 19, with most showing declines in excess of the U.S. market drop. In fact, when expressed in local currencies, the American market decline was actually the fifth smallest of twenty-three markets in developed countries.[9] Most of these other countries did not have active "portfolio insurance" programs; many didn't even have developed futures markets. Obviously portfolio insurance alone, acting through futures markets, was not the source of the worldwide market drop.

But while portfolio insurance strategies did not cause the 1987 crash in the United States, they undoubtedly exacerbated it. The large futures-related selling volumes identified in the SEC report were certainly of sufficient magnitude to do great damage in a market that was already extremely fragile. One market analyst said, "I don't know if Monday's drop would have been 50 points or 400 points without portfolio insurance, but it definitely made things worse."[10] The market decline was so severe that many insured accounts at first couldn't execute their insurance strategies effectively, then were forced to unwind their mangled positions at a loss when prices rebounded. One "insured" portfolio manager admitted that it was "questionable how well portfolio insurance worked this week."[11] An investment banker predicted (correctly) the "end of portfolio insurance as a strategy. It's really turned out to be portfolio destruction."[12]

In the final analysis, the impact of portfolio insurance selling in 1987 appears to have been similar to that of margin-call selling in 1929. Both were blamed for "causing" the respective crashes. While this extreme conclusion was overstated, it is apparent that both did make situations that were already bad considerably worse.

If "portfolio insurance" selling only accelerated a decline that was already occurring anyway, the obvious question becomes: What actually triggered the 1987 crash? More than a decade later, no one has been able to point to a single decisive news event that could or should have caused the precipitous fall in prices. This has caused considerable embarrassment to advocates of the efficient market theory, which allows for major market moves only in response to significant news. One such advocate was Eugene Fama, who in the mid-1960s originally coined the phrase "efficient market." By analyzing past data Fama had found that, depending on the period examined, a given year's stock market returns explained 50% to 70% of the variance of the following year's GNP growth. Thus it seemed logical to assume that the October 1987 drop represented a forecast of declining real economic activity. But Fama admitted his "frustration," which, he said, came "from not being able to identify the news that gave rise to the forecast."[13]

William Sharpe, another of the godfathers of the efficient market hypothesis, admitted he was "perplexed" by the market's volatility. "It's possible that a well-informed forecast of future market events moved the market as it did: you can't prove it one way or the other," he said. "On the other hand," he conceded, "it's pretty weird."[14]

Fischer Black pointed to increased volatility in the stock market in the months preceding the crash. He reasoned that this might have caused investors to perceive the market as being more risky, and thus caused them to demand a higher "risk premium." In this scenario, investors would have sold stocks down to levels where expected future returns were high enough to compensate for the new level of perceived risk. But, Black admitted, "the only insight that the [efficient] market theory provides is that stock prices are going to be more volatile than they have been. But, we don't know in what direction."[15]

The persistent mispricing of equity futures contracts during the crash period provided ammunition for critics of the belief that the market was efficient. The futures had traded at discounts of 10% to 20% below "fair" value for considerable intervals of time; in a truly efficient market, this, by definition, could not happen. Defenders of the efficient market hypothesis protested that this critique was not fair, in that the discounts that seemed to exist were at least in part illusory, since they were calculated using stock price indices that included many stocks that were not trading because of order imbalances. Had these stocks actually traded at market-clearing levels, the inclusion of their prices in the index would have resulted in an overall index value that was much lower, and much closer to the futures prices that actually prevailed.

The efficient market advocates also pointed to the decision by New York Stock Exchange authorities to cut off the automated order system after Tuesday morning, October 20. This effectively short-circuited the mechanism by which index arbitrage kept futures pricing "efficient." Economist Merton Miller said, "Efficiency is affected by the cost of transactions, and the big overload of the system [during the crash] meant that those costs became very high—not just the real cost of executions, but the uncertainty." Miller claimed that the crash period was not a "fair test" of market efficiency.[16]

The narrow issue of possible short-term mispricings in the futures market obscured a more fundamental question. How could a truly "efficient" stock market have lost 30% of its value in the four-day period concluding on October 19, with most of the decline occurring on one day? Since no news development can be identified that could so decisively have changed investor expectations over so short a time span, it seemed intuitively obvious that the overall market must have been badly mispriced, either before or after the crash. This is the essence of the case made by critics of the efficient market hypothesis. It is based on the same reasoning employed by the economist Robert Shiller, who, as discussed in chapter 13, found that stock prices have been far more volatile over time than can be justified by changes in underlying fundamentals.

After the 1987 crash, Robert Shiller wrote scathingly that "[the] efficient market hypothesis is the most remarkable error in the history of economic theory. This is just another nail in its coffin."[17] Harvard professor Lawrence Summers, later to be treasury secretary, agreed, noting, "If anyone did seriously believe that price movements are determined by changes in information about economic fundamentals, they got to be disabused of that notion by Monday's 500-point movement."[18] The reasoning of Shiller and Summers has been expanded on by other scholars, who seek to replace the efficient market theory with what can best be called "behavioral" explanations of market movements.

Shiller, Summers, and other "behavioralists" argue that patterns of not entirely rational behavior by investors influence stock prices in ways inconsistent with the efficient market theory. Specifically, they believe that investors must have either bid up stock prices irrationally before the 1987 crash or sold them down irrationally during the crash. For the most part, the behavioralists have focused on the notion that stock prices were "too high" in late summer 1987 after the sharp run-up in the first half of the year.

But was this really true? As demonstrated in earlier chapters, one way to determine whether a specific stock or group of stocks, or the overall market, was overpriced before a crash is to examine the long-term performance of those stocks from that point forward. If it can be shown that individual stocks on a risk-adjusted basis achieved a rate of return comparable to that of the overall market going forward, then it is hard to argue convincingly that they were overpriced. Likewise, if the overall market achieves a rate of return going forward that is comparable to or better than the long-term average rate of return stocks have provided historically, it is difficult to say that the market as a whole was overvalued.

The fact of the matter is that an investor who bought the market (as measured by the S&P 500) at the August 1987 market top and held it over the ensuing ten years would have earned a compounded return of approximately 13% (including dividends), significantly above the historical long-term average return the stock market has provided. Perhaps the market was overvalued in 1997, creating this favorable return comparison. Perhaps not. But whatever the case, given the subsequent returns earned by the 1987 investor, it certainly cannot be said that on a *relative* basis stocks were overpriced at the 1987 high.

This finding is consistent with those of chapters 10 and 12, where it was shown that the market was not overpriced before the 1962 crash, and that even the so-called Nifty Fifty stocks were not really overpriced at their 1972 highs. At each successive peak, valuations measures (such as P/E ratios) were extremely high by historical standards. Yet each peak was eventually followed by a still higher peak. Clearly an underlying trend toward increasing market valuations was at work, a trend missed by observers who rely only on historical standards and therefore constantly see evidence of "bubbles" and irrational overpricing.

It is important to emphasize that the "peaks" referred to here are peaks in *valuations*, such as P/E ratios, not just peaks in stock prices. Obviously stock prices tend to rise over time as the economy grows and corporate profits increase. But over the course of the century (at least since the 1920s), *valuations* have also increased dramatically. It is the summing together of these two trends—growth in the economy and profits, and increases in valuations—that has generated the impressive returns provided by stocks over most of the past hundred years.

Even if a "bubble" did not exist before the 1987 crash, the scope and suddenness of the crash itself is hard to reconcile with the efficient market theory; the arguments of the behavioralists become very appealing. The behavioralists search for ways that human psychology affects stock prices, causing erratic market action like the crash. Much more will be said on this subject in chapter 16. But suffice it to say that the crash of 1987 was a seminal event that catapulted the behavioralists into the spotlight. For the first time since the efficient market hypothesis was developed in the 1960s, a radical new theory of market behavior had been produced by academia.

The supporters of the efficient market did not sit silently in the face of mounting criticism. To defend the notion that stocks are always priced "efficiently," they needed to show that the sharp drop of October was the result of a rational reappraisal by investors of economic prospects, albeit one that happened with great abruptness. Economist Merton Miller took up the argument. His contention was that relatively minor, and quite rational, changes in the assumptions included in the standard, highly nonlinear valuation models for stocks could result in big stock price moves. He employed a simple example to illustrate his point. Recall from previous chapters that the long-term value of a stock must in theory be equal to the discounted present value of the future dividends a stockholder expects to receive. Two variables determine this "present value": the anticipated growth rate of the dividends, and the interest rate (discount rate) that is used to discount future dividends back to the present. Taking values typical of late summer 1987, Miller calculated that the then current average dividend of 3% would be justified, given a discount rate of 10%, if the market expected dividends to grow at a 7% annual rate indefinitely.

But what would happen if investor expectations changed? Miller assumed that investors revised downward their expected rate of dividend growth to 6.5%, from 7%, and revised upward the rate required to discount future dividends to 10.5%, from 10%. In this case, he calculated, the "value" of stocks would drop by a precipitous 25% (almost exactly the amount the market declined on October 19).[19]*

As mentioned previously, interest rates had been rising in mid-1987. Studies have shown that stock prices in the weeks before the 1987 crash were highly correlated with interest rates, much more so than normal.[20] It does not seem unreasonable to assume that investors may collectively have raised the rate at which future returns were to be discounted by one-half of

---

*For the mathematically inclined, the fact that large changes in theoretical valuations can result from relatively small changes in inputs can be seen from the following equation, which is valid if dividends are assumed to grow indefinitely at a constant rate.

V = Theoretical value of stock
D = Current dividend
R = Discount rate at which future dividends are discounted back to present, which in turn is simply the current risk-free interest rate (government bond interest rate) plus the equity risk premium
G = Rate at which dividends grow over time

$$V = \frac{D}{(R - G)}$$

Small changes in R and G can cause large variations in V.

1%. Dividend growth projections are somewhat more problematic, but it is not outside the realm of possibility that expectations of future dividend increases declined for some legitimate reason. If all this happened at once, according to Miller, a "crash" could be produced that was not irrational. It would be a "rational panic."

Eugene Fama made a similar argument. He compared average dividends before and after the crash with changes in what is called the default spread between very high quality and lesser quality corporate bonds. The default spread is the yield differential between bonds of differing quality, and is a measure of the amount of risk perceived in the economy by bond investors. When times are expected to be bad (risky), the possibility that companies of lesser credit quality will default on their bonds is greater. Therefore the lower quality bonds must pay more interest relative to higher quality bonds to compensate investors for that risk. The default spread increases. The opposite occurs when times are expected to be good (less risky).

Fama calculated that immediately before the crash, the average dividend payment for the S&P 500 stocks was 2.7%, compared with a norm in the 1957–1986 period of about 3.8%. After the crash, the average dividend jumped to 3.71% because share prices had fallen. This was close to the 1957–1986 mean. At the same time, the default spread increased from 27 basis points to 50 basis points (.27% to .50%), also close to its 1957–1986 mean.

Fama concluded that the perception of "risk" in the economy, as measured by the default spread, had increased to levels close to the historical norm, and that dividends had also reverted to their long-term average. He interpreted this to mean that investors had shifted their economic outlook, now expecting that the future would only be "average" instead of "good."[21] Such a change in expectations, when plugged into the discount model used to value stocks, could produce the results Miller had derived from his hypothetical example.

The crucial assumption underlying this argument is that investor expectations change over time, sometimes quite rapidly and without any readily apparent trigger. If this is true, then the large, seemingly "irrational" market moves behavioralists cite as evidence against the efficient market theory can in fact be reconciled with that theory. Unfortunately, as

William Sharpe admitted after the 1987 crash, "You can't prove it one way or the other."[22]

Alan Greenspan spoke publicly on this question in 1998 when he observed:

> *The United States experienced . . . a sudden change with the decline of stock prices of more than 20% on October 19, 1987. There is no credible scenario that can readily explain so abrupt a change in the fundamentals of long-term valuation on that one day. Such market panics do not appear to reflect a simple continuum from the immediately previous period. The abrupt onset of such implosions suggests the possibility that there is a marked dividing line for confidence. When [it] is crossed, prices slip into a free fall—perhaps overshooting the long-term equilibrium—before markets will stabilize.*"[23]

Greenspan had earlier referred to the 1987 crash as "an accident waiting to happen."[24] As chairman of the Federal Reserve System, he knew he would have to deal with the economic consequences of such catastrophic swings in stock prices. For this reason he sought to better understand why they occurred, and what (perhaps) could realistically be done to mitigate the worst of them. It was a tricky subject, hotly debated among scholars and market professionals. Yet it was a subject he could not afford to ignore.

16

GREENSPAN'S DILEMMA

W HEN WE MOVED on February 4, I think our expectation was that we would prick the bubble in the equity markets." So said Federal Reserve chairman Alan Greenspan in March 1994, recorded in transcripts made public five years later. The "move" Greenspan referred to was an increase in the Fed's target for short-term interest rates—one of a series of increases that would take rates from 3% in January 1994 to 5.5% in January 1995. Before Greenspan's move, the stock market, measured by the Dow Jones Industrial Average, had been on a tear, closing in on the 4,000 mark. But the rate increase took the steam out of the rally; in subsequent weeks the Dow fell 10%. "We partially broke the back of an emerging speculation," Greenspan later claimed to associates. "We had a desirable effect." When the market later recovered part of its loss, Greenspan expressed continuing concern. "The stock market," he said, "in my judgment is still a little rich, although off its price-earnings ratios of a while back."[1]

Not since William McChesney Martin in the 1960s had a Fed chairman been so openly concerned with the level of stock prices. And not since the late 1920s, when the Fed clumsily attempted to prick another so-called bubble, had Fed policy been so specifically motivated by a desire to curb stock speculation. Greenspan's worries about high stock prices would not be easily assuaged. He would spend the rest of the decade agonizing about how much Federal Reserve policy makers should take high stock prices into account.

Dow Jones Industrial Average, 1990–1999

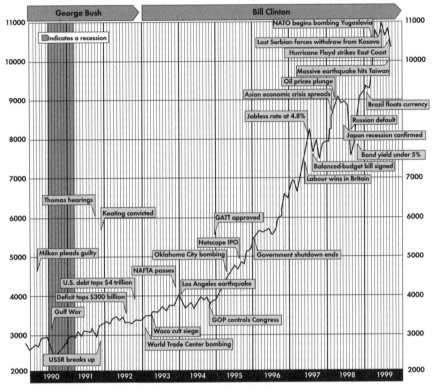

George Bush   Bill Clinton

■ Indicates a recession

NATO begins bombing Yugoslavia
Last Serbian forces withdraw from Kosovo
Hurricane Floyd strikes East Coast
Massive earthquake hits Taiwan
Oil prices plunge
Asian economic crisis spreads
Brazil floats currency
Jobless rate at 4.8%
Russian default
Japan recession confirmed
Bond yield under 5%
Balanced-budget bill signed
Labour wins in Britain
Thomas hearings
Keating convicted
GATT approved
Netscape IPO
Milken pleads guilty
Oklahoma City bombing
Government shutdown ends
NAFTA passes
U.S. debt tops $4 trillion
Los Angeles earthquake
Deficit tops $300 billion
Gulf War
GOP controls Congress
Waco cult siege
World Trade Center bombing
USSR breaks up

© 2000 Dow Jones & Company Inc.

The matter again came to a head in December 1996. The Dow Industrials were up nearly 30% for the year, trading well above 6,000. Attempting to make sense of the market's phenomenal rise, Greenspan summoned "experts" who held sharply opposing views to present their opinions to the Fed's board of governors. One was Abby Joseph Cohen, chief equity strategist for Goldman, Sachs & Company. Cohen laid out the "bull" case, justifying higher stock prices. In her view, fundamental changes in the economy, such as reduced inflation and increased productivity, were driving stock prices higher. Old parameters used to value stocks no longer applied.

The opposing view was presented by two academic economists, Robert Shiller and John Campbell. They did not directly rebut Cohen's argument, but instead relied heavily on a detailed analysis of market history stretching back to 1871. The lessons of the past, Shiller and Campbell argued, did not bode well for the market. Historically, whenever the dividend yield on stocks had been low, and the P/E ratio high, the return to stockholders over the subsequent ten years tended to be low. In late 1996 the dividend yield on the Standard & Poor's 500 stood at 1.9%, an all-time low, while the P/E ratio was approaching an all-time high. Based on these facts, Shiller and Campbell predicted that between 1997 and 2006, the stock market would lose 40% of its real value.[2]

Greenspan seemed to heed the Shiller-Campbell warning. Two days later he delivered a speech that posed a memorable question: "How do we know when irrational exuberance has unduly escalated asset values? . . . And how do we factor that assessment into monetary policy?" Stocks around the world immediately sold off after Greenspan spoke. Ironically, while the U.S. market, the presumed target of Greenspan's remarks, opened 2% lower the next day, it ultimately held up better than many overseas exchanges. Professor Shiller was reportedly troubled that his presentation to Greenspan might have triggered the international market turmoil. According to his wife, Shiller was concerned "that he may have caused a worldwide stock market slide."[3]

Shiller is a leading advocate of what has become known as the behavioral school of finance, which argues that nonrational behavior by investors in financial markets often causes the markets to diverge substantially from "intrinsic" value. The behavioralists think that real-world investor behavior makes markets *inefficient*, thus allowing massive overvaluations, such as Shiller believed existed in late 1996, to occur. The behavioral school developed from a growing body of academic research, commencing in the 1970s, that uncovered "anomalies" that apparently contradicted the efficient market hypothesis.

Recall that Eugene Fama, who originally coined the term "efficient market," proposed that a market could be defined as "efficient" if it was impossible to devise trading strategies based on publicly available information that would enable an investor to earn a risk-adjusted rate of return greater than the market rate of return. Taking up Fama's challenge, scholars searched for such anomalous returns and soon began to find likely candidates. As discussed previously, Fischer Black found in a 1973 study that an investor could have earned above-market returns simply by acting on publicly disseminated advice provided by the *Value Line Investment Survey*. His work was soon followed by a study showing P/E ratios were useful in predicting future stock market returns; specifically, stocks with low P/E's tended to do better than stocks with high P/E's. Both of these results called into question Fama's efficient market theory, which held that publicly available data on stock "fundamentals" was useless in predicting future returns.

Shiller's landmark work on stock volatility in 1981 further advanced the behavioralist critique, although the term "behavioralist" had not yet been invented. The efficient market hypothesis required that stocks move only in response to new information. But Shiller's work seemed to show that stocks were far more volatile than they should be if this were true.

A veritable cascade of academic studies poured forth in the 1980s and 1990s, identifying other instances in which the efficient market theory was apparently contradicted by empirical observations. These studies, usually published in scholarly journals, received little public attention until the 1987 crash finally put the behavioralists on the map. It was very difficult to square the October 19 collapse in stock prices with the notion that the market was efficient. Some other explanation for investor behavior seemed to be in order.

Behavioralists believe that "noise trading" accounts for the divergence between what is predicted by the efficient market theory and the observed reality. "Noise" is defined as extraneous information (such as rumors, uninformed guesses, and so forth) that distracts investors from the real information useful in valuing stocks. Because investors often cannot distinguish between noise and hard information, they trade much more frequently than they would in a perfectly efficient market. This tends to make the market more volatile, and more active, than it should be. Fischer Black first defined the term "noise" in 1986, contending that were it not for noise trading, markets would be relatively inactive.[4] It is noise traders—acting on an almost unlimited number of small bits and pieces of information they believe might be important—that account for most stock trading.

The behavioralists believe that because noise traders cannot distinguish between legitimate information and noise, they are forced to develop rules of thumb to guide them in making investment decisions. These rules of thumb, or patterns of behavior, are similar to patterns psychologists have observed in studies of the general population. Behavioralists seek to use the work of psychologists to better understand how the behavioral biases of noise traders distort the financial markets.

One bias the behavioralists believe exists is the tendency to unduly stereotype stocks as "good" or "bad" performers, causing stock prices to ultimately overreact to sustained good or bad news. Others include overconfidence (where market participants mistakenly exaggerate their ability to predict future results) and an unjustifiable reluctance to abandon past beliefs when confronted with changed circumstances.

Behavioralists also believe that investors place too much emphasis on the original cost of an investment, leading to an unwillingness to take losses. Another bias they have identified is what might be called a regret syndrome, where investors overemphasize past mistakes and make nonrational decisions in their attempts to avoid repeating them. Also included in the list of behavioral biases is the "money illusion," which refers to investors' inability to adequately take inflation into account when comparing real and nominal values.[5]

Research has uncovered empirical evidence that behavioral biases such as these may be influencing the stock market. One of the most important studies was performed in 1985, by Werner De Bondt and Richard Thaler, using stock price data going back to 1933.[6] For each year, two portfolios of stocks were constructed—one for the best performers over the preceding three years, and one for the worst performers over that period. Then the returns for the portfolios over the subsequent five years were calculated and compared.

The study concluded that the worst "losers"—the stocks that had performed the poorest over the preceding three years—outperformed the best "winners" by a wide margin in the subsequent five years. This was true even when the results were adjusted for beta risk. The conclusion seemed to be quite damning for the efficient market theory, suggesting that a strategy based simply on past price performance (picking the worst-performing stocks over a three-year period and buying them) could beat the market by a significant amount.

Behavioralists contend that these results reflect a pervasive tendency on the part of investors to overreact to past performance. Investors become excessively discouraged by "losers," expecting those stocks to continue to perform badly, and become excessively enamored of "winners," anticipating that they will continue to do well. As a result, the "losers" become cheap and the "winners" become expensive. Over time, when the true economic condition of the firms becomes evident, the "losers" tend to rebound from the abnormally cheap levels, while the "winners" underperform because their prices were too high.

Another example in which behavioral biases may be influencing stock prices can be seen in the empirically observed tendency of stocks that have announced positive earnings "surprises" to do better than the market for a prolonged period of time, while stocks that have negative earnings "surprises" tend to do worse.[7] The efficient market theory requires that all information (such as earnings announcements) be instantaneously incorporated into stock prices; there should be no continuing drift over time in the direction of any surprise news. Behavioralists believe that the observed drift is the result of excessive conservatism on the part of investors, who do not adequately adjust their expectations for a particular company in response to good or bad news. Thus investors are surprised again when the next earnings announcement occurs, causing the stock price to continue to move in the direction predicted by the first surprise.

Behavioralists also believe they have found support for the notion that irrational "bubbles" exist in stock prices. They cite research showing return correlations over three- to five-year time horizons that subsequently slowly decay, eventually reversing themselves.[8] In other words, stocks often move significantly away from fundamental values over long periods of time, only to fall back eventually, much as would be expected after a speculative bubble or fad.

Other studies indicate that a short-term momentum effect exists, in that individual stock price movements over six to twelve months tend to predict future short-term movements in the same direction.[9] Significantly, unlike the long-term "bubble" pattern that tends to reverse when the "bubble" bursts, the short-term moves tend to continue.

One of the most significant findings appearing to undermine the notion of market efficiency was published in 1992 by Eugene Fama himself.[10] Fama and a colleague found that both book-to-market ratios and the size of a company could be used to predict future returns. (The "book" value of a company is the value of its assets minus its liabilities. The book-to-market ratio is simply book value per share divided by the market price per share of the stock.) Stocks in companies with low book-to-market ratios tended to outperform other stocks, and smaller stocks tended to outperform larger stocks, adjusted for beta risk. On the face of it, this result seemed to flat-out contradict Fama's notion of market efficiency. If readily available information like the book-to-market ratio and the size of a company could be used to predict future returns, then the traditional concept of an efficient market would be essentially meaningless.

How did the efficient market proponents respond to the blizzard of data that seemed to contradict their theory? The case was stated best by Fama in 1998.[11] In spite of his own 1992 research, he was not at all willing to concede the field to behavioralist critics. He made a comprehensive case against what he called "the attack of the anomalies." He noted that in some instances (such as the losers-winners overreaction study) the behavioralists argue that the market overreacts to news, while in others (such as the earnings "surprise" studies) they contend that the market underreacts. Looking across all the published research, Fama concluded that the instances of overreaction and underreaction largely cancel each other out. Market efficiency, he points out, allows for the fact that overreactions and underreactions will occur; it simply requires that the overreactions and underreactions be the result of chance and thus be unpredictable.

With regard to his own 1992 conclusions that book-to-market ratios and company size are predictors of future returns, Fama has a very straightforward explanation, although one that requires him to abandon once and for all the notion that beta is a good measure of risk. (Recall that "beta" simply measures how fast a given stock moves relative to the market as a whole. High-beta stocks are riskier because they are more volatile than low-beta stocks, and vice versa.) Fama argues that the reason stocks of small firms and firms with high book-to-market ratios outperform the market going forward is that they are *riskier* than the rest of the market. In an efficient market, risk is correlated with return; to increase expected return, it is necessary to take more risk. Fama concludes that beta is an inadequate measure of the risk inherent in small firms and in firms with high book-to-market ratios. He believes that regardless of their specific betas, these firms are riskier than the overall market, which accounts for their tendency to earn above-market rates of return.

The notion that stocks with a high book-to-market ratio are riskier than other stocks seems reasonable. In such firms, the book-to-market ratio is usually high because the market price of the stocks is low, often because the company is not doing very well. Hence, more risk. Likewise, small companies tend to be either unproven firms with short histories or established firms that have fallen on hard times. Either way, it is logical to assume that these small firms are inherently riskier than the large firms that make up most of the market's capitalization.

Fama argues that appropriate (non-beta) risk adjustments might explain away some of the other "anomalies" cited by behavioralist researchers. Specifically, the results of the 1985 winners-losers study by De Bondt and Thaler can be made consistent with the efficient market hypothesis if it is assumed that the "loser" stocks studied are in fact much riskier than the "winners," therefore justifying higher future returns. De Bondt and Thaler themselves provided unwitting anecdotal evidence of the riskiness of the "losers." In an interview with *The Wall Street Journal*, Thaler admitted, "It's scary to invest in these stocks. When a group of us thought of putting money on this strategy last year, people chickened out when they saw the list of losers we picked out. They all looked terrible . . ." De Bondt added, "The theory says I should buy them, but I don't know if I could personally stand it."[12]

Is this extra risk sufficient to account for the extra returns the stocks of such firms seem to have provided? Unfortunately, neither Fama nor the behavioralists can provide a definitive answer. The crux of the problem in assessing so-called anomalies is that in order to establish that a given stock or group of stocks outperforms or underperforms the market on a risk-adjusted basis, it is necessary to develop a means of making the risk adjustment itself. The original beta method was beguilingly simple, in that the researcher only needed to measure the rate at which a stock moved relative to the market, taking this as the appropriate measure of risk. With beta dethroned, however, the process of adjusting returns for risk becomes painfully complicated. This makes it possible to dispute the existence of almost any "anomaly" in market returns simply by disputing the method used to adjust the results for risk.

Methodological questions aside, there is plenty of anecdotal evidence to suggest that the behavior patterns identified by the behavioralists occur frequently among stock market participants. Professor Shiller and other researchers have conducted organized surveys that bear out the anecdotal observations. Since the efficient market theory assumes that investors behave rationally in the aggregate, does not the obvious existence of nonrational behavioral patterns fatally compromise the hypothesis?

Not necessarily. The efficient market theory does not require that every investor act rationally. Instead, it makes two crucial assumptions. First, the theory assumes that while many investors may act irrationally, transacting on "noise," their actions are not correlated with each other and hence tend to be random. These random irrationalities, over a very large population of market participants, cancel each other out.

Second, even if the behavioralists are correct in arguing that systematic biases mean that noise trading is not random and thus does not cancel out, the efficient market theory still provides a mechanism to correct any mispricings. That mechanism is arbitrage. Arbitrage in this context is different from index arbitrage, discussed in chapter 14, which takes advantage of discrepancies in the pricing of stock index futures versus the underlying stocks. It is also different from the merger-related risk arbitrage engaged in by the likes of Ivan Boesky. The arbitrage necessary to keep markets efficient attempts to capitalize on pricing discrepancies created by irrational investors. Simply put, the arbitrageurs sell short stocks that are overpriced and buy stocks that are underpriced, until "irrational" prices are brought back into line.

Unlike index arbitrage or merger arbitrage, however, efforts to arbitrage broad market mispricings suffer from an inherent lack of specific events that create a date-certain at which the arbitrageur can cash in his position. The index arb who sells equity index futures versus buying index stocks knows that he will be able to unwind his position when the futures contract expires. To liquidate his position at that time, he sells his stocks at the expiration day's closing prices (the so-called witching hour), knowing that he will also be cashed out of his futures contracts based on the same closing prices. Likewise, the merger arbitrageur unwinds his position when the merger he is betting on is consummated. While there is more risk in the merger arbitrage than the index arbitrage, in both instances the arbitrageurs have a specific time horizon over which their bets will be paid off.

The market participant who attempts to arbitrage other types of mispricings has no such advantage. For example, if he thinks that technology stocks are expensive compared with "old economy" stocks, he can sell short technology stocks and buy "old economy" stocks. He may be right in theory, but there is no specific date (such as a futures expiration or the closing of a merger) by which time the mispricing must be resolved. Technology stocks may become even more expensive than "old economy" stocks, and the mispricing can persist for years.

Since most professional arbitrageurs (such as hedge fund managers and traders employed by investment banking firms) manage money for other people, and are evaluated on an annual basis, they often cannot endure long periods in which their arbitrage positions go against them. If a particular trader seems to be losing money, his managers and investors are often not very patient. Using the previous example, if technology stocks keep rising relative to "old economy" stocks, creating ever-mounting paper losses, eventually the managers and investors will require that the arbitrage trader cut his exposure, forcing him to take a loss. Ironically, this often happens when the mispricing the arbitrageur was attempting to exploit is at its widest point. The arb has a substantial paper loss because he got in too early, and the mispricing continued to worsen rather than shrink. Because there is no date-certain when the mispricing will resolve itself, the arb is forced to abandon his strategy. In this way, the behavioralists claim, the arbitrage mechanism breaks down, allowing inefficient market pricing to persist.

A high-profile example cited by the behavioralists as a failure of arbitrage can be found in the stunning collapse of Long Term Capital Management in 1998. LTCM was a "hedge fund" designed to take advantage, on a massive scale, of worldwide mispricings between securities. The term "hedge fund" is derived from the notion that such funds both buy and sell short securities, theoretically insulating, or "hedging," themselves from general market moves. For example, a hedge fund such as LTCM would buy one bond and simultaneously sell another, similar bond short, betting that the relationship between the two was out of line and would eventually return to what it should be. When that occurred, the fund would be able to close out its position at a profit.

LTCM was the proverbial mother of all hedge funds. It would be the biggest, with the brightest people employed to run it. Two Nobel laureates—Myron Scholes and Robert Merton, developers of the early options pricing theory—joined other Wall Street "stars" to manage the new entity. A minimum commitment of $10 million was required of anyone seeking to invest. There was no shortage of applicants.

In essence, the strategy of LTCM was to seek out and exploit pricing inefficiencies in all financial markets throughout the world. Relatively little of its activity directly involved the U.S. stock market. However, LTCM's trading strategy does serve as a good example of the type of arbitrage believed by efficient-market theorists to enforce market efficiency. Whenever "noise" traders in any given market forced prices out of line, LTCM traders (and other arbitrageurs like them) intervened to take advantage of the opportunity and through their actions moved prices back to where they should be.

But were there really enough market inefficiencies to enable LTCM and other, similar hedge funds to earn large profits for their investors? Ironically, even though Scholes and Merton were believers in the efficient market theory, they clearly thought that a sufficient number of exploitable opportunities existed to make LTCM viable. When Scholes was making a presentation to a potential investor (a Midwestern insurance company), he reacted sharply to a questioner who implied that the markets were too efficient to allow LTCM to earn excess returns. Scholes declared that "as long as there continue to be people like you, we'll make money."[13]

The insurance company's managers remained unconvinced, but there were plenty of other potential investors who had no such qualms. The money flooded in; by early 1994, LTCM had raised $1.5 billion. The amount continued to grow rapidly as the fund generated impressive results, producing better than 40% returns for investors in 1995 and 1996. But 1997 returns were disappointing—only 17% compared with a 31% gain shown by the unexotic S&P 500 index. LTCM's capital balance by late 1997 was over $7 billion.[14] The obvious question could not be avoided: Were there simply not enough market anomalies to exploit? In effect, were all the worldwide markets LTCM traded in becoming too efficient, preventing the fund from continuing to earn exceptional returns?

The principals at LTCM never really addressed this possibility. To do so would have required them to rethink the justification for the fund's continuing existence. Instead, they resorted to a bold strategy, ratcheting up the "leverage" of the fund by returning capital to investors without reducing the size of the positions the fund held. LTCM returned $2.7 billion to its investors at the end of 1997, reducing the fund's equity capital to approximately $4.9 billion. Many of the investors who got their money back vigorously complained about being involuntarily cashed out of what they believed was still a fabulous money machine. But their protests were ignored. The LTCM principals accomplished their objective; the balance sheet leverage of LTCM increased from 18.3 to 27.7, meaning that the firm now owned securities worth 27.7 times the amount of its equity capital.

The money necessary to fund these huge positions was borrowed. This meant that there was now much less margin for error; if some of LTCM's big market bets went bad, there was less of an equity cushion to absorb the losses. Apparently none of the LTCM principals had qualms about the increased risk involved. One later commented, "We decided to go for leverage and we didn't think it would be much of a problem."[15]

It was a problem. By midsummer 1998, many of LTCM's carefully calculated bets were simultaneously moving against the firm, something that in theory should not have happened. A large part of the trouble, as seen with the benefit of hindsight, was that LTCM was not alone; there were many other hedge funds using the same models and attempting to implement the same arbitrage strategies. When unexpected exogenous shocks hit the market, many of the competing funds had the same types of positions

LTCM had. When these funds were forced to reduce their exposure by unwinding those positions, they simply made matters worse. Everyone was trying to sell the same instruments at the same time.

As a Goldman Sachs trader put it, "If many arbitrage traders have similar trades and the aggregate position sizes are very large, it is like dry grass building up and just needs a match to ignite it."[16] A series of matches were struck around the world in the late summer of 1998, beginning with the economic collapse of Russia. LTCM would not survive the conflagration.

By the third week of September, LTCM's doom seemed sealed. Not much sympathy was expressed for the LTCM principals, who were seen as haughty and arrogant. But it quickly began to dawn on observers that an LTCM collapse might bring down other market participants as well. Beyond the highly leveraged positions on LTCM's balance sheet, there were huge derivatives contracts "off balance sheet," totaling to an astronomical amount in excess of $1 trillion. In theory, these contracts were offsetting and fully collateralized, but in the uncertain environment of September 1998 no one could be quite sure. Major Wall Street firms were "counterparties" to LTCM, meaning that they held many derivatives contracts with LTCM. What if LTCM were to fail, enmeshing the firms in tangled bankruptcy proceedings?

On Wednesday, September 23, a group of senior executives of leading Wall Street firms assembled in the fortresslike building housing the Federal Reserve Bank of New York. Fed officials were deeply concerned about the potential impact of an LTCM collapse; they hastened to act as intermediaries in efforts to arrange a refinancing of the fund. A solution seemed to be within grasp, as Goldman Sachs proposed an arrangement in which a Warren Buffet–led group of investors would take over LTCM for $4 billion, with Goldman Sachs traders managing the fund's myriad positions. To all those present, it seemed like an ideal solution to the problem. The Wall Street investment bankers were confident that most of the LTCM arbitrage positions were ultimately viable, if only a secure financing base could be provided that allowed the markets to return to normalcy.

The solution may have appeared ideal to the Wall Street executives, but it was certainly less than ideal for the LTCM principals. Since most of them had their entire personal net worth invested in the fund (many had actually borrowed money to invest in LTCM), they would effectively be wiped out by the arrangement, which gave them nothing in return. In short order, the LTCM principals rejected the plan.

The LTCM principals were playing a high-stakes game. It was the same game the Hunt brothers had played in 1980 when their silver scheme collapsed. They implicitly threatened to commit financial suicide if an arrangement to their liking could not be worked out, knowing full well that an uncontrolled collapse of their interests could jeopardize the entire financial system. The Hunts believed that they were too big to be allowed to fail. The LTCM principals, like steely-eyed players in a high-stakes poker game, made the same bet.

They were correct. The deal was renegotiated to allow the fund's investors (including the principals) to keep a 10% stake in the fund, with a chance to later recoup some of their losses.

As in the wake of the Hunt silver debacle, the Federal Reserve denied having officially brokered the deal, pointing out that no government money was involved. But regardless of whether or not the Fed intervened in an official capacity, it is unlikely that the solution to the LTCM problem could have come about without at least the tacit approval of the central bank.

The crisis in the markets did not end with the announcement of the LTCM deal. As it had after the 1987 stock market crash, the Fed pumped money into the financial system, eventually reducing short-term interest rates by three quarter-percent increments. That, and the resolution of the LTCM imbroglio, ultimately turned the trick. Worldwide financial markets stabilized, and the U.S. stock market resumed its seemingly inexorable climb.

Behavioralists point to the LTCM example as the kind of arbitrage failure that allows markets to remain inefficient. If a star-studded management team, including two Nobel laureates, had been overwhelmed by the "irrational" vagaries of the markets, was not the overall effectiveness of arbitrage in doubt? And without effective arbitrage, would not the systematic biases of "noise traders" inevitably taint the markets, making them inefficient?

There is another explanation for the LTCM debacle that is more consistent with the notion that markets are efficient. LTCM did not fail simply because of a series of bad bets on arbitrage relationships. It failed because it was excessively leveraged. The decision to employ so much leverage was made in direct response to the fact that by 1997 the fund was no longer able to earn the exceptional returns its principals hoped for. The markets it dealt in were becoming more efficient, as many other hedge funds attempted to implement similar arbitrage strategies. Competition was removing the market discrepancies LTCM sought to exploit. The only way the fund could continue to earn large returns was to take on more risk. This is precisely what it did by returning some investor capital, thereby increasing leverage.

LTCM would not have failed had it not increased its leverage (risk). In this sense the LTCM experience is remarkably consistent with the notion that markets tend toward efficiency. According to the efficient market theory, to make superior returns, it is necessary to take more risk. The LTCM principals did just that, and paid a very high price.

William Sharpe summed up the LTCM experience, and the fate of his former Stanford University colleague and LTCM principal Myron Scholes, in an interview with *The Wall Street Journal*. "Most of academic finance is teaching that you can't earn 40% a year without some risk of losing a lot of money," Sharpe said. "In some sense, what happened [at LTCM] is nicely consistent with what we teach."

There is reason to believe that the same tendency toward increasing market competitiveness that made it difficult for LTCM to earn excess returns in worldwide markets is also making the American stock market more efficient. For example, the previously cited evidence advanced by Shiller and others to support the notion that "bubbles" (long-term, slowly decaying departures from fundamental values) exist disappears when the years 1926–1940 are removed from the data.[17] This suggests that the statistical evidence of bubbles is an artifact of the Great Depression period and has not been seen since. Likewise, other anomalies cited by the behavioralists, such as the winners-losers effect and the tendency of small stocks to earn excess returns, seem to have vanished in the last fifteen years.

Significantly, many of the anomalies that have not yet disappeared tend to be concentrated in small stocks. In assessing the importance of these anomalies, it should be remembered that in the data sample used for most studies, "small stocks" were defined as the smallest 20% of the companies listed on the New York and American Stock Exchanges and the NASDAQ market system. While the absolute number of small firms is large, they make up only about 1.5% of the total capitalization of the stock market.[19]

Much of the superior performance of Value Line recommendations was concentrated in small stocks. The difficulty in generalizing from these results to the overall market is evident in the performance of the Value Line Centurion Fund, a mutual fund that invests in stocks favored by Value Line. The fund has been unable to generate above-market returns over the long run, in spite of the statistical success of Value Line Investment Survey recommendations.

Another of the anomalies mentioned earlier—the "surprise" earnings drift effect—also comes from the small-stock portion of the data sample. Furthermore, most of the stock price movement in the direction of the "surprise" comes in the three days immediately following each earnings announcement.[20] This suggests that stock prices of relatively obscure companies do not instantaneously adjust to unexpected earnings news. Instead, it takes approximately three days on average for the market to incorporate the new information on these companies into the stock price. While this is technically a violation of the pure definition of market efficiency, which assumes that the market adjusts instantaneously to new information, it does not seem unreasonable to "bend" the efficient market hypothesis slightly in the case of small, relatively unknown firms that are not as widely followed as the large-capitalization companies that make up most of the stock market.

While "behavioralism" is rooted in academic research that uncovered the market anomalies discussed above, its ultimate significance comes from the belief that the narrow anomalies discovered are merely symptoms of much broader market mispricings that cannot be tested for empirically. The 1987 crash, which in one day cut market valuations by more than 20% in the absence of any dramatic news, is one example. The stunning bull market of the late 1990s, which raised stocks to allegedly "irrational" levels, is another. According to the behavioralists, the existence of relatively minor, but statistically verifiable, anomalies makes the existence of large-scale irrationalities, like marketwide speculative bubbles, more plausible.

Alan Greenspan continued to wrestle with the notion of market irrationality after his "irrational exuberance" remarks in 1996. He assigned

Fed analysts the task of developing computer models that sought to explain past market crashes, with the hope of discerning patterns with predictive value. He studied the "anomalies" data presented by behavioralists. But, by his own admission, his efforts to understand why the market behaved as it did ended in frustration. Finally, he abandoned the project altogether, commenting wryly that the models his staffers had designed predicted "eight of the last three" market collapses.[21]

Greenspan slowly became more receptive to the notion that the 1990s bull market was more rational than he had first thought. In June 1998 he again invited outside stock market experts to present their views; the principal arguments in favor of historically high market valuations were thoroughly aired. One argument was based on fundamental changes seen to be occurring in the economy, while the other centered on changes in investors' perception of risk.

The "fundamentalist" case was (is) essentially that persistently low inflation, combined with improvements in corporate profitability, has created an environment in which historically high valuations are justified. Specifically, low inflation encourages higher P/E ratios because the quality of corporate earnings is good in a low-inflation environment. Illusory profits that come from pricing flexibility, and marking up existing inventory, do not exist. Because reported earnings are "real" (not artificially swollen by inflation), investors are quite right to pay more (higher P/E's) for those earnings.

In addition, structural changes in the economy, the application of new technologies, and a variety of "just in time" corporate strategies have fundamentally altered the way business is done. Sometimes this constellation of positive factors is referred to as a "new paradigm." Enhanced corporate profitability, and higher stock prices, are the expected results.

The other principal "bull" argument is that rising stock prices at the turn of the twenty-first century reflect a belated recognition by investors that stocks have been badly underpriced in the past. This argument is made most fervently by James Glassman and Kevin Hassert in their book *Dow 36,000*. Glassman and Hassert believe that the "equity risk premium"— the extra return, above the rate paid by risk-free government bonds, that stock investors receive as compensation for taking the risks inherent in investing in stocks—has historically been much too high. This is another way of saying that stocks are not as *risky* as they have seemed to be, or that they have become *less risky* over time, or both. Pointing out that there has never been a twenty-year period in American history in which the return on stocks has been less than the return on bonds, adjusted for inflation, Glassman and Hassert reach the very controversial conclusion that stocks (at least over the long run) are no riskier than bonds and thus do not deserve *any* risk premium.

Such an extreme assumption can justify stock prices that are astronomical by historical standards. Recall the example given in chapter 15, where mere half-percent changes in the expected rate of growth in future dividends, and in the discount rate used to value those future dividends, caused the theoretical value of a stock to move by an astounding 25%. Since the discount rate used in calculating the present value of future dividend flows is simply the risk-free government bond interest rate plus the risk premium, making a change in the assumed risk premium changes the assumed discount rate. Evidence suggests that the historical equity risk premium has been approximately 7%. As stock prices have risen, the implied risk premium has fallen; the best current estimates place it around 3%. It is by reducing this number to zero that Hassert and Glassman reach the startling conclusion that the Dow Jones Industrials should be at 36,000.

There are of course obvious reasons that the stock market should now be less risky than in the past. Greater transparency (better information), the elimination of manipulation, an understanding of how diversification can reduce risk, and the ability of individuals to invest in diversified portfolios through mutual funds and retirement plans all make the market less risky than it was years ago. Greater sophistication on the part of economic policy makers, safety-net regulations like bank deposit insurance, and the ability of the Federal Reserve to act as the lender of last resort in a time of crisis all reduce the chance of exogenous shocks to the market that create instability, and risk. And finally, not to be underestimated, the willingness of many institutional and individual investors to buy into the notion that stocks are sound *long-term* investments, not to be quickly discarded in the face of temporary volatility, has effectively increased the risk tolerance of market participants.

Market bears, of course, reject the Glassman-Hassert argument that stocks are no riskier than government bonds, contending that while the equity risk premium may have been too high in the past, it should certainly not fall to zero. (Some bears argue that the risk premium has fallen too far already.) The bears also dispute the notion that a "new paradigm" exists, pointing out that similar reasoning was employed to justify high stock prices in the past (notably in the 1920s), only to end in disaster. The bears believe that there are basic limits to the rate at which the economy and corporate earnings can grow, and that these long-term limits have not really changed much.

Only the future will tell whether the bulls or the bears are correct. But behavioralist bears like Shiller do more than simply argue that the bulls are wrong. They say, in effect, that the bulls are "irrational." It is the behavioralist bears' passionately held belief that the stock market is subject to mammoth speculative bubbles and that irrational behavior by investors, which cannot be corrected by arbitrage, is the source of the bubbles.

Whatever one thinks of the case made by bulls such as Abby Joseph Cohen, James Glassman, and Kevin Hassert, however, their arguments are certainly not irrational. The bulls are arguing that fundamental changes have occurred in the economy—and/or in the way risk is perceived in the stock market—that irreversibly change the way stocks are valued. If these arguments themselves are not inherently irrational, why is it that investors who accept this reasoning are presumed to be acting irrationally?

Bears such as Shiller rely heavily on historical data to make their case. In his 1996 presentation to Greenspan, Shiller analyzed price, earnings, and dividend data going all the way back to 1871 to show why stocks in late 1996 were badly overpriced. In his book *Irrational Exuberance*, published four years later, Shiller uses much the same reasoning, and data, updated to include the staggering rise in the market that occurred since he made the bearish 1996 pronouncements. That Shiller was wrong in 1996 does not necessarily mean he will be wrong again in the future. But it does warrant a closer examination of his methodology.

From the perspective of the events and trends described in the preceding chapters, it should be clear that the history of the stock market over the past hundred years has been *dynamic*, not static. Any attempt to use historical data to analyze the *current* state of the market is therefore suspect, if allowances are not made for the far-reaching changes that have obviously occurred. Shiller, and many others who rely on historical data to analyze current market conditions, make no such allowances. Instead they simply accept historical data as is, juxtaposing it against the present to reach their conclusions.

For example, Shiller places great emphasis on the fact that dividends are extremely low now compared to the past. But surely he cannot be suggesting that the relationship that prevailed prior to 1958, when dividend yields were always higher than bond interest rates to compensate for the presumed riskiness of stocks, should still apply today. And yet he freely uses data derived from the pre-1958 period to compute a historical average dividend, compared to which today's dividends seem very low. This comparison is essentially meaningless because it does not recognize the fundamental changes that have occurred in the way investors perceive risk in the stock market, and the much reduced importance of dividends as a means of offsetting that risk.

The same problem crops up in the "anomalies" data that Shiller and other behavioralists employ to show that the market is inefficient, and thus susceptible to irrational pricing. Because the statistical techniques used to uncover the anomalies are relatively weak, many years (often many decades) of data are required to generate a statistically significant result. But the "efficiency" of the market has not been static over those long periods. It should be clear from the events and trends described in this book that the market has been *evolving toward greater efficiency* over the past century. Clearly the conditions for a truly efficient market were not met in the past, when accurate financial information was not available, and when the market was routinely subject to manipulation. But Shiller and other behavioralists use data from these periods when testing for anomalies. In many ways, their results tell us more about the market in the past than about the market today. It is likely for this reason that many of the discovered anomalies have disappeared in current data, and the rest are largely confined to the smallest stocks. In a market that is *evolving toward efficiency*, this result would be expected.

Finally, Shiller and the other behavioralists make frequent references to the 1929 crash as an example of what can go wrong when historical measures of evaluation are abandoned in favor of new, forward-looking standards. But, as was demonstrated in chapters 6 and 7, the crash of 1929 was extraordinary only in that it preceded the Great Depression. It was the

Depression of the 1930s that wiped out stock values, not the bursting of an inflated speculative bubble in 1929. By holding up the 1930s as a cautionary example for contemporary investors, the behavioralists implicitly argue that another Great Depression (or similar catastrophe) is possible, and that such a possibility must be actively discounted today in valuing stocks.

But there has been no depression for nearly 70 years. It is not illogical (or irrational) to assume that greater sophistication on the part of economic policy makers (and built-in safety nets like federal bank deposit insurance) has made such calamities much less likely. In fact, the accompanying chart, "Fluctuations in Real Gross Domestic Product: Annual Percent Change, 1900–2000," illustrates how the American economy has become much more stable over the past half century. The business cycle has

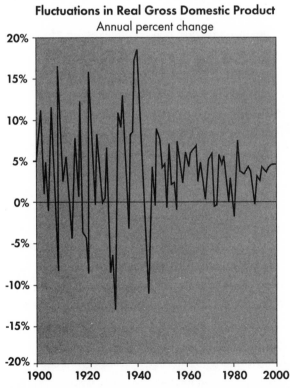

Fluctuations in Real Gross Domestic Product
Annual percent change

From *The First Measured Century: An Illustrated Guide to Trends in America, 1900–2000* (2000) by Theodore Caplow, Louis Hicks, and Ben J. Wattenberg. Reprinted with the permission of the American Enterprise Institute for Public Policy Research, Washington, D.C.

moderated substantially, which in turn means that the earnings streams of corporations (and therefore the stocks of those corporations) should be less volatile (risky). While new, unexpected macroeconomic disasters may loom undetected just beyond the horizon, the likelihood that the old-fashioned "busts" typical of the nineteenth and early twentieth centuries will recur has been significantly reduced.

As the debate raged on between behavioralists and the advocates of the efficient market theory, Alan Greenspan continued his effort to better understand how the market works, and how it affects the economy. Significantly, his views appear to have evolved substantially since he uttered his famous "irrational exuberance" remark in 1996. Greenspan's new interpretation was unveiled in 1999; he said then that the market represented the sum total of the "judgments of millions of investors, many of whom are highly knowledgeable about the prospects for the specific companies that make up our broad stock market indexes."[22] He concluded that the Federal Reserve should let investors set stock values; it is not the function of the central bank to do it for them.

According to *The Wall Street Journal*, Greenspan was one of the first economists to suspect that private sector productivity was surging, taking note of rapidly increasing investment in capital equipment and rising profit margins at a time of relative price stability. He has therefore become much more receptive to the "new paradigm" idea that rapidly accelerating earnings growth may justify higher P/E ratios.

Similarly, Greenspan is now apparently more receptive to the argument that stocks are not actually as risky as they have appeared to be (or actually were) in the past. He seems to be willing to consider the possibility that the equity risk premium has been too high historically, which is another way of saying that stock prices in the past have been too low. A declining equity risk premium can account for much of the spectacular rise in stock prices at the end of the twentieth century.

The evolution of Greenspan's views parallels, with a substantial lag, the evolution of the stock market itself. Recall from chapter 9 that as early as 1959, Greenspan warned of the danger of "overexuberance" in the market that could create a "speculative bubble" that would inevitably burst. After the 1987 crash, he referred to the market break as "an accident waiting to happen," implying that the drop occurred because stock prices had been unjustifiably inflated before the crash. His musings on "irrational exuberance" in 1996 reflected the same concerns; it was only after that date, as the market continued its relentless climb, that Greenspan finally began to question the notion that rapidly rising stock prices reflected "irrational" behavior by investors.

There is no question that many investors at the turn of the twenty-first century have been exuberant, bidding up stocks to unprecedented levels. This stock-price action has been, and will continue to be, a source of great controversy. But it is quite significant that the most powerful man in the American economy, after a great deal of painstaking analysis, now seems to feel that those exuberant investors may not have been so "irrational" after all.

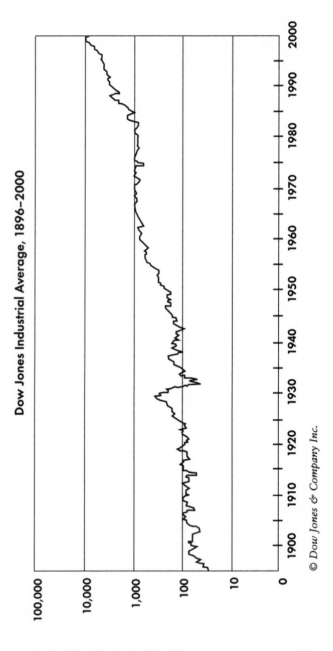

Dow Jones Industrial Average, 1896–2000

© *Dow Jones & Company Inc.*

17

RATIONAL EXUBERANCE

W HY IS ALL this important? Why should the average investor be concerned about arcane academic debates about market "efficiency" and valuations? And why has Alan Greenspan struggled so mightily to understand the stock market's behavior? The answer is very simple: the stock market plays a far more crucial role in today's economy than it ever has in the past. For the first time in history, over half the American population owns stocks, either directly or indirectly, meaning that to an unprecedented degree the financial well-being of the populace is tied directly to stock prices. Many millions of people depend on stock market returns to fund their retirement, and the notion that even Social Security funds should be invested in stocks has gained a degree of acceptance that would have been unthinkable not long ago. But if the market is subject to irrational bubbles that will inevitably end badly, as many behavioralists believe, potential disaster looms for baby-boom retirees, and for the federal government that might be required to bail out a crash-induced Social Security fund shortfall.

Similarly, since the stock market is the primary means by which equity capital is allocated in the economy, understanding how the market works is essential to understanding the process through which businesses secure the financing that is the very lifeblood of their existence. If the market is subject to large, irrational swings, then American business will inevitably suffer. Wasteful funding will be provided in boom times to favored companies that don't deserve it (as some observers suggest has happened with many immature Internet firms), or, after a market bust, funding will be denied to sound companies with legitimate needs. Either way, the economy is hurt by a nonoptimal allocation of resources.

And of course irrational stock prices pose a potentially dangerous problem for the Federal Reserve. The crash that will presumably occur if and when a speculative bubble bursts may severely test the ability of the central bank to keep the financial system, and the economy, afloat. As has occurred all too often in the past, stock market panics may in the future destabilize the broad economy, with disastrous consequences.

In short, if the behavioralist critique is valid, its troubling implications cannot be ignored. But fortunately, while behavioralism certainly provides interesting fodder for academicians debating economic theory, its practical usefulness is highly doubtful. Much of the empirical basis for behavioralism comes from research that has found anomalies that seem to contradict the notion that markets are efficient. But, as demonstrated in chapter 16, most of the so-called anomalies are found primarily in small-company stocks representing a tiny fraction of the market's capitalization, or have largely disappeared as the stock market has evolved to its present state. In an academic context, the fact that anomalies exist that undermine the efficient market theory may be interesting. But in the real world, where professional market participants recognize that perfect efficiency can never really exist, all the quibbling over "anomalies" takes on the practical significance of medieval theologians debating the number of angels that can stand on the head of a pin.

The question is not whether the efficient market theory is perfect, or has always held true in the past, but whether it best describes the state of the American stock market *today*. Ironically, one of the most telling comments on this subject has been provided by a leading behavioralist—Santa Clara University finance professor Hersh Shefrin. In his book *Beyond Greed and Fear*, Shefrin purports to offer advice directly to market practitioners, including portfolio managers, security analysts, and investment bankers. Recognizing that allegedly "irrational" behavior by investors is often hard to predict and therefore difficult for savvy market participants to exploit, and that many of the mispricings resulting from irrational behavior are relatively minor, Shefrin admits that investors "would be better off acting as if . . . markets are efficient."

To be sure, other behavioralists do believe that exploitable opportunities are created by irrational investor behavior. Some have even set up investment management firms, soliciting investors who seek to take advantage of these opportunities. (Richard Thaler, who coauthored the 1985 winners-losers study, is one such entrepreneur.) If they are successful, however, these academics turned portfolio managers will ultimately confront the same problem Benjamin Graham faced when his style of "value" investing became popular. Realizing that the actions of like-minded investors had competed away the market mispricings he had earlier exploited, Graham said in a 1976 interview shortly before he died that "I am no longer an advocate of elaborate techniques of security analysis in order to find superior value opportunities. This was a rewarding activity . . . but the situation has changed . . . I doubt whether such extensive efforts will [now] generate sufficient superior selections to justify their cost . . . I'm on the side of the efficient market school of thought."[1] To the extent that behavior-related mispricings can be shown to exist, behavioralist arbitrageurs like Richard Thaler will quickly compete them away.

If the behavioralist critique of the efficient market theory is of little practical significance, then the notion that the stock market is subject to large, irrational bubbles is also suspect. In fact, over the course of the twentieth century, there is no real evidence of *any* speculative bubbles affecting the large-capitalization stocks that dominate the market. This is not to say that speculative bubbles have not existed, or cannot exist, in certain segments of the market at certain times (as in start-up Internet companies recently). The market for small, relatively unknown firms is arguably less efficient than that for established companies; to the extent that bubbles appear, it is likely that they would be found in the "small stock" segment of the market. But whatever the case, these firms make up only a fraction of the overall market, and should not be used to make the more general argument that the entire stock market is frequently subject to "irrational" speculation.

Even if the existence of market-wide speculative bubbles is discounted, however, words of caution are still in order. Stock prices have risen over much of the past century in large part because the risk premium investors require has declined; this process cannot go on forever. Once the market completes the adjustment to the "new" risk premium, it will no longer rise faster than the rate of growth in corporate earnings. And unless the most optimistic "new economic paradigm" advocates prove correct, that rate of earnings growth will be considerably less than the recent rate of stock price increases. Hence, it is likely that the returns earned by stock investors in the future will be significantly less than those earned by investors in the recent past.

Of course, if *Dow 36,000* authors Glassman and Hassert are right in claiming that the equity risk premium should continue to fall to zero from its current level of approximately 3%, large increases in stock prices still lie ahead. Unfortunately, a closer examination of their methodology reveals that Glassman and Hassert make a mistake in interpreting historical stock price data not unlike the errors of their behavioralist critics. Glassman and Hassert base their case largely on the fact that there has never been a twenty-year period in American history in which the stock market has not outperformed the bond market, adjusted for inflation; therefore, they believe that over the long term, stocks are no riskier than bonds. But, like Shiller and other behavioralists who simply present historical data without really attempting to understand it, Glassman and Hassert misuse the data, failing to recognize that their reasoning is inherently circular. They argue (correctly) that the stock market has risen over time because the equity risk premium has fallen. But then they cite that very rise in stocks, compared with bonds, as evidence that stocks are no more risky than bonds, thus justifying further declines in the risk premium, and further increases in stock prices.

Even if stocks have done well relative to bonds over very long time horizons in the past, there is no guarantee that this pattern will persist in the future, particularly when the risk premium readjustment process that has been driving much of the stock market's rise has been completed. More important, there is no way to get around the fact that stocks are more volatile than bonds, even if bulls disguise that fact by smoothing out the volatility over long periods of time. As noted in chapter 15, the dividend discount model that Glassman and Hassert (along with most other analysts) employ to value stocks is subject to sharp moves given only relatively minor changes in its input variables. It is very difficult to argue that stocks are no more risky than bonds when relatively small changes in model inputs can create extreme changes in theoretical value, such as that which apparently occurred at the time of the 1987 crash.

There is also a possible demographic influence on the equity risk premium that is ignored by Glassman and Hassert. It is quite likely that the transition from defined-benefit to defined-contribution retirement plans that has occurred over the last twenty years has accentuated the process by which investors have lengthened their time horizons and thus become less sensitive to short-term market risk. An investor at age 30 or 40 who buys stocks through a 401(k) plan, for example, will by necessity have a long time horizon, since he or she is still many years away from retirement. That investor should be quite receptive to the Peter Lynch argument (reinforced by writers like Glassman and Hassert) that stocks have always been good long-term investments, regardless of short-term volatility. In other words, people making long-range investments to fund their retirements should be (and likely have been) willing to accept a lower equity risk premium.

But as those same investors approach retirement, their time horizons change. Short-term risk becomes more significant to people who are more interested in capital preservation than capital appreciation. As the massive baby-boom generation nears retirement, it is quite likely that members of that generation will demand *higher*, not lower, risk premiums. This has negative implications for stock prices, and certainly undermines the Glassman-Hassert argument that the equity risk premium will continue to decline. (Note that this reasoning is significantly different from the oft-repeated prediction that the stock market will falter once baby boomers begin to consume their retirement savings rather than accumulating more. Well before the boomers actually begin to draw down their savings, they may become more risk averse. Thus pressure could be exerted on the risk premium—and stock prices—at a much earlier date.)

Of course, all speculation about the future of the equity risk premium—and thus about the rate at which stocks will rise in the future—is largely academic if the market is truly efficient. Since an efficient market incorporates the best judgments of all market participants into a determination of stock prices, there is by definition little point in trying to outguess that consensus opinion. All factors—including possible trends in the risk premium—will already have been considered by current investors.

The investor who believes that the stock market is efficient (or at least that the efficient market hypothesis comes closest to describing the state of the market today) will buy equity index mutual funds* in an effort to mimic the market. He recognizes that the best he can expect to accomplish by doing this is to roughly match the performance of the specific market index chosen—such as the Standard & Poor's 500. In spite of this limitation, however, the dollar amount invested in equity index mutual funds has grown dramatically over the last two decades, indicating that many people have come to accept the idea that it is very difficult, if not impossible, to consistently "beat" the market. But what if all investors took this advice, and simply invested in index funds? Would the market still be efficient?

The answer is clearly no, and represents an interesting paradox. For a market to be efficient, most participants must believe that it isn't. The diligent work of sophisticated analysts like Benjamin Graham is required to search out stocks that are mispriced; their buying and selling of these stocks then moves prices back into line. But if the Ben Grahams of the world become convinced that few such opportunities exist (that is, that the market is largely efficient), they will cease their efforts. Hence stocks can become mispriced again, with no mechanism to correct the mispricings.

There is no evidence that this has yet occurred; by all accounts, there are still plenty of analysts, portfolio managers, and individual investors who believe they can beat the market. Two trends in the 1990s provide compelling evidence of this. First, the turnover rate on the New York Stock Exchange (the number of shares traded in a given year as a percentage of the total number outstanding), which had fallen to below 15% at mid-century, has risen sharply in recent years, approaching 100%. Second, the ability of individual investors to transact quickly and cheaply over the In-

---

*An index fund is a mutual fund that rigidly attempts to mimic the performance of a specific market index, like the Standard & Poor's 500. The fund accomplishes this by holding only the index stocks, in the exact proportion in which they are included in the index.

ternet has increased individual participation in the market. By the 1980s, the percentage of trading volume attributable to individuals, as opposed to institutions, had declined to approximately 20%; since then, however, it has rebounded to about 30%. Clearly, investors and portfolio managers who trade stocks actively do not believe the market is efficient, whatever the consensus wisdom of academic experts may be. Many of these participants transact on the basis of careful analysis, while others are essentially noise traders as defined in chapter 14 (so-called day traders would be an example of the latter).

Whatever theory of market behavior an observer chooses to accept, it is impossible to deny the unprecedented importance of the stock market to the modern American economy. As shown in chapter 16, Fed chairman Greenspan is acutely aware of the market's significance. While he has abandoned his efforts to determine whether current levels of stock prices are "rational" or not, he cannot ignore the need to cope with the economic effects of the stock market boom.

Specifically, Greenspan and other Fed officials are worried about "imbalances" in the economy created by "rising asset prices." The problem is the "wealth effect"—whereby escalating stock prices cause enriched investors to spend more on consumption. Rising stock prices, even if justified by long-term economic trends or a reduction in the equity risk premium, do not in and of themselves increase the supply of goods and services. As a result, a stock market–induced increase in consumer demand, unchecked by increased supply, could push up consumer prices, causing inflation.

The Fed's response to fears of the wealth effect has been to raise short-term interest rates in an effort to slow the economy and, implicitly, the rise in stock prices. Greenspan defined the issue in a presentation to Congress in February 1999. "How the current wealth effect is finally contained," he said, "will determine whether the extraordinary expansion . . . can slow to a sustainable pace, without destabilizing the economy."[2]

Greenspan describes the importance of the modern stock market to the economy in no uncertain terms. "I could readily stop talking about the stock market," he admitted to a Fed staffer. "But if I do, I will not be explaining how the process is working . . . There is no way to understand what is going on in this economy without reference to [stock] prices."[3]

NOTES

1. STEEL

1. Jean Strouse, *Morgan: American Financier* (New York: Random House, 1999), p. 406.
2. Ibid., p. 405.
3. Ibid.
4. Frederick Lewis Allen, *The Lords of Creation* (New York: Harper Bros., 1935), p. 30.
5. Alexander Dana Noyes, *The Market Place* (Boston: Little Brown, 1938).
6. Alfred Cowles, *Common Stock Indices* (Bloomington, Ind.: Principia Press, 1939), p. 372.
7. Ibid.
8. Richard Schabacker, *Stock Market Theory and Practice* (New York: B. C. Forbes, 1930), p. 407.
9. Peter Bernstein, *Capital Ideas* (New York: Free Press, 1992), p. 19.
10. Ibid.
11. Ibid., p. 22.
12. Ibid., p. 18.
13. Ibid., p. 20.
14. Allen, p. 25.
15. Ibid., p. 27.
16. Dan Bowmar, *Giants of the Turf* (Lexington, Ky.: The Blood-Lines, 1930), p. 103.

2. AN INDIAN GHOST DANCE

1. H. J. Eckenrode and P. W. Edmunds, *E. H. Harriman* (New York: Greenberg, 1933), p. 23.

2. Ron Chernow, *The House of Morgan* (New York: Atlantic Monthly Press, 1990), p. 91.

3. Edwin Hoyt, *The House of Morgan* (New York: Dodd, Mead, 1966), p. 244.

4. Peter Collier and David Horowitz, *The Rockefellers* (New York: Holt, Rinehart and Winston, 1976), p. 53.

5. Robert Sobel, *Panic on Wall Street* (New York: Macmillan, 1968), p. 286.

6. Ibid., p. 290.

7. Ibid., p. 292.

8. Ibid., p. 293.

9. Ibid., p. 294.

10. Michael Malone, *James J. Hill* (Norman: University of Oklahoma Press, 1996), p. 214.

11. Ibid., p. 210.

12. Ibid., p. 215.

13. Stanley Jackson, *J. P. Morgan* (New York: Stein and Day, 1983), p. 213.

14. *New York Times*, 10 May 1901.

15. Theodore Roosevelt, *Autobiography* (New York: Macmillan, 1913), p. 439.

16. Andrew Sinclair, *Corsair* (Boston: Little, Brown, 1981), p. 141.

17. Jackson, p. 220.

18. Sinclair, p. 141.

19. Ibid.

20. Joseph Bishop, *Theodore Roosevelt and His Time* (New York: Scribner's, 1920), p. 184.

21. Malone, p. 220.

3. LENDER OF LAST RESORT

1. Robert Sobel, *Panic on Wall Street*, p. 300.

2. Ibid., p. 303.

3. Frederick Lewis Allen, *The Lords of Creation*, p. 115.

4. Ibid.

5. Edwin Hoyt, *The House of Morgan*, p. 258.

6. John A. Garraty, *Right-Hand Man: The Life of George W. Perkins* (New York: Harper & Brothers, 1957), p. 172.

7. Jean Strouse, *Morgan: American Financier*, p. 578.

8. Stanley Jackson, *J. P. Morgan*, p. 270.

9. Lester V. Chandler, *Benjamin Strong: Central Banker* (Washington, D.C.: Brookings Institution, 1958), p. 28.

10. Edward Lamont, *The Ambassador from Wall Street* (Lanham, Md.: Madison Books, 1994), p. 38.

11. Ibid., p. 39.

12. Ida H. Tarbell, *The Life of Elbert Gary: The Story of Steel* (New York: D. Appleton, 1925), p. 202.

13. Andrew Sinclair, *Corsair*, p. 226.

14. Hoyt, p. 307.

15. Sobel, p. 349.

4. WAR

1. Robert Sobel, *Panic on Wall Street*, p. 338.

2. Alfred Cowles, *Common Stock Indices*, p. 405.

3. Paul Sarnoff, *Jesse Livermore: Speculator King* (Palisades Park, N.J.: Investors' Press, 1967), p. 55.

4. James Grant, *Bernard M. Baruch* (New York: Simon & Schuster, 1983), p. 146.

5. *New York Times*, 4 January 1917.

6. Frederick Lewis Allen, *The Lords of Creation*, p. 197.

7. Gardiner Means, "Diffusion of Stock Ownership," *Quarterly Journal of Economics*, August 1930.

8. H. T. Warshow, "The Distribution of Stock Ownership in the United States," *Quarterly Journal of Economics*, November 1924.

9. Alexander Dana Noyes, *The Market Place*, p. 184.

10. Warshow, p. 37.

11. Noyes, p. 225.

12. Cowles, p. 405.

13. Grant, p. 131.

5. A NEW ERA

1. John Brooks, *Once in Golconda: A True Drama of Wall Street* (New York: Harper & Row, 1969), p. 1.
2. Robert Sobel, *The Great Bull Market* (New York: W. W. Norton & Co., 1968), p. 99.
3. Kenneth Van Strum, *Investing in Purchasing Power* (New York: Barron's, 1925), p. vii.
4. Paul Sarnoff, *Jesse Livermore: Speculator King*, p. 7.
5. Ibid., p. 51.
6. Ibid., pp. 70–71.
7. Ibid., p. 71.
8. Ronald Kessler, *Sins of the Father* (New York: Warner Books, 1996), p. 34.
9. Brooks, p. 81.
10. Ibid., p. 110.
11. Sobel, *The Great Bull Market*, p. 57.
12. John Kenneth Galbraith, *The Great Crash, 1929* (Boston: Houghton Mifflin, 1979), p. 10.
13. Martin Fridson, *It Was a Very Good Year* (New York: John Wiley & Sons, 1998), pp. 55–56.
14. Sarnoff, p. 78.
15. Ibid.
16. Sobel, *The Great Bull Market*, p. 113.
17. Harold Bierman, *The Causes of the 1929 Stock Market Crash* (Westport, Conn.: Greenwood Press, 1998), p. 30.
18. Ibid., p. 31.

6. CRASH

1. Harold Bierman, *The Great Myths of 1929* (New York: Greenwood Press, 1991), p. 31.
2. Harold Bierman, *The Causes of the 1929 Stock Market Crash*, p. 43.
3. John Kenneth Galbraith, *The Great Crash, 1929*, p. 42.
4. Ibid., p. 44.
5. Joseph S. Lawrence, *Wall Street and Washington* (Princeton, N.J.: Princeton University Press, 1929), p. v.

6. *Barron's*, 10 June 1929.

7. Bierman, p. 47.

8. Galbraith, p. 99.

9. Ibid., p. 75.

10. Ibid., p. 105.

11. Frederick Lewis Allen, *Only Yesterday* (New York: Harper Bros., 1931), p. 330.

12. Galbraith, p. 107.

13. *Saturday Evening Post*, 28 December 1929.

14. James Grant, *Bernard M. Baruch*, p. 240.

15. Robert Sobel, *Panic on Wall Street*, p. 387.

16. Ibid., p. 384.

17. Paul Sarnoff, *Jesse Livermore: Speculator King*, p. 89.

18. Galbraith, p. 70.

19. Grant, p. 236.

20. Irving Fischer, *The Stock Market Crash—and After* (New York: Macmillan, 1930), p. 69.

21. John Brooks, *Once in Golconda: A True Drama of Wall Street*, p. 82.

22. A. A. Berle and Gardiner C. Means, *The Modern Corporation and Private Property* (New York: Harcourt, Brace & World, 1968), pp. 568–571.

23. Milton Friedman and Anna Schwartz, *A Monetary History of the United States, 1867–1960* (Princeton, N.J.: Princeton University Press, 1963), p. 290.

24. J. Pederson, "Some Notes on the Economic Policy of the United States," in *Money, Growth and Methodology*, H. Hegeland, ed. (Stockholm: CWK Gleerup, 1961).

7. REVOLUTION

1. John Brooks, *Once in Golconda: A True Drama of Wall Street*, p. 62.

2. John Kenneth Galbraith, *The Great Crash, 1929*, p. 156.

3. Brooks, p. 14.

4. Robert Sobel, *The Big Board* (New York: Free Press, 1965), p. 284.

5. Arthur Schlesinger, *The Coming of the New Deal* (New York: Macmillan, 1959), p. 468.

6. Galbraith, p. 157.

7. Sobel, *The Big Board*, p. 299.
8. Ibid., p. 293.
9. Ibid., p. 294.
10. Ibid., p. 298.
11. William Atkins, George Edwards, and Harold Moulton, *The Regulation of Securities Markets* (Washington, D.C., 1946), pp. 70–71.
12. Roger Lowenstein, *Buffet: The Making of an American Capitalist* (New York: Doubleday, 1995), p. 37.
13. Peter Bernstein, *Capital Ideas* (New York: Free Press, 1992), p. 33.
14. Ibid., p. 36.
15. Ibid., p. 38.
16. Robert Sobel, *NYSE: A History of the New York Stock Exchange, 1935–1975* (New York: Weybright & Talley, 1975), p. 34.
17. Galbraith, p. 169.
18. Brooks, p. 278.
19. Ibid., p. 276.
20. Sobel, *NYSE*, p. 72.
21. Ibid., p. 67.
22. Ibid., p. 127.
23. Paul Sarnoff, *Jesse Livermore: Speculator King*, p. 102.
24. Ibid., p. 122.

8. PEOPLE'S CAPITALISM

1. Edwin Perkins, *Wall Street to Main Street* (Cambridge: Cambridge University Press, 1999), p. 163.
2. Ibid., p. 10.
3. Robert Sobel, *NYSE: A History of the New York Stock Exchange*, p. 127.
4. Perkins, p. 173.
5. Ibid., p. 205.
6. Sobel, *NYSE*, p. 136.
7. Gene Smith, *The Life and Death of Serge Rubenstein* (Garden City, N.Y.: Doubleday & Company, 1962), p. 41.
8. Ibid., p. 49.
9. Sobel, *NYSE*, p. 153.
10. Smith, p. 67.

11. Ibid., p. 82.
12. Sobel, *NYSE*, p. 163.
13. Ibid.
14. Charles Ellis and James Vertin, eds., *Classics: An Investor's Anthology* (Homewood, Ill.: Dow Jones–Irwin, 1989), p. 261.
15. Sobel, *NYSE*, p. 171.
16. Robert Sobel, *The Last Bull Market* (New York: W. W. Norton & Co., 1980), p. 29.
17. Ibid., p. 30.

9. THOSE DAYS ARE GONE FOREVER

1. Peter Bernstein, *Capital Ideas*, p. 60.
2. Ibid.
3. Ibid., p. 44.
4. Ibid., p. 47.
5. Ibid., p. 50.
6. Peter Bernstein, *Against the Gods* (New York: John Wiley & Sons, 1998), p. 248.
7. Ibid., p. 252.
8. Bernstein, *Capital Ideas*, p. 48.
9. Marshall Blume, Jeremy Siegel, and Dan Rottenburg, *Revolution on Wall Street* (New York: W. W. Norton, 1993), p. 95.
10. Robert Sobel, *The Last Bull Market*, p. 130.
11. Blume, Siegel, and Rottenburg, p. 97.
12. Ibid.
13. Ralph Smith, *The Grim Truth About Mutual Funds* (New York: Putnam & Sons, 1963), p. 9.
14. Robert Sobel, *NYSE: A History of the New York Stock Exchange*, p. 205.
15. Martin Fridson, *It Was a Very Good Year*, p. 139.
16. Ibid., p. 223.
17. Ibid., p. 149.
18. Sobel, *NYSE*, p. 224.
19. Ibid., p. 229.
20. Sobel, *The Big Board*, p. 341.
21. John Brooks, *The Seven Fat Years* (New York: Harper, 1958), p. 146.

22. Ibid., p. 151.
23. Ibid., p. 153.
24. Bernstein, *Capital Ideas*, p. 94.
25. Ibid., p. 95.
26. Ibid., p. 96.
27. Sobel, *NYSE*, p. 232.
28. Ibid.
29. Ibid., p. 235.
30. Sobel, *The Big Board*, p. 355.
31. Benjamin Graham, *Analysts Journal*, June 1958.
32. Ibid.
33. Ibid.

10. THE KENNEDY MARKET

1. Robert Sobel, *NYSE: A History of the New York Stock Exchange*, p. 265.
2. *Barron's*, 28 May 1962.
3. Sobel, *NYSE*, p. 243.
4. John Brooks, *The Go-Go Years* (New York: Allworth Press, 1998), p. 27.
5. Robert Sobel, *Panic on Wall Street*, p. 408.
6. Roy Hoopes, *The Steel Crisis* (New York: John Day & Co., 1963), p. 116.
7. Ibid., p. 136.
8. Robert Sobel, *The Last Bull Market*, p. 86.
9. Hoopes, p. 77.
10. Ibid., p. 67.
11. Ibid., p. 140.
12. Sobel, *Panic on Wall Street*, p. 414.
13. Sobel, *The Last Bull Market*, p. 98.
14. Sobel, *Panic on Wall Street*, p. 419.
15. Sobel, *The Last Bull Market*, p. 97.
16. Sobel, *Panic on Wall Street*, p. 419.
17. Ibid., p. 424.
18. Robert Sobel, *The Big Board*, p. 371.
19. Ibid., p. 407.
20. William Beaver and Dale Morse, "What Determines P/E Values?" *Financial Analysts Journal*, July/August 1978.

21. *Barron's*, 2 July 1962.
22. Sobel, *The Last Bull Market*, p. 87.
23. Sobel, *NYSE*, p. 270.
24. Harold Bierman, *The Great Myths of 1929*, p. 148.
25. *Barron's*, 11 June 1962.
26. Sobel, *Panic on Wall Street*, p. 420.
27. Irwin Friend, Marshall Blume, and Jean Crockett, *Mutual Funds and Other Institutional Investors* (New York: McGraw-Hill, 1970), p. 24.
28. Norman Miller, *The Great Salad Oil Swindle* (New York: Coward, McCann, 1965), p. 169.
29. Ibid., p. 170.
30. Ibid., p. 174.

11. ORANGUTANS

1. Peter Bernstein, *Capital Ideas*, p. 78.
2. Ibid., p. 77.
3. Ibid., p. 127.
4. Ibid., p. 130.
5. Marshall Blume, Jeremy Siegel, and Dan Rottenburg, *Revolution on Wall Street*, p. 89.
6. *Institutional Investor*, March 1967.
7. Bernstein, *Capital Ideas*, p. 133.
8. *Institutional Investor*, June 1969.
9. John Brooks, *The Go-Go Years*, p. 132.
10. Ibid., p. 153.
11. Ibid.
12. Robert Sobel, *The Last Bull Market*, p. 152.
13. Brooks, p. 136.
14. *Institutional Investor*, April 1967.
15. Dilip Mirchandi, *One Way Up Wall Street* (New York: Fred Alger & Co., 1999), p. 52.
16. Ibid., p. 63.
17. Ibid., p. 126.
18. Martin Mayer, *New Breed on Wall Street* (New York: Macmillan, 1969), p. 57.

19. Ibid.
20. Ibid., p. 58.
21. Brooks, p. 140.
22. *Institutional Investor*, March 1970.
23. *Institutional Investor*, December 1968.
24. Mayer, p. 58.
25. *Institutional Investor*, January 1969.
26. Brooks, p. 267.
27. *Institutional Investor*, January 1969.
28. Sobel, *The Last Bull Market*, p. 138.
29. *Institutional Investor*, June 1969.
30. *Wall Street Journal*, 24 February 1969.
31. Ibid.
32. *Business Week*, 18 August 1986.
33. *Institutional Investor*, June 1969.
34. Brooks, p. 269.
35. *Institutional Investor*, March 1970.
36. *Barron's*, 19 November 1986.
37. Ibid.
38. *Wall Street Journal*, 1 October 1986.
39. *Institutional Investor*, April 1967.
40. Irwin Friend, Marshall Blume, and Jean Crockett, *Mutual Funds and Other Institutional Investors*, p. 24.
41. Brooks, p. 213.
42. *Institutional Investor*, September 1971.
43. Ibid.
44. Ibid.
45. Bernstein, p. 75.
46. Ibid., pp. 142–143.

12. BURSTING APART

1. John Brooks, *The Go-Go Years*, p. 1.
2. Ibid., p. 23.
3. *Institutional Investor*, October 1970.
4. Ibid.

5. Eugene Fama and G. William Schwert, "Asset Returns and Inflation," *Journal of Financial Economics* 5 (2), 1977.

6. *Institutional Investor*, September 1971.

7. Ibid.

8. Ibid.

9. Ibid.

10. Ibid.

11. Ibid.

12. *Institutional Investor*, April 1977.

13. Burton Malkiel, *A Random Walk Down Wall Street* (New York: W. W. Norton, 1999), p. 193.

14. *Institutional Investor*, April 1977.

15. Peter Bernstein, *Capital Ideas*, p. 292.

16. Bernstein, *Journal of Portfolio Management*, Fall 1974.

13. CRUNCH

1. Stephen Fay, *Beyond Greed* (New York: Viking Press, 1982), p. 235.

2. *Barron's*, 15 October 1979.

3. *Barron's*, 10 May 1980.

4. Fay, p. 14.

5. Ibid., p. 212.

6. Ibid., p. 218.

7. *Institutional Investor*, June 1980.

8. *Institutional Investor*, January 1979.

9. *Institutional Investor*, June 1980.

10. Marshall Blume, Jeremy Siegel, and Dan Rottenburg, *Revolution on Wall Street*, p. 92.

11. Sanjoy Basu, *Journal of Finance* 32 (3), 1977.

12. Robert Shiller, *American Economic Review*, June 1981.

13. Peter Bernstein, *Capital Ideas*, p. 211.

14. RETURN OF THE BULL

1. Peter Bernstein, *Capital Ideas*, p. 69.

2. Hayne Leland, *Journal of Finance* 35 (2), May 1980.

3. Peter Lynch, *One Up on Wall Street* (New York: Simon & Schuster, 1989), p. 34.

4. Ibid., p. 35.

5. Ibid., p. 34.

6. Ibid., p. 13.

7. Ibid., p. 19.

8. Ibid., p. 44.

9. Jeremy Siegel, *Stocks for the Long Run* (New York: McGraw-Hill, 1998), p. 277.

10. Lynch, p. 36.

11. Bernstein, *Against the Gods*, p. 299.

12. Burton Malkiel, *A Random Walk Down Wall Street*, p. 377.

13. Mark Stevens, *The Insiders* (New York: G. P. Putnam's Sons, 1987), p. 56.

14. Ibid.

15. Ibid., p. 14.

16. James Stewart, *Den of Thieves* (New York: Simon & Schuster, 1992), p. 345.

17. Ibid., p. 347.

18. Ibid., p. 340.

15. AN ACCIDENT WAITING TO HAPPEN

1. *Wall Street Journal*, 20 November 1987.

2. *Wall Street Journal*, 20 October 1987.

3. Ibid.

4. Ibid.

5. *Wall Street Journal*, 20 November 1987.

6. Peter Lynch, *One Up on Wall Street*, p. 12.

7. *Wall Street Journal*, 20 October 1987.

8. Ibid.

9. Roger Kamphuis, Robert Kormendi, and J. W. Henry Watson, eds., *Black Monday and the Future of Financial Markets* (Homewood, Ill.: Dow Jones–Irwin, 1989), p. 5.

10. *Wall Street Journal*, 22 October 1987.

11. Ibid.

12. Ibid.

13. Kamphuis et al., p. 72.
14. *Wall Street Journal*, 23 October 1987.
15. Ibid.
16. Ibid.
17. Ibid.
18. Ibid.
19. Merton Miller, *Financial Innovations and Market Volatility* (Cambridge, Mass.: Basil Blackwell, 1991), p. 100.
20. Kamphuis et al., p. 18.
21. Ibid., p. 75.
22. *Wall Street Journal*, 23 October 1987.
23. Bradford Cornell, *The Equity Risk Premium* (New York: John Wiley & Sons, 1999), p. 190.
24. Miller, p. 89.

16. GREENSPAN'S DILEMMA

1. *Wall Street Journal*, 8 May 2000.
2. Hersh Shefrin, *Beyond Greed and Fear* (Boston: Harvard Business School Press, 2000), p. 40.
3. *Wall Street Journal*, 8 May 2000.
4. Fischer Black, *Journal of Finance* 41, 1986.
5. Discussed at length in Shefrin.
6. Werner De Bondt and Richard Thaler, *Journal of Finance* 40, 1985.
7. Victor Bernard and Jacob Thomas, *Journal of Accounting Research* 27, 1989.
8. Lawrence Summers, *Journal of Finance* 41, 1986.
9. Narasimhan Jagadeesh and Sheridan Titman, *Journal of Finance* 48, 1993.
10. Eugene Fama and Kenneth French, *Journal of Finance* 47, 1992.
11. Eugene Fama, *Journal of Financial Economics* 49 (3), 1998.
12. *Wall Street Journal*, 7 January 1988.
13. Nicholas Dunbar, *Inventing Money* (New York: John Wiley & Sons, 2000), p. 130.
14. Ibid., p. 180.
15. Ibid., p. 188.
16. Ibid., p. 205.

17. Fama and French, *Journal of Finance* 47, 1992.

18. Robert Hagen, *The New Finance* (Englewood Cliffs, N.J.: Prentice Hall, 1995), p. 71.

19. Eugene Fama, *Journal of Finance* 46 (5), 1991.

20. Hagen, p. 71.

21. *Wall Street Journal*, 8 May 2000.

22. Ibid.

17. RATIONAL EXUBERANCE

1. Burton Malkiel, *A Random Walk Down Wall Street*, p. 193.

2. *Wall Street Journal*, 8 May 2000.

3. Ibid.

INDEX